CONFLICT MEDIATION
across
CULTURES

Also by David W. Augsburger

Pastoral Counseling Across Cultures

CONFLICT MEDIATION

across

CULTURES

Pathways and Patterns

DAVID W. AUGSBURGER

Westminster John Knox Press
LOUISVILLE • LONDON

Book design by ediType

First edition

Published by Westminster/John Knox Press
Louisville, Kentucky

This book is printed on acid-free paper that meets the American National Standards Institute Z39.48 standard. ∞

PRINTED IN THE UNITED STATES OF AMERICA

19 18 17 16 15 14 13 12

Library of Congress Cataloging-in-Publication Data
is on file at the Library of Congress, Washington, D.C.

ISBN-13: 978-0-664-25609-8
ISBN-10: 0-664-25609-0

Contents

Foreword

Interest in the subject of conflict has increased dramatically over the last fifteen years. This includes scholarly as well as practical interest, and addresses questions such as how to prevent or decrease conflict in schools, hospitals, churches, businesses, families, and so on. Scholars want to know how to prevent nuclear war, what causes conflict, what techniques are effective in arriving at "settlements," and how people in different cultures approach the problem of conflict. The how-to books abound, more often than not promising on the cover more than they deliver inside. Book racks in airports, drugstores, and supermarkets provide a substantial range of manuals on the subject, some of which are very good. These days I pick up new (to me) works on conflict with a modicum of trepidation; much of what I see is repetitive of what is popular these days, and some of it is ridiculous, promising reconciliation through good works and effective technique.[1]

Because I have had a good deal of exposure to other writings by David Augsburger, I was confident what I would read in this work would be fresh, interesting, and helpful. My expectations were met, and more so. Augsburger's approach to his subject is both sagacious and entertaining. He begins each chapter with folktales from a wide range of cultures and sprinkles his text with aphorisms from around the world. Just as a collection of captivat-

---

1. Not all the popular literature propounds what I have here called "good works"; some of it, like Robert Ringer's *Winning Through Intimidation*, is, according to my lights, malicious in intent and delivery.

ing stories, this book is a treasure. Augsburger presents tales and stories that I have never encountered and that abound with wisdom and insight. However, the depth and interest of this work are not merely contained in the perceptive sayings of others: From his own knowledge and experience, Augsburger brings discernment and wisdom to a subject that baffles and confuses.

The insights in this book are still ringing in my head several weeks after having read it. Many writers have seen the value of low-level conflict in organizations and relationships and have looked for ways to describe a healthy organization not as avoiding or denying or suppressing conflict, but as "managing" or "utilizing" it in some way. These words seem to imply that dealing with difference is simple enough, if you just understand how to do it. Augsburger has found a new way to talk about this process — he talks about conflict "transformation." Here is a word that connotes a deeper dimension of experience than conflict utilization or management.

Conflict management is not simple; there is much that can go wrong, much that is out of our control, much that strikes terror in normal human beings. "Transformation" implies that the management is not all in our hands, and it points to one of Augsburger's key assertions: The task of dealing with conflict is not just to end the fighting; nor is it merely to get enemies to be friends; there is more to it than that. Augsburger helps us aim beyond these worthy goals to re-create the broken relationship, indeed, to reopen the future for the parties to the dispute in a way that empowers them both to move back into responsible relationship. In other words, conflict transformation assumes (or demands) that the parties to the dispute not act unilaterally, but join together in a search for their future. Obviously, this goal of transformation will be beyond the reach of the disputants in some conflicts: Are you going to seek a transforming relationship with the people who have made a low offer on your house? And what of the guy who just cut too close in front of you in traffic or the out-of-control schizophrenic who is unable to differentiate between reality and delusions? Augsburger recognizes that some of our efforts will fall short due to our own "stuff," the situation, or the other(s) with whom we are in conflict. Yet the larger goal — the vision, the hope of transformation — permeates the book so readers set their sights high, taking a measure of the situation from a perspective that does not exclude at the beginning the possibility of new life *together* for the disputants.

From my perspective the chapter on reconciliation and forgiveness is the pièce de résistance. By looking at forgiveness from the perspective of many cultures, Augsburger helped me to see dimensions of this Christian goal that I had either not taken seriously, had misunderstood, or had no idea of before reading this book. Augsburger offers us this gift of understanding in a way that is both respectful and empowering, helping those of us who are Christian to learn from other cultures' experiences.

The title of the book may at first be misleading to some readers. My first impression of the book from its title was that it was going to help me understand how to do cross-cultural conflict resolution as a mediator. This is not that kind of book. The reader will find here helpful models and maps for reflecting on anger, conflict patterns and processes, triangling (drawing allies into the dispute), and mediation. These clear and perceptive models would be useful to any organizational leader or to any person caught up in a dispute with a neighbor, with a spouse, with a government agency, or within a church. However, this book is not essentially a manual or guidebook on mediating or managing (or transforming) conflict. Readers will find suggestions and models here, but will be disappointed if they are looking for a step-by-step guide for mediators with chapters on how to analyze the dispute, gain entry into the system, develop rapport with the disputants, and so on. The book is deeper and broader than that. Augsburger is dealing with fundamentals of the human condition here. He is helping us get perspective on our own culture by standing outside of it for a moment in order to better appreciate its values and better recognize its limits.

Perhaps the subtitle says it better: This book is about pathways and patterns of dispute resolution. From it readers will learn about themselves, their culture, and other cultures; from it readers will come to understand, just a little bit more, about the nature of conflict *and* transformation, frustration *and* hope.

SPEED LEAS

Alban Institute

Acknowledgments

In writing a book in a field little explored — in this case, conflict patterns across cultures — the contribution of counselors, mediators, and consultants is as great as that of the written sources. Among those whose influence and insights have instructed and enriched this study, I am most indebted to the following: in England, Chris Sugden, David Atkinson, Michael Nazir Ali, Wendy James, Kenneth Cragg, and T.R. Ranger; in America, John Paul Lederach, Roelf Kuitse, Daniel Schipani, Lillian Asoera, Ahmed Ali Haile, Paul Hiebert, Mary Schertz, and Marcus Smucker; in Asia, Dayanand Pitamber, Mesach Krisetya, Philemon Choi, John Williamson, Allen Harder, Takio Tanase, and Kenneth Dale.

Colleagues in South and Latin America, Africa, the Middle East, and Australia have offered me more than I have been able to assimilate. To all these I am profoundly grateful, as I am to my mentors in the study of human relationships, Frank Kimper, Howard Clinebell, Jr., Jan Chartier, Myron Chartier, and Murray Bowen.

Many of my co-travelers in a life of practice, scholarship, and teaching deserve gratitude and recognition. Among these are many of my students who taught me from their rich experiences across cultures and their boundless good humor.

To all of the above persons and to many who must remain unrecognized, I offer my thanks.

Introduction

FOLKTALE: THE COMING OF PEACE
Basotho Tribe, Africa

This is a story that the old people tell.

One day the hen flew to the top of the stack of wheat to find food. From where she stood on top, she could see far over the fields. Across the fields a jackal was approaching. When the jackal came near, he spoke to the hen.

"Good morning, mother of mine," the jackal greeted her.

"Yes, I greet you."

"Are you still living?" he asked according to customary greetings.

"Yes, I am still living. And you? Are you still living also?" she asked.

"Yes, I am still living, mother. Did you wake well this morning?"

"Yes, I woke well," she answered as is proper.

While he was talking, the clever jackal was admiring the hen, seeing that she would taste very sweet. But he could not reach her. So he asked her, since he was a man of many plans: "Mother, have you heard that there is peace among every-

body on earth? Now one animal may not catch another animal anymore, because of that peace."

"Peace?" she asked.

"Yes, mother, peace. The great chiefs called together a big meeting, and at that pitso they decided this business of peace on all the earth."

"Oh yes," said the hen, but she wondered whether this jackal could be telling the truth, since his many clever stories were many times nothing but lies.

"You say there is peace now?"

"Yes, mother, the big peace. There has never been such a big peace. You can safely come down from that stack of wheat. Then we can talk about the matter nicely. We shall take snuff together. Come down, mother! Remember the peace."

But the hen was not quite as stupid as the jackal thought. She wanted to be sure of his story, and she turned and looked far over the fields.

"What is it you see from up there that you stare so?"

"What do I see? It does not matter, for there is no more danger to any animals on earth. Is it not peace among the animals? It is only a pack of dogs that is running toward us."

"Dogs! A pack of dogs!" he cried. And his fear was very great. "Then I shall have to leave you, mother. I am a man who has a lot of work waiting."

"Kekekekeke," the hen laughed. "Remember the peace. I thought it was peace among all the animals. Have you forgotten it? Why do you run away, grandfather?"

"I don't think this pack of dogs was at the meeting of the peace." And the jackal ran so fast that dust rose in great clouds behind him.

"Kekekekeke," laughed the hen. She knew that the story of the big peace was a lie. And if she had taken snuff with that fellow he would have caught her. Instead she had caught him.

"Kekekekeke!" she laughed. "I caught the storyteller with another story!" And this is the end of this story.

(Postma 1964, 115–17, abridged)

FOLKTALE: THE PEACE-BRINGER
Iroquois Nation

Before the Peace-Bringer came, the Iroquois were a fierce and violent people, constantly at war with neighboring tribes. Their braves were raised to be warriors; their tribes were organized for waging war; their culture was shaped by the mythology and values of the raid, the ambush, the valiant act, the violent victory.

Then came the Peace-Bringer. He walked through the village to the house of the greatest and bloodiest hero, the Man-Who-Eats-People, and he climbed to the top and looked down through the smoke hole.

The Man-Who-Eats-People was preparing a ritual feast from the cut-up body of one of his victims; he would absorb the victim's power by eating him. A large pot sat on the fire, and the face of the Peace-Bringer, looking in at the smoke hole, was perfectly reflected on the oil on the surface.

The Man-Who-Eats-People froze as he saw the reflection, astonished by the nobility he saw in it.

"That is my face," he said to himself, "and it is not the face of a man who kills others and eats their flesh to steal their power. That is the face of one who draws people together, the face of one who makes peace, not war."

He seized the pot and emptied it outside. "Never again shall I take a life or seek to take another's spirit and strength," he told all those who came running.

Then the Peace-Bringer came forward to meet him, and the man said, "Here is the face of peace. I have seen it in my own face. I see it in another's."

And the two became as one. The Man-Who-Eats-People became Hiawatha the hero, the healer, the maker of peace.

―――――――

CONFLICT AND DIVERSITY

If you cannot remove conflict from life,
why not adjust your thinking about it?
If you can't beat it, join it.
Why not try and see conflict
as the salt of life,
as the big energizer,
the tickler,
the tantalizer,
rather than a bothersome nuisance,
as a noise in a perfect channel,
as disturbing ripples in otherwise quiet water?
Why not treat conflict
as a form of life,
particularly since we all know
that it is precisely during the periods in our lives
when we are exposed
to a conflict that really challenges us,
and that we finally are able to master,
that we feel most alive. (Galtung 1975–80, 3:501)

These words distill a Swedish scholar's experience from a lifetime of studying human conflict, and they echo the conclusions of thinkers from all over the world — from Japan and Korea, China and Tibet, India and Pakistan, Israel and the Muslim nations of the Middle East, England and Ireland, Latin and North America, the United States and Russia; and from South Africa and tribes such as the Yoruba and Hausa, the Basotho and the Zulu.

Conflict is essential to, ineradicable from, and inevitable in human life; and the source, cause, and process of conflict can be turned from life-destroying to life-building ends.

Our methods of resolving disputes and conflicts, especially the major ones, are still crude, ill-considered, inadequate, and frequently ineffective. There is a need for a fundamental shift in our thinking about and our approach to the resolution of all types of conflicts — from the interpersonal to the international.

In this book, the interpersonal and the intra- and intergroup conflicts will be the primary concerns, particularly when I am comparing conflict patterns within and between various cultures.

The first basic proposition that emerges from cross-cultural conflict studies is: Our much-loved patterns of either-or thinking, of argumentative and appositional disputation, and of competitive and win-lose forms of resolution must be superseded. When we are locked into traditional either-or thinking, the logic (no matter how tight and tidy) has a fundamental limitation. Any competitive and conflictual thinking about conflict blocks us from shifting over to a designing style of thinking, from moving into an exploratory mode of searching for an alternative solution.

The second basic proposition that becomes obvious in cross-cultural studies is that the parties most directly invested in a dispute are usually the least able, are in the worst position, and are the least equipped to settle the dispute constructively. So the traditional options of threatening and coercing, or litigating and adjudicating, must be expanded to include more effective means of mediating and negotiating — means such as creative design and constructive alternatives. These invariably come from third parties. In any dispute, rarely can the two opposing parties design a constructive way out or a creative way through. A third party becomes essential, an outsider who does not contrive to think in an either-or manner or to apply conflict to resolve conflict.

The third basic proposition is that, viewed across cultures, conflict confounds our theories, confuses our social contracts, and confronts us with our ignorance on human interaction.

One of the first learnings that confronts the student of conflict across cultures is that better solutions than our own have frequently been achieved by peoples with much less information than we have at our disposal. So-called primitive societies often have conflict solutions that are more effective in bonding adversaries and blending goals than those groups who designate themselves as advanced, developed, or possessing far more data about human relations.

The obvious conclusion is that, in most conflict situations, we are painfully ignorant. The most experienced mediators, theorists, or counselors are still, in a larger sense, conflict-ignorant. The confusion we experience as conflict breaks into the open reveals our ignorance of our own part as well as of the roles played by others in the interaction.

Socrates made the famous statement, "I know that I know nothing." In conflict, the beginning of wisdom is the recognition of the breakdown of our understandings, assumptions, and common knowledge about our relational, communal, or national social contracts; it is the recognition that these contracts are failing to meet the needs of all, are not providing justice to each, and are not opening equal opportunities for everyone. The first step for mediators and participants in every culture is recognizing that we do not possess the requisite data, cannot foresee the necessary process, and fear joining the opponent in an earnest search for a joint pathway. In traditional cultures, pathways exist in tribal wisdom for channeling the search for conflict resolutions. However, they often have been lost in the blending of cultures in modern society, a blending that reduces cultures toward the common denominator of legal social contracts.

A fourth initial proposition is that recognizing, enhancing, and utilizing each culture's conflict wisdom are preferable to creating a universal science of conflict and dispute negotiation. Enhancement, not elimination, of human diversity must be our goal.

Diversity can be a source of harmony, rather than a source of conflict. Uniformity can destroy rather than advance civilization. A single world culture is not a desirable goal.

Cultures embody the authenticity and unique purposes of each community. Each culture seeks to express a people's values, sensitivity, and spirituality. A little beaver carved from stone by a distant ancestor and passed hand-to-hand during a community assembly of Eskimos as a symbol of human warmth is charged with as high a voltage of meaning and emotion as a Flemish old master to the Dutch, a Michelangelo to the Italians, or a Ming vase to the Chinese. Continuity and congruence with their cultural history connect persons and groups to their own peculiar depths, their own unique wisdom, and their own particular configuration of human archetypes, religious symbols, and central values.

As human history records, people have learned to enlarge the circles of their allegiance, loyalty, and government from the family to the clan, to the tribe, to the village, to the town, to the city, to the city-state, to the nation-state. The interdependence of ecology and economics now calls upon us to make the final step to the global level. In the preceding transitions, we have not erased the uniquenesses of family, clan, tribe, village, town, city, or nation. But now, the scientific revolution, the homogenization of culture through communications technology, the parallel processes of modernization and urbanization, and the pressures of ecological survival and economic sufficiency threaten to minimize or even obliterate our diversity and reduce the provocative and pregnant variety of the human family of families.

Although threatened, cultural variety still buds and even flourishes. The overwhelming majority of societies at the end of the twentieth century are internally divided into ethnic, racial, linguistic, religious, and other groupings that lead distinctive lifestyles. In most cases, the cultural diversity is reinforced by economic gaps and power disparities. Pluralism — along with inequality and injustice — exists in every nation. It exists in marked degree in such places as South Africa and the United States, and in lesser degree in such places as Switzerland and Canada. This diversity increases both the possibility of conflict and the possibilities within conflict to reveal the richness of human society and its cultural treasures.

AN OVERVIEW OF THE ARGUMENT

Traditional cultures see conflict as a communal concern; the group has ownership of the conflict and context. Urbanized (Westernized) cultures, in contrast, focus on the individual issues and assume personal and private ownership.

Traditional cultures deal with conflict in preferred patterns of mediation through third parties so that the resolution is achieved in indirect, lateral, and systemic ways, while urbanized (Westernized) cultures prefer direct, one-to-one encounter between the disputants that utilizes a third party only in extremity or in legal process. Individualism in life shapes individualism in strife.

Traditional cultures follow conflict patterns embedded in the mores and customs of the group or people. Resolution processes are culturally prescribed. In contrast, urbanized (Westernized) cultures see conflict as situationally defined, with open options for pragmatic choice. What works in a situation today may be very different from what worked in a virtually identical situation yesterday.

Figure 1 sketches these initial contrasts and identifies the chapters in which they emerge most pointedly. The gender issues, the disparity of the allotment of power between the sexes, the contrast between the public and private conflict styles of women and men form the central nexus. The vertical dimension of creative versus destructive conflicts reveals patterns that turn conflict toward competitive and nonproductive ends in every human culture. The three central contrasts — situational versus cultural, individual versus communal, direct versus indirect — map three major areas of difference. Each contains a world of variations in pathways and patterns.

The goal of this study is to both sensitize and desensitize the reader.

The desensitization of our common sense about conflict (*common sense* is the expression of our particular cultural pool of assumptions) is necessary if we are to understand another culture's process "interpathically" — that is, if we are to perceive and experience another culture's content and context from within while coming from without.

Figure 1
Central Contrasts in Conflict and Dispute
Patterns Across Cultures

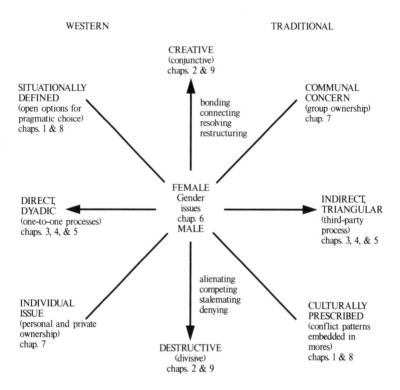

WESTERN   TRADITIONAL

CREATIVE
(conjunctive)
chaps. 2 & 9

SITUATIONALLY
DEFINED
(open options for
pragmatic choice)
chaps. 1 & 8

bonding
connecting
resolving
restructuring

COMMUNAL
CONCERN
(group ownership)
chap. 7

FEMALE
Gender
issues
chap. 6
MALE

DIRECT,
DYADIC
(one-to-one processes)
chaps. 3, 4, & 5

INDIRECT,
TRIANGULAR
(third-party
process)
chaps. 3, 4, & 5

alienating
competing
stalemating
denying

INDIVIDUAL
ISSUE
(personal and private
ownership)
chap. 7

CULTURALLY
PRESCRIBED
(conflict patterns
embedded in
mores)
chaps. 1 & 8

DESTRUCTIVE
(divisive)
chaps. 2 & 9

The sensitization of our "uncommon senses" about conflict invites us to learn from another culture as well as respect it. We have much to gain from each other. Every culture can be our teacher in some respect, offering some new perspective from the surprising and amazing disequilibrium that occurs on the boundary.

Who knows but one culture, knows no culture. We come to self-knowledge on the boundary.

Who knows only one way of dealing with disputes, knows little about conflict. We come to understand human relationships by encountering the other, by going beyond our own familiar ways of working through confusion, conflict, and change to see new pathways, new patterns, and perhaps new ways of creating peace.

Chapter One

Conflict: A Universal, Cultural, and Individual Process

There is no dipper which never strikes the kettle.
—Chinese proverb

UNIVERSAL INSIGHT
(The Bottom Line)

Conflict is a crisis that forces us to recognize explicitly that we live with multiple realities and must negotiate a common reality; that we bring to each situation differing — frequently contrasting — stories and must create together a single shared story with a role for each and for both.

FOLKTALE: THE PIG'S FLAT NOSE
AND THE BABOON'S BARE BUTTOCKS
Africa

Long ago, the pig and the baboon lived together on the hillsides. One day it was bitterly cold and a cutting wind was chilling them to the bone. As the pig and the baboon sat in the sun trying to get warm, the baboon turned to the pig and said, "This wind is enough to freeze one's nose off until it is a flat ugly stub." "Yes," said the pig, "it's really enough to freeze the hair off one's buttocks and leave a bare, dry patch."

"Look here," said the baboon crossly, "don't make personal remarks." "I did no such thing," replied the pig, "but you were rude to me first." This began a bitter quarrel and in the end they concluded that both despised the other's company, so they parted. The baboon went to the rocky ridges, the pig to the swampy lowlands, and there they remain to this day.

(Abrahams 1983, 191, adapted)

FOLKTALE: THE CREATION OF CONFUSION
Yoruba Tribe, West Africa

Once upon a time, two farmers were working their fields on either side of a road. As they worked they made friendly conversation across the road. Then Eshu, god of fate and lover of confusion, decided to upset the state of peace between them. He rubbed one side of his body with white chalk and the other with black charcoal and walked up the road with considerable flourish.

As soon as he passed beyond earshot, the two men jumped from their work at the same time. One said: "Did you notice that extraordinary white man who just went up the road?" In the same breath the other asked: "Did you see that incredible black man I have just seen?" In no time at all their friendly questions had turned into a violent quarrel and finally into a fight. As they fought they screamed, "He was white," or "He was black." Finally, exhausted, they returned to their fields in gloomy and hostile silence. No sooner had they settled down than Eshu returned and passed with greater flourish back down the road.

Immediately the two men sprang up again. "I am sorry, my good friend. You were right; the fellow is white." And in the same instant the other was saying: "I do apologize for my blindness. The man is indeed black, just as you said." And in no time again the two were quarreling and then fighting. As they fought they shouted this time, "I was wrong!" and "No, I was wrong!"

At last the two fighters were brought by their neighbors before the chief, where each told his story and insisted on his apology. The chief was dumbfounded. What confusion! Two men fight, then apologize, then fight over who dare apologize.

Then Eshu appeared and walked through the circle twice. At last he spoke: "Creating controversy and confusion is my favorite pastime."

(Achebe 1975, 20)

FOLKTALE: THE WISE ADVISER
Yoruba Tribe, West Africa

There was once a powerful king whose mad ambition was to rule without the advice of his elders. (Some people scratch out an eye because it itches.) The king did not realize that his strength came from the elders' wisdom. (After a man is cured he beats his doctor.)

The king called some ambitious young men, and said, "You have the brains and energy to rule the kingdom. Why sit and let your fathers talk? Go home, each of you, and kill your father, and come and have your share of the world." (The knife destroys its own house, thinking it is only an old sheath.)

The young men went home, and each killed his father. Except for one whose father said, "Spare my life. It is only in times of crisis that you will know how useful I am." (No one can appreciate his bottom until it has a boil.) So he hid his father in a remote hut.

The king kept his promise, and gave titles to the young men. But soon he grew weary of their interference and tired of their stupidity. So he called them all and said, "We shall build a new palace. All of you shall help. Any who refuse, shall die. To distinguish it from all other buildings, it shall start from the top down."

The young men were frightened, and did not know what to do. But the boy with a father went to his hiding place and told the story.

"What an old man can see sitting down, a young man can't see standing up," he said. Then he told him what to do.

The next day, when all had appeared at the building site in fear and trembling, the young man stepped forward. "Oh king," he said, "we are ready to begin the palace, but according to the custom, you, the king and landlord, must lay the first stone."

"Who taught you such wisdom?" asked the king, and the boy confessed that he had preserved his father. Then the king *called for the old man and installed him as the* bashorun, *saying: "Truly it is your wisdom that will guide my kingdom, for you see, seated, what we cannot see on our feet." And the old man replied, "It is the wisdom of the dead that prevents old men from making mistakes."*

(Gbadamosi and Beier 1968, 51–53, adapted)

Michel Foucault tells of a consciousness-shattering laughter that broke from him as he read a passage from Borges. The passage violated all the familiar landmarks of his thought, the thought that bears the stamp of our age and our geography. It broke up the ordered surfaces, the parallel planes with which we tame the wild profusion of things. It disturbed and threatened with collapse the age-old distinctions of *same* and *other*. Quoting Borges and then commenting upon the quoted material, Foucault writes:

In a "certain Chinese encyclopedia" it is written that "animals are divided into: (a) belonging to the Emperor, (b) embalmed, (c) tame, (d) suckling pigs, (e) sirens, (f) fabulous, (g) stray dogs, (h) included in the present classification, (i) frenzied, (j) innumerable, (k) drawn with a very fine camel hair brush, (l) *et cetera*, (m) having just broken the water pitcher, (n) that from a long way off look like flies." In the wonderment of this taxonomy, the thing that is demonstrated in the exotic charm of another system of thought, is the limitation of our own, the stark impossibility of thinking *that*. (Foucault 1970, xv)

What is it that arouses such conflict that it is impossible to think? Each of these categories can be assigned a precise meaning, a demonstrable content with distinct boundaries and with significant cultural referents and values. What transgresses the boundaries of our imagination, of our capacity to reason, is the alphabetical series (a, b, c, d) that links each of those categories to all the others. We cannot conceive of the context, the site, and the frame of reference that place these categories in sequential order. Yet a great culture existed that did so: "The fundamental codes of a culture — those governing its language, its schemas of perception, its exchanges, its techniques, its values, the hierarchy of its practices — establish for all of us, from the very first, the empirical orders with which we will be dealing and within which we will be at home" (Foucault 1970, xx).

Conflict exists in this tension between *same* and *other:* Conflict arises from the competition of *same* and *other;* conflict erupts as those who are *same* seek to control the *other* (and reduce its otherness), subordinate the other (and exploit its otherness), destroy the other (and annihilate its otherness), and exclude the other (escape from the threat of otherness).

But what if the other is necessary to us, part of us, completing us, redefining us, capable of transforming us? What if the other we fear is the bearer of our healing, our hope, and our health as a human race?

In this examination of conflict patterns across cultures, we will explore otherness and find within it both sameness and differentness, the surprise both of recognition and of the inconceivable and unknown. In the study of conflict we move into the mysterious sides of culture, the depths that are revealed in threat, emergency, competition, and confrontation.

Conflict practices and patterns are profoundly revelatory. They cut through the trunk of a culture and reveal the rings of its growth that in turn tell us much about the tiniest twig and the nethermost root. If we have some inkling of how a culture handles its conflicts, we are in touch with core values, with its roots and shoots.

Conflict provides an in-depth view of a culture's social construction of reality. When conflict situations are fully explored, they reveal that we live simultaneously in multiple frames of reference, multiple realities — superficial, social, psychic, elemental, and survival realities. In the conflicts of our social interactions, we must coordinate these multiple worlds and create connections between them.

Conflict is, at essence, the construction of a special type of reality. Most of the time we assume and take for granted that we share a single reality with others, but we do not. We simultaneously live in multiple realities. We accomplish this rather amazing feat because, "for all practical purposes, we assume we share a common definition of a situation with others at least sufficiently enough so that we can make sense of people and events in a coordinated fashion in order to act and respond appropriately. There are times, however, when our definitions clash, when suddenly we come to realize that what we assumed and took-for-granted was not shared by others" (Lederach 1988a, 38).

Suddenly, we are suspended in confusion. We must sift through the juxtaposed meanings in the search for a common meaning. "Conflict situations are those unique episodes when we explicitly recognize the existence of multiple realities and negotiate the creation of a common meaning" (Lederach 1988a, 39).

Social reality is constructed of networks of subjective realities; it may be defined as collective shared meaning. It is created by the interplay of consensus and conflict. As consensus breaks down, conflict emerges; as the conflict is resolved, a new consensus containing and reframing the old social reality emerges. The evolution of a culture's social reality, and each member's experience of it, unfolds through ongoing cycles of consensus, confusion, conflict, and clarification.

Among the trusted axioms of anthropology, Kluckholn's integrative statement of three levels of inquiry is a starting point for discussion of humanity, society, and personality: "Every individual is, in some respects, like all others, like some others, like no other" (Kluckholn and Murray 1948, 35). In parallel form, we can continue this hypothesis to affirm that every human conflict is, in some respects, like all others, like some others, and like no other. Conflicts are universally similar, culturally distinct, and individually unique — simultaneously, invariably, and intriguingly!

Universally, all humans experience anxiety and tension interpersonally, and live in some kind of network of fellow humans that experiences stresses and strains that result in conflict.

Culturally, all human groups have created their own pathways for channeling conflict. Since humans become more similar as we approach basic biological levels, we might expect some common-ality of interactions most affected by bodily arousal (anger, shame, fear), but this does not seem to be the case. Culture is, perhaps be-cause of the dangers these energies evoke, wonderfully varied in how even the most basic responses are expressed.

Individually, all human groups tend to have as much variation within as is found between groups, but the bell curve of cen-tral tendency shows accepted and nurtured patterns of behavior. Thus, there is a latitude of behavioral options possible in each per-son's developmental journey from childhood to maturity. When we speak of cultural groups and their conflict preferences, we must do it cautiously, heuristically, knowing that it is not accurately de-scriptive of persons but generally useful to understand tendencies, preferences, customs, and accepted practices.

CONFLICT IS UNIVERSAL

> The brass ladle now and then hits the iron pot.
> — Chinese proverb

Conflict is universal yet distinct in every culture; it is common to all persons yet experienced uniquely by every individual. These puzzling universals, these surprising cultural distinctions, these fascinating individual uniquenesses are the mysteries of human relationship explored in this study. The contributions and contra-dictions in the ways different cultures manage tensions will be gathered as we seek to discover patterns of resolution in its many and diverse forms.

Conflict is a visible sign of human energy; it is the evidence of human urgency; it is the result of competitive striving for the same goals, rights, and resources. Although it is a basic concern of all per-sons in all cultures, the literature on the nature of conflict patterns within (and thus between) cultures is surprisingly sparse. Perhaps the most universally practiced response to conflict — avoidance and denial — has limited both our behaviors while in conflict and our research on its nature and dynamics during the quiet periods of reflection that lie between its eruptions.

In many cultures, what counsel there is on how to manage differences is found in proverbs quoted, stories told, and cases recalled. Conflict theory is not easy to find, although the pathways for handling disputes, the processes of coping with power differentials, the role of mediator and go-between, and the means of achieving mutually satisfactory settlements are well known in particular societies.

Disputes, within groups and between theories, are found universally in human society, but the cultural variety of types, styles, patterns, and lengths of disputes, the contrasts in forms and significance, offer a rich field for seeking out commonalities and contrasts.

Disputes are not only universal; they also appear to be an inevitable and normal part of human existence, although they are sometimes destructive and sometimes constructive. Convergent and divergent currents among members flow through the most harmonious groups. If a group were found in which such ebb, flow, and counterflow did not exist, it would show no discernible life process.

But the patterns of dispute are a study in contrasts, as are the values that they express. In one society, unwelcome words or deeds may be met with immediate violence, in another with covert attack through sorcery or witchcraft or curse, while a third moves toward compromise or conciliation. In some, a wrong requires retaliation, in others, restraint. In one group, honor is regained by revenge; in another, honor is lost in retaliation since it lowers the avenger to the level of the offender.

The patterns of third-party involvement differ widely, indeed wildly: warn the wrongdoer on consequences or costs if the act is repeated, shame the offender with ridicule by public exposure and mimicry, cut off all association and cooperation as punishment, divert attention by raising a second conflict, channel the conflict into institutional or ritual pathways, initiate a go-between process of negotiation, summon a kinship group for violent retaliation, and so on and on. The goals of third-party intervention are many: support for one party, neutral assistance to both, destruction or execution of the wrongdoer, the return of equal injury, exact compensation, reduction of tension, modification of future behavior, restoration of harmony, or some other desired outcome.

In retaliation, an eye for an eye may be immediate in one society, or delayed in another. The East African Gisu wait to avenge the murder of a son until the son of the killer is of equal age of the man killed. Then the kinsmen strike (Roberts 1979, 37). Or retaliation may be contained and restricted by tribal rituals. The Minj-Wahqi peoples of western New Guinea deal with disputes between two kinship groups by use of an institution called the *tagba boz*. Members of opposing groups form lines with their hands clasped behind their backs and kick each other's shins until one side withdraws (Reay 1974, 198). The Eskimos practice a similar ritual in a buffeting contest. Two men in a dispute meet before an audience at a public gathering place and deliver alternate straight-arm blows to each other's heads until one is knocked down or yields. A variation is headbutting in which the disputants sit opposite each other and butt heads until one is unseated by the impact and thus ends the bout (Weyer 1932, 293). The Eskimo *nith*-song contest offers a vocal, not violent, dispute-resolution process. The two disputants confront each other before the assembled community and voice their grievances through the media of songs and dances improvised for the "trial." The accuser opens with a song pouring out all the abuse and rage felt; then the accused responds in musical ventilation. The antiphonal debate continues until the contestants are exhausted. The winner is given public acclaim for superior vocal, vituperative, or poetic skill (Weyer 1932, 226). Song contests, such as Wagner celebrated in *Tannhäuser* and *Die Meistersinger*, are found in other cultures as well. The Tiv of eastern Nigeria are famous for their song disputes (Bohannan 1957, 142–44).

A common assumption among students of conflict is that the phenomenon of conflict, in its rich and varied forms, is an inevitable and universal feature of human groups. Wherever there are scarce resources, divided functions in society, different levels of power, competition for a limited supply of goods, status, valued roles, or power as an end in itself, there conflict will occur.

All human populations exhibit social conflicts. The twentieth century has proven to be the bloodiest of all centuries; the twenty-first promises to continue the basic processes that accelerated conflict in the previous century — industrialization, urbanization, and technicalization. All these encourage contact among people, competition between interests, increased visibility of inequities and injustices, and inertia in social institutions. "Since competition, contact and visibility are prerequisites for conflict, the mathematical possibilities of conflict increase both within and between societies under industrialization" (Mack 1965, 395).

Conflicts are endemic and will continue to be so for the future we can project from the recorded past. Eliminating conflict is clearly impossible, and likely undesirable, because of the close link between conflict and creative, constructive change. Limiting conflict is undeniably necessary, inescapably crucial to our future on this planet, and inevitably a central agenda for all disciplines — economics, anthropology, psychology, political science, theology, education. It must be a central agenda for the next century.

Exploring differing perceptions of conflict within and between cultures is one small part of this larger agenda, but a part that is important to the whole. Whether it has been neglected, avoided, or taken for granted, the study of conflict across cultures has only begun.

CONFLICT IS CULTURAL

Two anthropological classics by Colin Turnbull present polar contrasts in conflict patterns in two African groups.

In *The Forest People* Turnbull describes conflict practices among the pygmies of the Ituri forest in Zaire, a people he came to know and love in his journey into their cool and restful world of the jungle. What emerges is the utterly sensible way in which conflicts and disputes are dealt with. First, the pygmies show their emotions so that everyone knows where they stand. Second, they achieve a compromise. They need and want to get on well together: Cooperation is the key to pygmy society. One can expect it, demand it, and claim it, and one has to give it. The sense of belonging to a community is so strong that troublemakers are punished simply by being ridiculed, ignored, or, at worst, banished to the forest alone for several hours (Turnbull 1961).

In contrast, *The Mountain People* describes the IK, a society in crisis, its members slowly starving to death. Turnbull studied the people in the mountains that form the barren boundary between Uganda, Kenya, and Sudan. The callousness to each other, even to their own children, the stealing, the jeering at the dying, and the ignoring of cries for help show the decay of traditional social order and the increase in inhumanity in a situation of extreme circumstances — famine and starvation.

The contrasts are striking. The pygmies help a disabled girl to walk on crutches by making a game of it. All make crutches and chase each other on one leg. The IK lock a disturbed little girl away to starve to death. The one group is the reverse of the other, its shadow. And, in an awful and awesome way, they mirror, shadow, and illuminate possibilities in all humankind (Turnbull 1972).

From culture to culture, each has developed its unique patterns of managing differences and resolving disputes. Each constructs its repertoire of conflict behaviors, its hierarchy of values, its code of laws. The study of conflict patterns is the study of contrasts. Out of the same basic needs, fears, and hopes, humans have created ways of dealing with competition, frustration, and aggression that reverse and reflect each other and that would, if brought together, complete each other.

Custom and tradition create a "pool of habits" for a society (not unlike the gene pool of a family) that induces the society's members into complementary, reciprocal habits. As these interlock, they create mutually fulfilling relationships. Each culture invites a wide range of habits, personality styles, and behavioral patterns for use in times of calm or in situations of conflict; and each culture also prohibits and seeks to limit the exercise of what it considers undesirable or unacceptable behavior.

Virtually all societies have laws for limiting conflicts and for achieving legal resolution of differences. However, the Andaman Islanders are the classic example of a group without the most rudimentary elements of law, with no means of resolving disputes, and with no specific sanctions that may be brought to bear on one who injures others. Careful anthropological work among them indicated that there was considerable violence in the frequent quarrels, but no one possessed the authority to intervene. There was no accepted process to deal with conflict situations. The injured family might seek revenge, or the offender might hide out until it seemed safe to return (Radcliffe-Brown 1964, 48).

Among the Zuni Amerindians, few laws or conflict-resolution processes existed because the sanction against any and all controversy was so powerfully believed and practiced that conflict rarely occurred. Among the Zuni one is not to stand up for his or her rights, is looked down on if involved in any sort of conflict, and is complimented highly if it can be said he or she is "a nice polite person, no one ever hears anything from him, or she never gets into any difficulty" (Redfield 1964, 339).

Among the Andaman, the absence of conflict channels created anarchy. Among the Zuni, the same absence led to a strict social control of conformity and cooperation. In the one, all did what was right in their own and their kin group's eyes; in the other, no one dared even to mention a wrong or to seek to right it if inconvenienced.

Both of these cases represent rare exceptions. Among humans, retaliation, revenge, and a demand for repayment are the norm, and means of channeling and limiting conflict have evolved in patterns unique to each group. The principle of equivalent retaliation — *lex talionis* — is often the first line of social control or custom for restraining unlimited revenge. But this is altered in most societies by elements of distributive justice that move beyond retributive justice whether out of values of harmony, equality, solidarity, hierarchy, or equanimity.

What comprises a conflict in one culture is a daily difference of opinion in another. A serious insult in one setting — crossing one's legs or showing the sole of one's foot, for example — is a matter of comfort in another. An arrogant challenge in one culture — putting one's hands on one's hips — is a sign of openness in another. A normal pathway for de-escalating a conflict in one society — fleeing the scene of an accident — constitutes a serious offense in another. Human boundaries are cultural creations — social boundaries, legal boundaries, and emotional boundaries are all drawn according to each culture's values, myths, and preferences.

These rules and norms defining when conflict is acceptable, how it may be expressed acceptably, and with whom it may be pursued are among the most crucial learnings we need when venturing into cultures strange to us.

In stress, we all regress to our earlier learnings, and since defensive conflict behaviors were often learned in fragmented, distorted fashion from experiences of high anxiety and tension, they may be our least functional behaviors. Regression to the conflict patterns that did not serve us well, even in our own culture, is no solution for coping with new conflicts in a foreign situation. In addition, our own emergency moves may only bring out the worst in the other party in an altercation.

The practices of resolving differences within various cultures, and the ways of facilitating interactions between cultures, have received inadequate research and development as a field. Individual studies have been done with outstanding quality, but they have not been brought together as a discipline, a field of study. And, perhaps, few things are as important, as crucial, as utterly necessary in our world.

Conflict in one's own culture is invariably confusing, and culture assists us in establishing some basic ground rules. The confusion experienced when involved in a second culture's conflicts is so great that mediators, consultants, and counselors tend either to withdraw helplessly or plunge in heedlessly. It has been written that every social encounter is an imminent disaster. Cues get mixed, signals scrambled, people become angry, embarrassed, or reduced to inaction by the failure of scenarios to come off as planned. Culture minimizes this uncertainty by setting rules on how we should behave, how we should act, what we can expect in every situation.

Conflict in all cultures is characterized by multilevel communication, alternate movement between subtle cues and visible behaviors, intricate combinations of covert responses and overt reactions, ambivalent feelings and polarized perspectives, defensive strategies of concealment and offensive attempts to provoke a crisis, and so on. All these multifactorial, multilevel, multiple-meaning signals, cues, and behaviors leave the knowledgeable participant confused and the outsider confounded. Attempted intervention or mediation by one external to the culture inevitably misses cues, scrambles data, and confuses primary and secondary issues at best. At worst such an outsider utilizes tactics least likely to facilitate an opening of communication that will clarify differences and enable conciliation.

CONFLICT IS UNIVERSAL, CULTURAL, AND INDIVIDUAL

A professor from an Asian country, educated in Europe, is teaching in West Africa. He is struggling with disowning his cultural past and embracing Western ways. Psychologically compelled to disown the values and customs of his youth, he is alienated from anything resembling his home culture. The Islamic host culture, where he is teaching, strongly resembles his home culture, but the alienation stimulated by his student experience in western Europe impels him to defy local mores. He becomes sentimentally attached to a female pupil, who is also not a national of the country. In defiance of local conventions, the two meet in his public office. This inevitably attracts attention from students who regard this as an affront to their religion, which forbids anything resembling public display of lovemaking. There is an outcry. Authorities express their disapproval and the question of resignation or dismissal is raised. At this point, European expatriates, who see nothing inappropriate with expressions of love in a quasi-public situation, indignantly organize a petition. This is perceived by the local community as defiance of and an attack on their standards of behavior. This only ensures the maximum penalties for the offender. In view of the publicity, no compromise or mitigation can now be arranged. Both sides have reached a state of intense mutual irritation that is culturally rooted, contextually blind, and totally unnecessary. The intransigence of the foreigners, with their imported attitudes, has only increased the difficulties for those who hold the prevailing opinion in the host culture (Daniel 1975, 70).

The individual rebellion of the lovers against the cultural expectations of the host country triggered individual expatriates to import their cultural values. A universal situation of adjustment to contextual conventions had now become a conflict on all three levels — for the host culture, for the strangers, and for the couple at the center of the controversy.

Doubtless all three levels can be identified in any human conflict. The danger lies in our making one or both of the following assumptions that were made by the expatriates: (1) the universal of loving relationships is more important than the cultural issues of social appearances, courtship rituals, and sanctions on male-female interaction; (2) the Western romantic notion of "affairs of the heart" justifies all, offering at least extenuating circumstances for overlooking an individual violation of public protocol.

This conflict (or compatibility) of values between the individual and the society is a complex, dynamic process. Every individual, group, community, society, and embracing culture holds a set of values that are ranked, prized, and obeyed. Each person's world of values exists within these surrounding value fields. All persons order their own value commitments with reference to the values of their group, which in turn is located within the value structures of the community. But each person ranks even commonly held values with different degrees of importance, so each is at the same time culturally similar to other members of the group and culturally unique.

A citizen of the United States may live in a culture that prizes individualism, equality, democracy, free speech, free enterprise, freedom of religion, tolerance of others, and pluralism of values while also belonging to a group that affirms individualism and equality for males and dependency and submission to hierarchy for females.

By use of multiple overlapping ellipses (fig. 2), Marshall Singer offers a picture of the complexity of values created by membership in multiple identity groups. Two persons, Mary and Margaret, members of the same culture and sharing almost identical group affiliations, are at the same time culturally similar and culturally unique. Although each is at the confluence of twelve specific identity groups (each group possessing a culture of its own within a common cultural field), each creates her world of values and thus her world of perceptions in her own unique way.

Each person is a member of a unique configuration of groups,

Figure 2
Values and Multiple Identity Groups

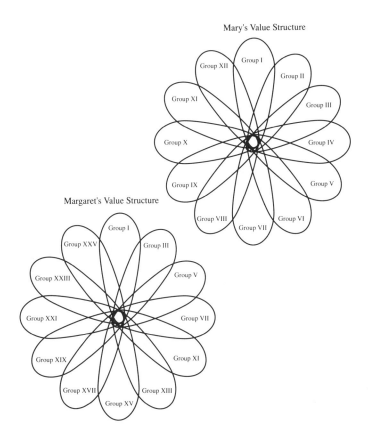

(Singer 1987, 23–24)

with an individually ordered value system that (1) ranks commitments to the particular groups, (2) ranks the values shared with each group, and (3) selects from the values of each group to form an individual value system. Every person stands at the confluence of such identity groups and perceives, orders, ranks, and prizes group values in her or his own way. Since each group has a culture of its own, each person is multicultural in identity. So each is culturally unique. A colleague belonging to the same series of groups would have a different order, preference, and construction of reality and identity.

CONFLICT: WHERE, WHY, WHAT, WHICH?

In a brief overview of contrasting conflict patterns across cultures, several crucial factors may be noted at the outset. We shall discuss these under the questions of where, why, what, and which.

First, the *where*. The context in which a conflict erupts or lies dormant may have high or low influence on its development and final direction. In cultures with low contextual influence, the individual shapes and determines the major part of the process; in settings where there is high contextual influence, the conflict interaction unfolds according to cultural and social controls.

Individualistic (low-context) cultures prefer directness, specificity, frankness in stating demands, confrontation, and open self-disclosure. Collectivistic (high-context) cultures tend toward indirect, ambiguous, cautious, nonconfrontational, and subtle ways of working through communication and relational tangles.

If a North American supervisor is unsatisfied with a subordinate's sales proposal, the response will probably be explicit, direct, pointed: "I can't accept this proposal as submitted, so come up with some better ideas." A Japanese supervisor, in the same situation, might say: "While I have the highest regard for your abilities, I regret to inform you that I am not completely satisfied with this proposal. I must ask that you reflect further and submit additional ideas on how to develop this sales program."

Tactfulness and indirect speech are valued in high-context cultures, while openness and directness are preferred in a low-context setting. As a result, a calculated degree of vagueness and circumlocution is employed as anxiety rises in the former; a spontaneous frankness or bluntness in confrontation signals mounting tension in the latter.

In a low-context culture — such as the United States — a conflict is more likely to be seen as a one-to-one difference. The opponents will seek to fractionate the conflict into the smallest possible slice of interaction. "The behavior you did was.... Its impact on me is.... And when you do this I feel...." Such linear and instrumental definitions of cause and effect seek to isolate the particular transaction and request an adjustment of behaviors. In a high-context culture — such as China — a conflict is experienced as a characteristic of ongoing relationships in a less mobile, more permanent and given context that cannot be readily left behind, challenged, or changed. Thus instrumental strategies are less appropriate. Since everything is related to everything else in the setting, a conflict tends to be seen in holistic terms. The causes and effects become virtually interchangeable. The logic is correlational in a spiral of associations and contrasts, connections and distinctions. The function of conflict, usually expressed through a third party or parties, is expressive and ventilating — a discharge of tension and frustrations allowing some readjustment and relaxation.

The second factor, the *why* (that is, the reason for the conflict), will differ sharply from one culture to another. Dividing conflicts between those that are *expressive* and those that are *instrumental* will sharpen the contrast. Expressive conflicts arise from a desire to release tension, to express frustration, and to discharge emotion and are usually generated from hostile or negative feelings. Instrumental conflicts arise from a difference in pathways or goals; they are directed toward actual ends and press for visible outcomes. Now the contrast: Members of individualistic, low-context cultures are more likely to perceive conflict as instrumental, while members of more collective, high-context cultures are more likely to perceive conflict as expressive. Strongly contextual persons are more sensitive to the interpersonal *meaning* of words and acts and more likely to assess their personal implications.

Triggering events for conflicts in different cultures are often sharply different. In Western cultures, conflict is more likely to be stimulated by an *individual offense;* in Eastern or third world cultures, the triggering event is often an act causing a *group offense.* As Stella Ting-Toomey argues, in low-context, individualistic cultures, it is the individual's expectations of what is appropriate behavior that, when violated, provoke conflict. These are likely to be overlooked in a high-context culture. But when a high-context group's normative expectations of accepted behavior are violated, then a legitimate conflict is allowed to emerge. In a high-context culture, the context plays a crucial role in providing meaning to and interpretation for all communication. In a low-context culture, the meaning must be specified by the message, so more information is given in the interchange. The less important the context, the more often conflict will be attached to actual interpersonal violations of individuals. But when the context is highly important, then collective, normative expectations must be honored, not ignored. Violations of group ethos are not overlooked; their meanings are read, their impact felt, their consequences dealt with.

In a Western setting, people in conflict say things like: "I am responsible only for myself, my perceptions, my feelings, my thoughts, my actions, and the consequences that follow." The opponent is equally responsible for hers or his. In a conflict, other members of the group need permission "to interfere." A difference is caused by another intruding into one's zone, one's privacy, one's area of responsibility. This violation of emotional, physical, or functional boundaries must be challenged, the cause identified, the situation corrected. Whether others agree is secondary; the person's subjective feeling of violation must be resolved.

In a high-context setting, such as Japan, an individual inconvenience will more likely be ignored, but as a person's behavior comes into conflict with group values, it will be engaged. On a Tokyo street, one pedestrian will rarely cross against the traffic signal, but a group walking together will disobey it readily.

In a low-context setting, one expects the necessary information to be supplied in any message. If the required details are not specified, the messenger is at fault. In a high-context setting, the sender and receiver are equally active. The host is aware of the guest's needs and offers the appropriate response without request. To ask for specification — "Would you like coffee or tea? cream or sugar? lemon?" — is an affront. One knows from the context what is appropriate and offers it without question. The gift is received without equivocation. When conflict occurs, the contextual data are assimilated with the content of communication, so the triggering event will be less a particular offense, more a sequence of situational, relational, and communal circumstances.

> People raised in high-context systems expect more of others than do the participants in low-context systems. When talking about something that they have on their minds, a high-context individual will expect his interlocutor to know what's bothering him, so that he doesn't have to be specific. The result is that he will talk around and around the point, in effect putting all the pieces in place except the crucial one. Placing it properly — this keystone — is the role of his interlocutor. (Hall 1976, 98)

In a high-context setting a rich and elaborate code system of metaphor and simile may communicate arguments with complex and colorful rhetorical content that serves profound social purposes. Such multilevel communication that utilizes metaphor to offer covert criticism is recorded by Evans-Pritchard from the Azande:

> A man says in the presence of his wife to his friend, "friend, those swallows, how they flit about there." He is speaking about the flightiness of his wife and in case she should understand the allusion, he covers himself by looking up at the swallows as he makes his seemingly innocent remark. His friend understands what he means and replies, "yes, sir, do not talk to me about those swallows, how they come here, sir!" (What you say is only too true.) His wife, however, also understands what he means and says tartly, "yes, sir, you leave that she (wife) to take a good she (wife), sir, since you married a swallow, sir!" (Marry someone else if that is the way you feel about it.) The husband looks surprised and pained that his wife should take umbrage at a harmless remark about swallows. He says to her, "does one get touchy about what is above (swallows), madam?" She replies, "ai, sir. Deceiving me is not agreeable to me. You speak about me. You will fall from my tree." The sense of this reply is "you are a fool to try and deceive me in my presence. It is me you speak

about and you are always going at me. I will run away and
something will happen to you when you try and follow me."
(Evans-Pritchard 1963, 211)

Rhetoric, the skill of using language to produce an impression
on the listener, is an art in high-context groups. Among the ancient
Chinese, the eloquent person was described by the terse proverb:
"Leaves mouth, becomes literature." African Americans have created a rhetoric of verbal skills and signs that define identity and
clarify boundary lines in community.

Many cultures do not separate rhetoric and logic, metaphor
and fact. The alternation between them may serve, as in the
Azande case cited, to avoid confrontation while communicating
indirectly, yet with impact.

The third factor, *what* the attitude and action of the participants
will be, is in stark contrast as to *what* is done with the emerging
conflict in different cultures. People in individualistic, low-context
cultures are much more likely to utilize a confrontational, direct-
address, one-to-one negotiating style, or at least believe that that
is the final way to resolve differences; people in high-context
cultures are more likely to possess a nonconfrontational, indirect, triangular resolution style. The factors involved here are
multiple, complex, and intertwined. High-context group values
of harmony, solidarity, interdependence, honor, and the maintaining of face, hierarchy, and status differentials contrast with
low-context values of individualism, autonomy, independence,
self-reliance, self-esteem, equality, and egalitarianism.

Interpersonal conflicts, in Western cultures, are seen as dyadic
issues that must ultimately be resolved by the two parties involved, and preferably without a mediator. Confrontation skills,
self-disclosure capacities, assertiveness in expressing demands,
flexibility in negotiation, and adaptability in compromise and collaboration are all highly valued. Deficits in any of these capabilities
protract the conflict and create secondary complications in the relationship. Direct address regarding difficulties and direct redress
of differences are seen as evidence of interpersonal-relationship
skills and personal maturity. The incorporation of third parties
in the early stages of a conflict is seen as avoidance of the other

party, as indication of unmanageable anxiety, as personal insecurity, or as a coercive strategy of colluding to gain support or power. Third-party resolutions are seen as appropriate when communication is blocked, the relationship has deteriorated, or the conflict is intransigent. The immediate common-sense reflex of Westerners is to confront the other party immediately, express demands assertively, and seek resolution directly.

In most of the cultures of the third world, such behavior is not only dysfunctional; it is considered maladaptive, and pragmatically endangers all hopes of resolving the conflict productively.

Third-party negotiations are a highly developed art in some cultures, a life-saving necessity in others, and a face-saving strategy in still more. They offer objectivity, emotional distance, protection of face and honor, a time delay to allow emotions to cool, mediation and negotiation skills, the experience of the larger community, balancing of power differentials, and witnesses to attest to the genuineness of the process and its appropriate resolution and termination.

A fourth factor in conflict styles is *which* pattern of communication persons use in dealing with differences. Three basic and pervasive styles used to resolve conflicts have been defined in research by Glenn, Witmeyer, and Stevenson (1977) as: factual-inductive (used by the scientist), axiomatic-deductive (used by the traditionalist), and affective-intuitive (used by the artist).

The *factual-inductive* method begins with the visible data and selection of important facts and inductively moves toward a conclusion in linear, sequential reasoning based on logical inferences.

The *axiomatic-deductive* method begins with a general principle or value and deduces the implications for specific situations. It seeks to apply a value that is held to be important and applicable to the given situation.

The *affective-intuitive* method is based on relational, emotional, and personal perceptions of the situation and on the hunches that arise from these perceptions.

Glenn and associates conclude that the factual-inductive method is the one most valued in Western cultures, where scientific methodology is seen as approximating truth. They observe that the other two styles predominate in what was the Soviet

Figure 3
Graphic Representations of Thought Processes
of Linguistic Groups

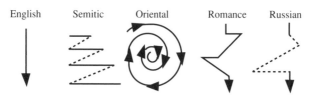

English   Semitic   Oriental   Romance   Russian

(Kaplan 1966, 15)

Union. Ting-Toomey argues that all low-context cultures tend to prefer and use the factual-inductive approach first and the axiomatic-deductive style second. But members of high-context cultures "are more likely to use affective-intuitive styles in conflict" (Ting-Toomey 1982, 11).

Conflict styles are also shaped by the choice of a pattern of logic and perception. Low-context cultures tend to use analytic, linear, sequential logic to define situations, while high-context cultures are more likely to use holistic, spiral, correlational logic (Ting-Toomey 1982, 8).

In an interesting article on the thought processes of different linguistic groups, Robert B. Kaplan observes that while English writing — and thinking — is linear (a statement with almost unanimous agreement among logicians, linguists, anthropologists, and other scholars), those who speak and write Semitic languages (Arabic and Hebrew) seem to use various kinds of parallels in their thinking, and the writing and thinking of Chinese and Koreans (whom Kaplan lumps together as Orientals in his study) are marked by indirection. Kaplan has graphically represented the major groups he studies (see fig. 3). One must not fall into believing that *all* Chinese and Koreans think by a process of indirection, that *all* English-speaking people think in a linear manner all of the time, and so on, yet the fact is that most probably do, much of the time.

Even within the linear-logic group, the processes may be strikingly different. Americans are known to prefer inductive reason, starting with the specific data and drawing inferences from them. Europeans, in contrast, prefer to reason deductively, beginning with a total logical or theoretical conceptualization and then reasoning from that logical construct, drawing in data only where they are appropriate to the logical argument. When two individuals in conflict prefer differing styles of reasoning, there will inevitably be greater misunderstanding and discontent with each other.

MEDI-ETIC OR MEDI-EMIC MEDIATION?

Mediation may be an imported process, a catered affair. It may bring theory, methodology, and praxis from another culture, another vocabulary, another world of thought.

Or mediation may begin with, build on, and construct from local insight, understanding, and experience. One can cook with local peppers knowing that they suit the palate better.

The starting point for understanding any particular person, group, or culture can be from within, utilizing the indigenous language or frame of reference; or from without, through application of structures and perspectives from other cultures. These two approaches are referred to as "emic" and "etic" in anthropological parlance (see table 1).

The "emic" approach describes a cultural phenomenon in terms of its own units. The "etic" approach imposes categories that are external to the phenomenon. For example, the Lakalai of New Britain have an ethno-psychology that categorizes people into distinct binary pairs contrasting "men of anger" with "men of shame," or "men of play" with "men of silence." These are clear emic categories. If, however, one sought to equate these with Western typologies and to combine the two systems, then one has constructed an etic structure; if one correlates two distinct emic systems, each can retain its own integrity (Valentine 1963, 441–47).

The mediator who takes an emic approach to understanding a conflict or dispute (a medi-emic mediator) bases all work on the assumption that the local understandings of conflict — the local language used to describe its process, the local pathways or strate-

Table 1
Comparison of Medi-emic and Medi-etic Mediation

MEDI-EMIC MEDIATION	MEDI-ETIC MEDIATION
("Emic" is taken from the linguistic designation "phonemics," which refers to a culturally unique vocal utterance.)	("Etic" is taken from the linguistic designation "phonetics," which refers to universal vocal utterances.)
In anthropology, "emic" refers to a unique concept, construct, or idea present in a given culture and not defined by the language or experience of another culture. It emerges internally, inherently, intrinsically from those in the situation.	In anthropology, "etic" refers to a concept, construct, or idea that is recognized and can be demonstrated as a universal or transcultural entity. It is etic because it is applied from without, externally and extrinsically, by those observing the situation.
IN MEDIATION:	IN MEDIATION:
In a medi-emic approach the mediator functions as a listener, learner, facilitator, mirror, and catalyst and observes the conflict patterns already in use. The mediator learns from the conflict wisdom of the culture; facilitates the clarification and implementation of these patterns in particular cases; mirrors what is taking place for the participants' evaluation and further development; and participates in the creation of further patterns that extend and enhance the traditional pathways for conflict resolution.	In a medi-etic approach the mediator brings a theory of conflict, a set of conflict models, and a fund of knowledge and practices for conflict management that are believed to be applicable cross-culturally. These models, theories, and processes are translated or transferred by teaching participants, opponents, or trainee mediators to acculturate and implement the mediation or resolution strategy.
CHARACTERISTICS:	CHARACTERISTICS:
Begins from unawareness. Works inductively, descriptively. Increases consciousness of trustworthy patterns. Discovers methodology and reinforces its use and refinement.	Begins from expertise. Works deductively, prescriptively. Provides information and demonstrates new models. Imports methodology and imparts the necessary skills.

gies for managing the conflict — are superior to any imported understandings, language, or pathways.

The medi-etic consultant or trainer tends to prefer the more "formal process" and "the specialist role" and thus intervenes through a structured setting, process, time frame, and final contract. These tend to be processes adapted from patterns of modern legal custom and are similar from one culture to another. The specialist intervenes as a neutral outsider bringing objective methodology and expertise.

Intercultural mediation trainer John Paul Lederach reports an intriguing experience in Metapán, El Salvador, that illustrates a medi-emic or, as he calls it, an "elicitive" approach.

"Are they talking?" a trainee asked twice about a role-play assignment of two neighbors who were "all entangled," as the Latin Americans say. When told, "No, they are not talking," he said to his co-mediator, "We better meet alone with each of them; they aren't talking." Then it dawned on the trainer that "they are not talking" was a common-sense (i.e., North American) category for a particular conflict stage in a Latin American setting. The trainee, thinking along the lines of a North American mediator, was using the category to locate the conflict and decide what the next steps should be for go-betweens.

> As we move in and out of a variety of contexts and cultures, our "trainer talk" can become an obstacle. I must remain open to new, more "appropriate" language. In Panama, after my first day of training, someone said that mediators were like "guides" leading people through complexities. The image stuck. By the end of the week, we almost never spoke of "mediators" and "mediation," but rather of "guides" and the "process of guiding." Language is not merely a means of communicating, but is an essential feature of the conflict experience. (Lederach 1988b, 10)

Lederach's approach model, in the language we are using, is a medi-emic approach that calls forth the cultural patterns and seeks to develop the alternate models implicit or explicit within the culture's norms and values. As Lederach concludes:

"Training" is not the transfer of knowledge, but rather its creation. We should aim to create an atmosphere in which the participants' own know-how about conflict is raised to an explicit level and can be used as a basis for constructing appropriate intervention models for the problems they face in their context. The model is not transferred; it is created. It is not prescriptive; it is elicitive. This is an especially important notion in cross-cultural settings, but also in work in one's own culture. (Lederach 1988b, 11)

When the mediator suspends or brackets the categories of his or her parent culture in the attempt to understand persons from another culture "emically," there is an unfolding process of perception, adjustment of what is found to be etic, renewed perception, and correction to move toward understanding what is truly emic. J. W. Berry describes such attempts:

Modification of our external categories must ... be made in the direction of the system under study, until we eventually achieve a truly emic description of behavior within that culture. That is, an emic description can be made by progressively altering the imposed etic until it matches a purely emic point of view; if this can be done without entirely destroying or losing all of the etic character of the entry categories, then we can proceed to the next step. If some of the etic is left, we can now note the categories or concepts which are shared by the behavior system we knew previously and the one we have just come to understand emically. We can now set up a derived etic which is valid for making comparisons between two behavior settings and we have essentially resolved the problem of obtaining a descriptive framework valid for comparing behavior across behavioral settings. (Berry 1966, 124)

The interpathic moderator seeks to begin from the counselee's culture and to observe the emic categories present within it. Correlation with one's own categories can follow with the likelihood of decreased distortion from external labels. The ongoing internal dialogue of interpathic listening alternates between perception and reflection, apprehension and attempted comprehension, accommodation to the new situation and assimilation into one's own means of constructing meanings.

> In every culture, social phenomena such as conflict have unique configurations of meaning. Two conflicts may seem similar in one culture but not in another. In view of this problem of cross-cultural relativity in the perception of conflict, one should regard with great caution superficial comparisons of the cumulative level of tensions and conflict in different societies. Harmony may be observed where there is, in fact, deep-seated antagonism. The emotional, verbal, and behavioral cues for signaling conflict are so different between cultures that outside observers may easily misjudge the intensity and character of conflict. (Krauss, Rohlen, and Steinhoff 1984, 10–11)

Although a consultant, development worker, or mediator may work infrequently as a conflict consultant in transcultural conflicts, there is no escape from involvement in interpersonal, marital, familial, and communal conflicts as they impinge on those being counseled. The growth of the counselee invariably results in the acquisition of new conflict behaviors, new interpersonal coping strategies, and new willingness to risk in larger conflict situations. Thus the conflict skills of the mediator and the awareness of the dynamics of conflicts on intrapersonal, interpersonal, intragroup, and intergroup levels — and beyond — are crucially important.

Methodologies and theories that are assumed helpful in one part of the world are useless in another. Assertiveness training, a popular methodology for growth from passive conflict behaviors to active negotiation, is widely used in Western countries and in urban settings in the third world. Its use, even in the West, has serious liabilities unless the assertiveness is balanced with an equal affirmativeness (Faul and Augsburger 1978). In many settings, it is counterproductive since a much more cautious, flexible, and affiliative approach is demanded by cultural values and practices.

The cross-cultural educator, mediator, consultant, or counselor must assess the appropriateness of any conflict model that includes confrontation, direct address on differences, self-disclosure of feelings, fair-fight training skills, and utilization of open-anger and individualistic conflict-management strategies, since each of these has strengths and weaknesses that may be exaggerated in a particular cultural situation. We shall explore and illustrate some of the significant contrasts in conflict styles and behaviors across various cultures in succeeding chapters. The goal is to stimulate self-reflection on one's own conflict assumptions and their cultural embeddedness, and to raise consciousness on the appropriateness and effectiveness of responses in other cultures that one might perceive as dysfunctional in one's own context.

CASE: WHO WILL PAY THE PIPER?
Guatemala

In the mountains of Guatemala, near Lake Atitlán, lived a retired American businessman named Sam Green. He had worked in Guatemala for his business career, and had fallen in love with the land and its people. He had learned the language, culture, and reality world of the Indians in his region and spent his evenings in the villages talking with people of their needs and dreams. He discovered that a major problem in meeting their basic needs — health, safety, food, security — was the lack of capital, so he set up a loan process to supply small loans for basic projects — building, digging a well, medical care. The schedule of payments was low, the process was by word of agreement, and the repayment record was 100 percent. He called it the Penny Foundation.

When Green returned from a visit to the United States, he was approached by a Guatemalan official for help in mediating a conflict. A village well had gone dry in an Indian community, so the government had arranged to pipe water from a neighboring village, and imposed a water tax to cover the costs. The villagers who had agreed to pay back the government for its help now refused to pay. Green agreed to mediate and rode out to the village to listen to the villagers' perspective.

"Yes, the well went dry," they said. "It was an act of God.

Now the government is attempting to charge us for water when everyone knows that God gives us the water free."

"Of course the water is free," agreed Green, "but the pipes are expensive. Would you agree to pay the government by installments for the pipes and their installation?"

The villagers had no objection to paying for the pipe, and the conflict was resolved.

(Singer 1987, 33–34, abridged)

Chapter Two

Conflict: Creative or Destructive Dynamics?

If you haven't fought with each other, you do not know each other.

— Chinese proverb

UNIVERSAL INSIGHT
(The Bottom Line)

"The harmful and dangerous elements [of any conflict situation] will drive out those which would keep the conflict within bounds" (Coleman 1957, 14). Hence, a destructive conflict needs containment; a confusing conflict requires clarification; a creative conflict can be utilized; all conflicts require transformation that does not eliminate or control the conflict, but channels, alters, and ultimately transforms the relationship.

FOLKTALE: WISDOM OF THE MEDIATOR
Trinidad

Once upon a time there was a poor devout man with an old, blind mother and a bitter, barren wife. His life was miserable, so each morning he rose early and went to the temple to pray for the blessing of God to relieve his family's suffering.

After twelve years of prayer, he heard a voice — the voice of God. "What one thing do you desire?" "I don't know," he said. "I really didn't expect you to ask. Do you mind if I go home and ask my mother and my wife?"

After receiving permission, he ran home, and first met his mother.

"Son, if you will ask God to restore my eyes so that I may see again, you will never be indebted to me for anything."

Then the man went to his wife and told her of God's promise. "Forget your mother; she is old; she will soon close her eyes for the last time. Ask for a son who may care for us, and perhaps bring us wealth."

The mother was listening, and she came with her cane and began to beat the wife. "No, it must be my eyesight." The wife fought back, pulling her hair, and a terrible fight ensued.

The poor man ran from the house to a wise adviser, an old man who had mediated many conflicts, and he told him his dilemma. "My mother wants eyesight, my wife wants a son, and I, I wish for a bit of money so we can eat everyday. What shall I ask? Whose needs come first?"

The adviser thought for a moment, then he answered: "Ah, my friend, you must not choose for any one of your family alone, but for the good of all. Although you may ask only one thing of God, ask wisely. Tomorrow morning you shall say,

'Oh Lord, I ask nothing for myself; my wife seeks nothing for herself; but my mother is blind, and her desire is, before she dies, to see her grandson eating milk and rice from a golden bowl.'"

(Dorson 1975, 511–13, abridged)

FOLK HISTORY: AINU WISDOM
Japan

In Hokkaido, the northernmost island of Japan, two Ainu tribes confronted each other across the shallows of the Saru River (also called Nupumatsu). The Ainu from that area (the Saru Ainu), from the village of Pipaushi, were a gentle, peaceful, and eloquent people. They lived on salmon, venison, and the trading of their fish and meat with the Japanese in the larger island to the south. Through trading they possessed a wealth of steel knives, axes, swords, and lacquer ware.

The Ainu from the Tokachi River, who lived far to the north, learned of this wealth and came attacking the peaceful people of Pipaushi.

When the villagers learned of the threat, they brought out their bows and arrows. These arrows, tipped with poison made from the root of the Torikabuto plant, and the bows were used only for the killing of bear and deer. So the men begged the understanding of the god who forbade use of their weapons against fellow humans, and leaving women and children in the village, they went out to face the invaders.

The Ainu custom first ruled that a charanke (negotiation) be held to show valid reason for the attack. The Tokachi Ainu presented a series of pretexts and rationales for their action. Both sides sent forward their most eloquent speakers. If either side could out talk the opponent, treasures could be demanded without battle. If neither prevailed, violence would follow. For three days and nights charanke *continued with no advantage for either side.*

In the village of Pipaushi lived Pikumueashi, the most eloquent person along the Saru River, but he was so old he could not stand or walk by himself and no one was allowed to address the charanke *without standing in the center of the two opposing forces. So one of the young men stepped forward with Pikumueashi on his shoulders. From the mouth of the old man poured such eloquence, as if a stream gushed out from a volcanic geyser in Akan. The voice of Pikumueashi rang with power and clarity. It seemed inconceivable that it issued from the gnarled man on the back of the youth.*

Hear me, O men from Tokachi. As you journeyed through the mountains from your distant land, you passed through the shadow of the great mountain Poroshiri. Two rivers spring from its twin peaks and create the Saru and the Tokachi rivers. These rivers, our own rivers, rise from a common source. We have shared one mother. You have drunk at one breast and we at the other. If this be so, then we are brothers. My brothers, why should we fight for no reason? Put up your swords, throw down your bows and arrows. Let there be peace between us.

As the Tokachi Ainu heard his words, they melted. "We have the same mother, we drink from the same breasts, we are brothers by birth," they said, and prepared to withdraw without bloodshed. Then the Saru Ainu brought out gifts of value, knives and lacquer ware, as gifts of peace, and the two tribes became friends.

When the Ainu teach their children they say: "Remember, no matter how well a sword may cut, or how strong the poison on your arrow tips, there is no weapon as powerful as the spoken word. Become people who speak eloquently and listen carefully. Those who make great efforts at talking through conflicts need never fight useless battles." This is what the Ainu children are taught.

(Kayano 1966)

"If you haven't fought with each other, you do not know each other." This Chinese proverb is likely to be interpreted in very different ways by Eastern and Western cultures. From a Western bias it promises deeper encounter and fuller understanding of the other as a positive benefit of conflict; from the oriental perspective, it is a warning that conflict reveals the negative side of the person when "face" is torn away.

Both of these attitudes exist in every culture; humans are ambivalent about conflict; conflict creates ambivalent feelings in human beings; the ambivalence creates conflict itself. Perfect circle. Ambivalence has many faces:

Will collaboration result in competition or cooperation?
Will competition trigger win-lose or win-win attitudes?
Will conflict connect us or reveal irreconcilable differences?
Will anxiety improve performance or frustrate it?
Will tensions alienate or affiliate a group?
Will the process go into a negative or positive spiral?
Will the conflict turn destructive or constructive?

No unified theory exists for examining conflict patterns in contrasting cultures, and a single paradigm that seeks to integrate the great variety would be of limited use. However, multiple models will help map out similarities in process, pathways, and problem-solving patterns.

CONSTRUCTIVE OR DESTRUCTIVE CONFLICT?

A conflict is destructive — has destructive consequences — if the participants in it are dissatisfied with the outcomes and all feel they have lost as a result of the conflict.

A conflict is constructive in its process and consequences if all participants are satisfied with the outcome and feel that they have gained as a result of the conflict. The more equally participant groups are satisfied, the more constructive the conflict (Deutsch 1969, 10).

This is clearly a value-laden judgment. The teleological value of "the pricing of constructive ends," the utilitarian value of "the greatest good to the greatest number," and the deontological value of "what extends justice in equal distribution" are being utilized to differentiate constructive and destructive processes (Augsburger 1986, 250).

The two directions of conflict can be defined operationally by examining its characteristic patterns. Productive conflict has four basic characteristics. The individuals or the groups are able to: (1) narrow the conflict in definition, focus, and issues in dispute, so that it can be clearly visualized and stated; (2) limit the particular conflict to the issues of origin and resist the introduction of secondary issues; (3) direct the conflict toward cooperative problem solving and controlled competition (parallel, not symmetrical, competition); and (4) trust leadership that stresses mutually satisfactory outcomes.

Destructive conflict is also characterized by four tendencies. In this case, the individuals or groups tend to: (1) expand the number of issues, participants, negative attitudes, and self-justifications; (2) emancipate the conflict from its initiating causes so it can continue after these are irrelevant or forgotten; (3) escalate into strategies of power and tactics of threat, coercion, and deception; and (4) polarize into uniform opinions behind single-minded and militant leadership.

These destructive processes are exaggerated by the cluster of emergency behaviors that accompany competitive confrontations: anxiety rises, perceptions become more selective, and thinking becomes total and consistent. The atmosphere of competition inevitably accelerates anxiety in the urgency for victory; as anxiety rises, misperception and biased perception increase; as these create conflicts within the person, the need to reduce dissonance creates a cognitive consistency by bending and blending thought and belief. These three emergency behaviors interlock, reinforce, and accelerate each other in a spiral of intensification.

It is inevitable, then, that "the harmful and dangerous elements will drive out those which would keep the conflict within bounds," as James Coleman has articulated in his "Gresham's Law of Conflict" (Coleman 1957, 14).

CONFLICT: COMPETITION OR COOPERATION?

Conflict is essentially competitive, but not all competition is conflictual. Symmetrical competition, where behavior is aimed at affecting the opponent, such as a boxing match, is won only by causing the opponent to lose. Parallel competition, for example, a foot race, is aimed toward achieving the same goal — a record time — and the other is free to win, lose, or draw.

At its best, a foot race is a cooperative process. Each gives the others space, helps set the pace, and stimulates to maximum performance. But a boxing match, even in friendly sparring, is intrinsically competitive in blocking, countering, evading, punching, and controlling, even in the clinch. The metaphor we use in conceptualizing conflict influences the model we follow (see the list entitled "Conflict Metaphors and Models").

When the atmosphere becomes competitively charged, the competition becomes bi-directional, both toward the goal and against each other, and then the urge to win may become secondary to the urge to make the other lose.

After several decades of studying conflict and cooperation, Morton Deutsch has summed up his bottom-line insight in what

Conflict Metaphors and Models

1. Duel: One wins, and lives. The other loses, is annihilated.

2. Boxing match: Usually one wins and one loses. Blows are exchanged, countered, and blocked.

3. Foot race: The competition is indirect. None blocks the others; each stimulates others.

4. Soccer or football: The goal is scoring goals or touchdowns. Rules govern play.

5. Auction or sale: There is direct competition on cost and payment.

6. Bargaining or trade: Both involve a trade-off or give and take.

7. Popularity contest: Each presents benefits; outcome is with judges or consumers.

8. Dividing the pie: One cuts, the other chooses.

9. Arm wrestling: A limited sample of strength is demonstrated.

10. Court of law: A formal setting, competing advocates, and a judge and jury are involved.

11. Arbitration: The decision is delegated to a third-party judge.

12. Pressure group: The goal is to raise consciousness, influence decision.

13. Nonviolent protest: It involves appeal to conscience, to guilt or shame.

he calls his "crude law of social relations." The law is: The atmosphere of a relationship will foster certain acts and processes. A competitive atmosphere induces threat, coercion, deception, suspicion, rigidity, faulty communication, and so on. A cooperative atmosphere, in contrast, induces perceived similarity, trust, open communication, flexibility, concern for the other, emphasis on mutual interests, and attraction between the parties.

The first corollary to this law, Deutsch reports, is that the processes and acts that are characteristic of a given social atmosphere will induce that very atmosphere if introduced into a newly forming relationship. First steps tend to induce a whole series of related perceptions, actions, and responses.

The second corollary to the law is that a firmly developed atmosphere can be rapidly changed to the negative if one party acts in a contradictory manner. A negative atmosphere can much more slowly be turned back toward cooperation since trust is rebuilt in small increments of trust and risk (Deutsch 1973, 365–69).

A constructive process of conflict can be identified with a cooperative social process; a destructive process has the social and psychological characteristics of competition.

Symmetrical, win-lose competition breeds the conditions of a destructive atmosphere and fosters further competition; parallel, cooperative competition, if indeed it is competition, engenders a constructive context and creates the conditions of further cooperation.

Competition is an either-or, win-lose process; it stimulates either-or communication, either-or solutions, and either-or attitudes and actions. Either-or communication is two-channel and highly selective. One hears what will support victory for oneself or defeat for the opponent; one communicates what will enhance one's image of strength and invulnerability and what will mislead or intimidate the other; one refuses direct communication that would encounter ambiguities and relies on indirect and circuitous means of gathering reinforcing data. As the competition escalates, the thinking becomes more concrete, the positions become more polarized, and the communication becomes more and more either-or.

Either-or solutions are envisioned in which the only desirable outcome is imposing a settlement by superior force, cleverness, deception, or majority domination. The enhancement of one's power and the minimization of the other's, the rallying of one's supporters and the belittling of the adversary — these divert the conflict from the immediate issue (what is right) to the power issue: that is, who shall define and decide. As competition accelerates, either-or solutions become the inevitable and exclusive goals.

Either-or attitudes and actions follow. Suspicion, hostility, sensitivity to threats, and projections of one's own anger, fear, and hatred all seem justified and inevitable. Behaviors that would be unacceptable or outrageous if directed toward those "like oneself" are now permitted toward those who are "so different"; the moral insensitivity of one side triggers and justifies the same from the other. Either truth and justice — our truth and justice — will prevail or falsehood and oppression will triumph. As competition increases, either-or attitudes take control, and unilateral actions follow.

Cooperation is a both-and process or, at its best, a neither-nor process (see table 2). Both-and communication processes tolerate and integrate ambivalence and create mutual understanding; both-and solutions seek mutually satisfactory goals; both-and attitudes and actions of negotiation, interaction, and integration result from the process.

Both-and cooperation requires a floor of common connections and conflict-limiting processes. These may include such factors as the number and strength of existing cooperative bonds; crosscutting identifications and commitments connecting the group in many ways; common allegiances and memberships in other groups or subgroups by conflicting parties; shared values, rituals, and institutions; recognized channels and procedures for limiting and regulating conflict; and awareness of the costs and consequences of intensifying conflict.

Both-and cooperative processes aid open and honest communication. Information is more freely shared; underlying assumptions surface; joint definitions are achieved; misperceptions are clarified; access to data becomes reciprocal; the legitimacy of each other's needs becomes visible; and the rationale for each other's positions becomes understandable.

Table 2
Comparison of Both-and and Either-or Conflict

BOTH-AND COOPERATIVE CONFLICT	EITHER-OR COMPETITIVE CONFLICT
Conflict is focused on desired goals, positive needs, and chosen ends and is more easily directed toward cooperation.	Conflicts instigated by fears, stimulated by aversions, and fed by negative feelings are more likely to turn competitive.
The less intense the feelings and the more detachment people can achieve from the goals in dispute, the easier it is to resolve the issues cooperatively.	The more intense the feeling and the more invested in and attached to a particular outcome, the more likely the conflict will become competitive.
Conflict negotiated as an issue unconnected to one's self-esteem can more easily be turned to cooperative ends.	Conflicts that are closely attached to one's self-esteem, in which self-respect is dependent on winning, are more likely to turn competitive.
Defining conflicts narrowly and neutrally with specific issues and cases in view increases cooperation.	Defining conflicts as large issues of principle in general terms with broad application heightens competition.
Conscious conflicts clearly expressed, openly discussed, and frankly owned are more easily resolved jointly.	Unconscious conflicts, rising from unexplored feelings and attributed to "personality problems," are invariably competitive.
Conflicts between parties who mutually perceive self and other as unequal in power and legitimacy more easily resolve cooperatively; thus recognized hierarchy encourages cooperation.	Conflicts between parties who mutually perceive self and other as equal in power and legitimacy more often provoke competition.
Cooperative conflicts tend to heighten the positive, bonding qualities of mutual trust, openness to hear, freedom of choice, and caring for joint solutions satisfactory to both parties.	Competitive conflicts tend to magnify and express the areas of dysfunction in participants: perceptual distortion, self-deception, unwitting involvement, unaware fears, or a need to win and see the other lose.

Both-and cooperation takes a positive interest in the other party's power. The stronger the cooperating partner becomes, the more resources, information, and skill will be available to us all. In cooperation, we seek to enhance each other's strengths and contribute to the well-being of each person's position in constructive ways. In the reverse situation, where each seeks to increase power differentials, a destructive process of bringing the relationship or conflict to an end creates a negative spiral of either-or, competitive interactions.

Further, both-and processes assume the existence of a mutually beneficial solution. The commitment to work jointly limits the strategies of influence to persuasion and debate and the options for bargaining to negotiation or compromise. The likelihood of achieving a mutually satisfactory solution is greatly increased.

In neither-nor cooperation, we move beyond both-and processes of combining perceptions and intended outcomes to co-creation of an alternative solution that neither party has envisioned or engendered. The parties involved neither own the solution nor claim any portion of it as a victory. The outcome is a joint creation — a mutually constructed, equally supported, communally concluded process.

The Javanese process of arriving at communal consensus is a neither-nor process. The pride of winning and the loss of face in losing are both eliminated in the shared creation of a third way that belongs to neither one party nor the other.

COMPETITIVE SPIRALS
VERSUS COOPERATIVE CYCLES

Unchanneled and undirected conflicts tend toward becoming self-perpetuating, vicious cycles. The cycle, as it intensifies, escalates until the conflict becomes detached from its original causes and becomes its own self-energizing cause. The originating causes may be no longer relevant, or may appear insignificant in light of interactional developments, and be essentially forgotten. The conflict has become its own raison de être, its own self-empowered, self-fulfilling cycle. As the escalation continues, the other's existence,

Figure 4
Competitive Conflict Spiral

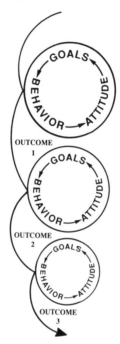

success, and future fulfillment become sufficient cause for the ongoing hostility and hatred. The conflict has now moved from injustice through rage to hate (see fig. 4).

Once the negative spiral has become longer-term conflict, the self-fulfilling prophesies lead to behavior that elicits reactions that confirm expectations, warp further perceptions, and destine the conflict toward obfuscation of motives and negativizing of the interactions between the parties.

In almost any extended, protracted conflict between two parties, both sides are always right, the other is hostile, the other has negative feelings: "He doesn't like me; she is treating me badly." And both sides would be right in their perceptions because they have set up a vicious, mutually confirming expectation. Each is treating the other badly because it feels that the other deserves to be treated badly because the other treats it badly and so on. (Deutsch 1987, 41)

A negative spiral becomes fully self-perpetuating as personal, positional, and relational investments are made. In the course of conflict, the parties become invested in evolving commitment processes. Each party's attitudes are shaped by personal investments in perceptions and explanations and in the personal story of the conflict, occasion, and events. Positional investments in stance, response, and future actions define each's behaviors. Relational investments in alliances made, coalitions committed, and networks constructed narrow one's options. So the parties are invested in particular positions taken; in beliefs about the other that have developed in the course of the conflict; and in promises made to self and others that are difficult to give up without sacrificing self-esteem or the respect of others, without a loss of "integrity."

Cooperative conflict behaviors are also cyclical, but in progressive experiences of testing, risking, and trusting.

Cooperative conflict moves through stages of consulting in joint problem solving, cooperating in the search for a creative solution, conciliating in resolution of differences, and contracting settlement, implementation, and future relationships. Chapter 8 will offer multiple models for cyclical, intentional, and cooperative conflicts that develop and elaborate the simple schema sketched in figure 5.

NEEDS, RIGHTS, AND POWER

A pair of stolen boots was the trigger for the explosion. One night a miner discovered that his boots had been taken from his clothes-basket hanging in the bathhouse. He could not go down into the mine without boots.

"It ain't fair!" he complained to the shift boss. "Why should I lose a shift's pay and the price of a pair of boots because the company can't protect the property?"

Figure 5
Cooperative Conflict Cycle

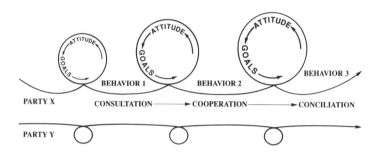

"Tough luck," the shift boss replied. "Read the regulations; the company is not responsible for personal property."

"I'll show them. If I can't work this shift, neither will anyone else," the miner replied. He convinced his group of buddies to walk out with him, and in union solidarity all the others followed.

The superintendent of the mine admitted later that he often replaced stolen boots, and the shift boss should have done the same: "If he had said, 'I'll buy you a new pair and loan you some meanwhile,' we wouldn't have had a strike."

Three ways of resolving a dispute are present in this case: reconciling the needs and interests of the parties, determining who is right, and seeing who is more powerful.

When the miner first discovered that his boots were missing (need and interest), he reacted by pressing his rights ("It ain't fair . . ."). The shift boss, rather than responding to the needs and interests, reacted by defining rights, rules, and regulations. The confrontation escalated as the miner turned to the use of power ("I'll show them"). The superintendent's focus was on needs and interests — the miner's interests in his boots and his pay and the company's interest in all the miners' working their shifts productively (Ury, Brett, and Goldberg 1988, 3–5).

Reconciling needs and interests — the desires, concerns, fears, and wants — resolves the conflict at the most basic human level.

This is not easy since it requires listening for deep-seated concerns, devising mutually satisfactory alternatives, and negotiating trade-offs, concessions, or joint outcomes.

Determining who is right or possesses the rights to a victory or advantage in the dispute is a process of appealing to a legitimate standard, contract, or law. Persons may also apply precedent, seniority, reciprocity, or equality as criteria for demanding their rights. The miner, in the case of the boots, had no contractual right, but he felt that standards of fairness and reciprocal concern for interests should lead the company to protect personal property. Conflicting standards, contradictory precedents, contrasting interpretations of contract, and competing values of fairness and equal distribution make negotiation of rights complex and exceedingly difficult, requiring not only mediation, but also adjudication.

Discovering who is more powerful is a competitive process of imposing costs, coercing outcomes, or damaging benefits or profits for either side. Often the question of who is more powerful turns on who is less dependent. The more alternatives one possesses, the less dependent one will be on the opponent. Defining who is more powerful may be done in power negotiations, but more often it becomes a contest of wills, of force, of courage to resist, compel, and coerce.

All three processes may occur in cycles, in spirals of escalation and de-escalation. The focus may shift from needs to rights, to power and back again. The more creative process focuses more on the former and leads toward collaboration and cooperation; the more destructive process focuses on the latter and becomes increasingly competitive (see fig. 6).

Reconciling interests is less costly than determining who is right, which in turn is less costly than demonstrating who is more powerful (Ury, Brett, and Goldberg 1988, 15).

FROM COMPETITIVE
TO CREATIVE THOUGHT

If you want the window open, and I want it shut, and if we keep phrasing our desires in terms of an open or shut window, then one

Figure 6
Three Ways of Resolving a Dispute

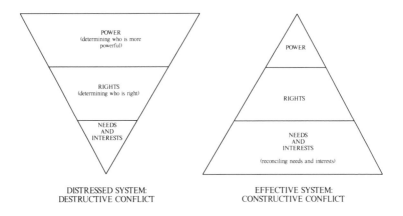

DISTRESSED SYSTEM:
DESTRUCTIVE CONFLICT

EFFECTIVE SYSTEM:
CONSTRUCTIVE CONFLICT

Most disputes are resolved through reconciling needs and interests, some by
determining who is right, and the fewest through demonstrating who is more powerful.
The effective designer guides the conflict in such a way that it becomes constructive.

of us must win, the other lose, or there will be some sort of only
partially satisfactory, perhaps chilly, compromise.

But if we discover that what you really want is fresh air, and
what I am concerned about is avoiding a draft, a creative alternative may be possible: Opening a window or door in an adjoining
room could provide fresh air without a draft. *Either* open *or* closed,
the window debate remains deadlocked; but *both* fresh air *and* freedom from draft can be envisioned. Each person *neither* wins *nor*
loses, yet both are satisfied.

Competitive thought processes — argument — have a serious
handicap in helping resolve conflicts. Argumentation is, in itself,
conflictual thinking, and although it has been the mainstay of conflict processing, it is not simply fighting fire with fire; more often
it is adding fuel to the fire.

There are conflicts, of course, in which dialectic thought is
quite useful. A thesis is put forward by party A, its antithesis by
party B, and from the clash and contradiction of the argument a

synthesis emerges that combines the best of both. However welcome such meeting in the middle may be, it occurs less frequently than is desirable; it is fraught with complexity and difficulty. Since both sides are focused on what is objectionable in the other, it is hard for them to see what is best in the opposite point of view; since each side is defending its own perspective, it is hard for each to judge what is truly important in its own position; since each is holding to what seems indispensable in its perspective, it is not unlikely that the compromise may combine less than the best parts of each side so that the solution accepted may not satisfy the real needs of either group in the end. The synthesis is, too often, a grudging compromise or a face-saving retreat from a position. The strengths of both sides may be combined, but not the excellence of each; the power positions are protected, but what is actually important is lost. Exploration ends as rigidity increases, and creative options are unexamined since the two defensive positions become more and more entrenched. The stronger elements, not necessarily the better elements, survive into the compromise.

There are cultures, the Japanese and the Javanese, to name two obvious examples, that do not value dialectic argumentive patterns. Where harmony and cooperation are basic values, verbal contradiction is not the automatic first choice in conflict. A more accepted process is to affirm the strengths of each other's position, let them stand without attack, and then join in exploring other options. Both parties search for superior options. In an argumentive idiom, the time spent dismantling or demolishing the old positions is nonproductive effort; in an exploratory idiom the energy is turned toward constructive investigation (see table 3). If a superior alternative is not found, the previous positions remain undestroyed. Frequently the old positions are essentially good — they cannot be simply discredited, but they are no longer necessary. When a creative alternative emerges, a choice can be made on the basis of values rather than on destruction of the past before reconstructing a future. This process of exploration tends toward combination and invention by collaboration. There are times when argumentation is superior, when what has been must end and the new must come. But to as-

Table 3
Comparison of Argumentation and Exploration

USES OF ARGUMENTATION

Negative:
In arguing a case, the disputant debates:
1. Against a position/proposition to prove something is wrong; to prove B does not follow A; to prove the logic inconsistent; to point out all possible sources of error, distortion, partial truth, potential effects, and so on.
2. Against a person/personality to discredit the opponent; to expose an area of weakness and thereby invalidate the whole; to undermine the other's credibility with others or his or her self-esteem; to impugn motives and integrity; to show the other's ideas are not better than his or her persona.

Positive:
In arguing, one may debate:
1. For a position/proposition as an alternative explanation; by showing its consistency in inference vis-à-vis the other; by proving its logical order or necessity; by demonstrating its superiority to competing options.
2. For the person/personality by expressing respect for the opponent; but the intention is to bring about a change of view in the other by identification and persuasion.

USES OF EXPLORATION

Negative:
None. Exploration suspends negation and puts existing options on hold while other possibilities are designed.

Positive
1. Exploration seeks to open up both your own and the other's view by:
a. pushing both views forward into the future, widening them to embrace parallels and deepening their value base.
b. uncovering similarities, commonalities, and complementarity that may allow both views to co-exist in a new setting.
c. identifying shared goals that now exist, making the dialogue possible, and identifying further goals to be jointly affirmed.
d. expressing affect and interests, sharing feelings, preferences, attractions, and aesthetics.
2. Exploration utilizes creative thinking tools and exercises such as:
a. The 3-D thought map. Construct a map of options by drawing out: *dreams:* What are your hopes (pluses)? *doubts:* What are the fears (minuses)? *desires:* So what do you want (interests)? Arrange on a decision map.
b. The 3-R thought process. Experience seeing the issues from the other side by:
Reversing positions: each side takes the opposing position.
Role playing: each expresses and defends.
Reporting perspectives: after returning, reflect and report discoveries.
c. The three-story universe. Explore three possible stories:
Worst-case scenario: together write/tell the story of possible failure.
Best-case scenario: tell the story of possible success.
Likely case scenario: tell the story of probable outcomes.

sume that either-or thought with its conflict and contradiction, its clash and competition, is the inevitable or preferable option is to limit ourselves needlessly. Dialectic, hypothesis, experimentation, and proof are essential in scientific advance; exploration, cooperation, synthesis, and collaboration are crucial in human relationships.

The exploration process takes many forms across cultures. A typical pattern is as follows: (1) The present position, idea, or vision is not attacked or discredited; it is put on hold. (2) Both parties either cooperate on exploration of further creative options, or delegate the problem to a third party (or to third parties) to design further directions. (3) Since fault finding is suspended, each other's face protected, and defensiveness reduced, it is possible to envision change in an idea or position that is already good, valued, and useful. (4) Since all are committed to the process, there is a sense of joint ownership, joint participation in decision and evaluation. (5) The solution is not either-or or both-and but neither-nor or some combination of all of the above.

Exploration does not need to be logically consistent at each step; argument does. Exploration can be provocative, provisional, speculative, and emotional; argument is rarely so. Exploration can be optimistic, hopeful, and positive; argument may be all of these, but more often is negative, pessimistic, and guarded. Thus, in conflict situations where anxiety is high, threat is real, and fear is a basic motivator, the imagination must walk tediously; it cannot leap or fly in new directions.

Two Hong Kong women, arguing over the ownership of an orange, each made a strong case for sole ownership. The mediator, a neighbor, heard each side as equally compelling, and recommended that a compromise be struck. The orange was divided into equal proportions. When each had received her half and returned home, the one peeled her half, threw away the peel, and ate the flesh. The other peeled her half, discarded the flesh, and julienned the peel for a stirfry.

If the focus is on interests, not positions, the persons can move beyond an either-or compromise to a creative both-and or neither-nor solution that meets the needs of all concerned.

FROM COMPETITIVE TO CREATIVE GOALS

In most cultures in the first and second worlds, traditional views of conflict end in win-lose solutions. The predominant notion is that conflict involves objective differences of interest, scarce resources, or fundamentally conflicting belief systems. With such definitions any expectation of win-win outcomes is seen as utopian and naive.

Yet this utopian view is the position to which we are being led by contemporary thinking. Conflict is not over objective differences of interest that involve scarcity, at least not the kind of conflicts that are of concern in the international system. It is over more fundamental values of security and identity that are not necessarily in short supply. (Burton 1984, 137)

The need for security and identity — the elemental drive beneath social and political conflicts — cannot be resolved in win-lose processes with win-lose solutions. So much of the law-and-order framework on which we rely for social stability and so much of the coercive deference we trust to suppress deviance are destined to fail.

At the international level, if the competitive problem is not due to scarcity of resources, and if threat does not deter when there are important values at stake, then the strategic policies of deterrence on which world society appears to rely, are unlikely to contribute to peace, and are more likely to promote conflict to the extent that they frustrate the pursuit of human goals. (Burton 1984, 138)

The basic human needs that are both universal and ontological have been described as "the vast pools of energy known as wants, needs, aspirations and expectations" (MacGregor Burns 1977, 267) or as "a natural law springing from men and women's own humanity which must be incorporated into the positive law of the state" (Scarman 1977, 37). Political scientists and psychologists, anthropologists and theologians are moving toward a consensus:

There are basic needs, values, and interests that are essential to humanness. What these are is not commonly and unanimously defined, but they are recognized as universals that are more basic than cultural values or individual interests (Augsburger 1986, 50). One effective summary is that of P. Sites, who isolates eight basic needs: "a need for response, a need for security, a need for recognition, a need for stimulation, a need for distributive justice, a need for meaning, a need to be seen as rational (and for rationality itself), and a need to control" (Sites 1973, 43).

Conflict, on all levels, may be only secondarily due to scarce resources, and primarily rooted in social values that are not in short supply but may instead increase as they are exercised. They are non-zero-sum (not zero-sum) values. An increase for one party does not require a decrease for the other. The more security one group experiences and expresses creatively, the more secure are its neighbors; the clearer and more positive the identity of one people, the more clearly they perceive and experience the identities of those who adjoin them.

Thus, what political realists once called utopian views are becoming behavioral realism, and what was thought impossible, win-win solutions in conflicts are both inevitable and necessary goals.

PROMOTING COOPERATION

Promoting cooperation is a central goal in virtually all conflict resolution (see table 4). Robert Axelrod, a game theorist and political scientist, has suggested five basic factors in increasing mutuality; he has derived these from his research in competitive and cooperative game theory.

1. Enlarge the shadow of the future. Mutual cooperation can be stable if the future is sufficiently important relative to the present. An effective threat of retaliation in the future or the promise of continuing rewarding interaction can both enlarge the shadow of what is to come. In a mobile society the expectation that the other will move, leave, die, or distance himself or herself reduces commitment to the future. Durability in interactions, increased

Table 4
Comparison of Productive and Nonproductive Conflict

PRODUCTIVE CONFLICT	NONPRODUCTIVE CONFLICT
1. When parties can call a time out when a conflict process is out of control, and can discuss what is going wrong with more insight than feeling. Each partner is more committed to achieving mutually satisfactory solutions than to winning at the other's expense. This involves the ability to (1) channel the conflict by a prior agreement to try a new process, (2) call "time out" to redirect the process, (3) request a rematch and take it once more from the top, and (4) reflect and learn from what occurred.	1. When parties feel stuck in a conflict style that continues in spite of all efforts to change it. The participants feel the relationship is out of control. Each party reports a deep interest in improving the relationship, yet their individual styles interlock so tightly that once the cycle is initiated, both are powerless to interrupt it. The conflict rituals produce only increased tension, suspicion, powerlessness, and unhappiness with self and other.
2. When parties are achieving personal goals that also contribute to or support their joint goals. The productive fulfillment of individual and shared goals with reduced expenditures of energy for both crisis resolution and maintenance leaves increased amounts of energy available for separate and united goals.	2. When parties feel cheated of reaching personal goals, with one or both feeling that individual goals are being usurped by the other, or both are losing to the waste or consumption of energy in maintaining an exhausting relational cycle. When one partner feels powerless, helpless, and optionless, then decisions are beyond reach and the relationship has become nonproductive.
3. When parties feel valued, supported, excited, and energized by the relationship so each attempts tasks that will provide individual and joint fulfillment and serve to increase the self-esteem of both, leading to deepening trust and greater satisfaction with the relational contract or covenant.	3. When parties feel used and struggle with feelings of wanting to "get" or to "get even with" the other person. Vengeful, violent, or hostile impulses indicate that self-esteem is being undermined and that goals are being blocked by the other or by the constraints of the relational covenant or contract.

frequency of exchanges, interdependency in development, reciprocity in rewards all darken the shadow.

2. Change the pay-offs. Cooperation can be supported by transforming the pay-off system in the relationship, the family, or the group so that there are fewer private incentives and more

balancing social incentives that profit the whole as well as the individual's own part. Even a relatively small transformation can promote an increase in solidarity and mutual concern. The goal is to build a long-term incentive for mutual cooperation that is greater than the short-term incentive for defection.

3. Teach people to care about each other. Teaching persons to value the welfare of others and to prize creative altruism is a goal for all human communities. As persons serve, give, and share out of concern for the welfare of the recipient — not out of strategies to gain social approval, to reduce personal guilt, or to create obligation in others — then cooperation is grounded in the more stable motivation of concern for mutuality.

4. Teach reciprocity. Tit for tat may be an effective strategy for an egoist to use, but it is not useful moral strategy for a person, group, or society interested in cooperation. This does not suggest that unconditional cooperation is the basis of creative resolution; rather that reciprocity is the bottom line, with the goal of reciprocity being the ultimate achievement of unconditional cooperation. So tit for tat reciprocity, tempered by the willingness to reduce recrimination to invite correction of the negative and to increase recrimination to reinforce the positive, can lead from minimal equal rewards to more unconditional trust and cooperativeness.

5. Improve recognition abilities. The ability to recognize other persons, recall past interactions, appreciate individual identities, and welcome future cooperation opportunities will invite a widening world of associations, a broader field of trust, and a richer community of collaboration (Axelrod 1984, 124–44).

CONFLICT COMPETENCE

To summarize the key rules for developing conflict competence, consider the following terse injunctions: Stay centered; do not polarize. Stay creative; do not negativize. Stay calm; tolerate ambivalence.

Stay centered; do not polarize in feelings, in actions, or in basic positions. Maintain contact with the other party. Do not withdraw or cut off relationship. Attempt dialogue rather than isolating from or fighting with the opponent. Immediately challenge the intrusion of either-or thinking, traditional stereotypes, and reductionistic explanations of the other's motives as simple while seeing your own as complex. Sustain the conflicting images of reality, one from the antagonist and one of your own, in parallel co-existence within your mind. Be open to a third, centered perspective that may bring a new synthesis into view. To suppress one of the images is to remove a creative polarity that may be the source of creative ferment and eventual creative breakthrough.

Stay creative; do not negativize. There is no necessary, inevitable, or logical connection between the presence of conflict and the emergence of destructive attitudes or behavior. Only the linking of cultural patterns and prejudices, of models and teachers, and of earlier experiments and failure connects conflict and chaos in our innards. Conflict and creativity can be paired in our attitudes and actions. Conflict can be actualized as a bond not a barrier between actors, as a unifier not a wedge, and as a demonstration of how our circumstances, plights, fates, privileges, and opportunities are intermingled.

Stay calm; tolerate ambivalence. Do not homogenize. Discard the childhood pattern of concrete thinking, either-or judgment, necessary retaliation, and immanent justice that springs up as we regress under stress. The urges to be "consistent," clearly right, and self-justified are remainders of unfinished developmental stages. Maturity emerges as there is recognition of ambiguity in all situations, admission of ambivalence in the self, and tolerance of contradictory impulses and insights. Authoritarian personalities project ambivalence outward, into the opponent, in phobic flight from their own bipolar human feelings; the fully functioning person can admit such complex thoughts and feelings into consciousness and allow them to enrich the inner conversation.

Conflict is, to choose a simile, like sex. Victorians saw sex as something one must tolerate, learn to live with, but not enjoy. Most persons voice the same negative mindset toward conflict. Like sex, conflict should happen between persons committed to be present with continuity, occur with appropriate frequency, be mutually exciting to both, activate both parties equally to contribute their best selves, and be prolonged until mutually satisfactory climax is possible for each. When it is over, both should feel better as a result. And its energy should then empower other areas of life with vitality and creativity. Like sex, conflict is a source of joy, fulfillment, empowerment, and celebration.

COMPETITIVE OR COOPERATIVE CONFLICT SITUATIONS?

It is useful, at times crucial, to diagram what appears obvious, to clarify boundaries in human interactions, and to strategize interventions. The conflict triangle offers a basic set of boundary definitions — both intrapersonal and interpersonal boundaries — that allows us to draw fundamental distinctions between the conflict situation, the conflict attitudes and perceptions, and the conflict behavior (see figs. 7 and 8).

The conflict situation is any moment when two parties discover that they possess mutually incompatible goals, such as when two children simultaneously want exclusive possession of a single toy.

The conflict attitudes are those perceptions that create negative variations: the wish for the toy, the sibling rivalry and competition, the wish to deprive the other of the toy, the wish to demonstrate strength or stubbornness, and the claim to third-party, unconditional support.

The conflict behavior or actions are those visible, measurable steps taken to fulfill the perceptions and move toward the goals. For the children, this may include struggling, grabbing, name calling, crying, appeals to an adult as a third party, as well as escalation of anger within and hostility between.

The same dynamics occur among adults, such as when divorcing parents quarrel over custody of a child, appeal to third parties, file for court involvement, or resort to kidnapping and flight in order to claim custody or deny possession to the other parent. At the international level, the contested object may be the Falkland Islands desired by both Britain and Argentina; or the Senkaku Islands claimed by Japan, China, and Taiwan; or Palestine, claimed by both Israel and the Palestinians.

Figure 7
The Conflict Triangle

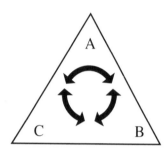

2

Attitude
(perceptions).
The parties' frustration
creates or reinforces
a negative attitude
(competition or
elimination).

1

Conflict
(situations).
Two parties discover
their goals collide.

3

Behavior
(actions).
Actions ensue that
seek to deprive the
other of the goal or to
eliminate the competitor.

1. The cycle may start at any point: with *A* triggered by an attitude
   from ideology or tradition, with *B* triggered when a behavior creates a conflict situation or stimulates a conflictual perception, and with *C* triggered
   when goals collide.

2. The cycle may move in either direction, clockwise or counterclockwise.

3. The cycle can be stopped, interrupted, or regulated at any of the three
   points: by intervening at *A* through clarifying conflict perception, at *B*
   through conflict management, and at *C* through negotiating conflict
   resolution.

4. The conflict *(C)* can become a positive or negative situation. If the
   attitudes and perceptions *(A)* are competitive, the behaviors *(B)* will
   become destructive; if *(A)* is cooperative, *(B)* will be collaborative
   and constructive.

Figure 8
Complexities of the Conflict Triangle

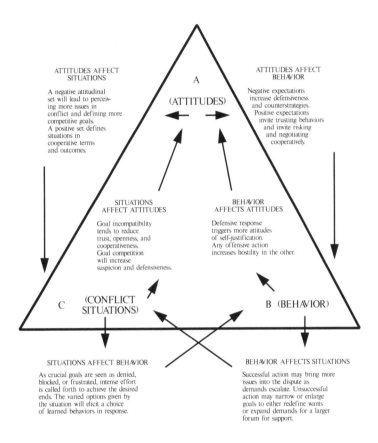

By charting these three components — attitudes, behavior, and the conflict context — in triangular interdependence, one can see the systemic interrelatedness of all three intrapersonally and interpersonally. Each affects every other aspect, but each conflict experience has its own unique configuration and sequence.

The culturally sensitive mediator develops the skills of breaking open a conflict situation and looking at its basic dynamics. By untangling the attitudes within each party, the behavior going on between the parties, and the conflict that enmeshes them, the mediator can help them see what is confusing with new clarity.

The mediator seeks to separate people (their attitudes and actions) from the problems (the conflict situations). The negotiator can then be supportive of persons as they clarify their own views and values while being confrontational with the conflict situation itself. The negative spiral can be interrupted by setting mutually agreed on limits to the conflict process; a positive cycle can be encouraged by contracting for a process that will assist each in clarifying attitudes and cleaning up behavior so that trust increases and the conflict is transformed into a productive negotiation.

This conflict transformation — not "conflict management" or "conflict resolution" — occurs as there is a metamorphosis in each of the three elements.

1. Transforming attitudes, by changing and redirecting negative perceptions, requires a commitment to see the other with goodwill, to define the conflict in terms of mutual respect, and to maintain attitudes of collaborative and cooperative intent.

2. Transforming behavior, by limiting all action to collaborative behavior, can interrupt the negative cycle. This requires a commitment to seek noncoercive processes of communication, negotiation, and dispute resolution even when there has been intense provocation. The commitment on both sides to act with restraint and mutual respect changes the dynamics of the negotiation from mistrust to trust.

3. Transforming conflict, by seeking to discover, define, and remove incompatibilities by creative design, can invent options for mutual gain (see the lists on pp. 160–63 and 198, and table 11 below). In negative conflicts, incompatibilities are seen as essentially problematic, so attitudes become destructively negative, and behavior is divisive and alienating. Such negative modeling of conflict is present in most person's behavioral repertoire from early childhood, but each element can be relearned and reframed into a positive metaphor and reexperienced in mutuality.

Conflict can be unifying, precisely because most of our weaknesses and fears are common to us all, connecting us like an invisible bond of similarity beneath the surface of contrasts and differences. Conflict can be transformed; attitudes can be altered

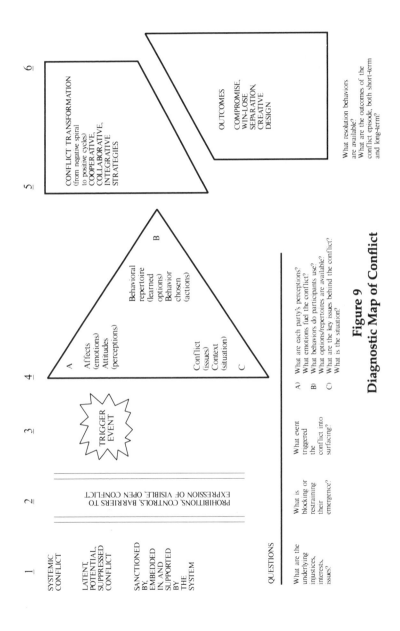

Figure 9
Diagnostic Map of Conflict

to seek mutual outcomes; and behavior can be focused toward reconciliation and cooperation.

In summary, the "Diagnostic Map of Conflict" (fig. 9) offers an integration of the theoretical skeleton of this chapter. Cooperative goals, collaborative values, and integrative strategies can emerge when *conflict transformation* is the goal, *creative design* is the methodology, and *mutually satisfactory outcomes* are the ends pursued.

When you have "fought" with each other creatively, as the proverb at the opening of this chapter affirms, you truly come to know and respect each other.

Chapter Three

Conflict: The Power
of Honor, Dignity, and Face

Do not remove a fly from your neighbor's face with a hatchet.
— Chinese proverb

UNIVERSAL INSIGHT
(The Bottom Line)

"Facework" is the primary experience of interpersonal conflict; it
is a universal human process, a ubiquitous concept present in the
thought and life of all cultures.

STORY: THE DEATH OF A CIVIL SERVANT
Russia, Chekhov

One fine evening, an office worker, Ivan Dimitrich Krupikov, sitting in the second row of stalls at the opera, was overcome with an impulse to sneeze. Not at all embarrassed, he simply wiped his nose, and looked about to see if he had disturbed anyone. Then he did have cause for embarrassment. He saw that the little old gentleman in front of him was wiping his bald pate with his glove and muttering something. He recognized him as General Shpritsalov, a Number 2 in the ministry of communications.

"I spattered him. It's awkward. I'll have to apologize," he thought, so he coughed, leaned forward.

"Please excuse me, your excellency, for spattering you, it was quite unintentional."

"That's all right. That's all right."

"Please, please forgive me. I—I didn't mean to."

"Oh, do sit down, please. I can't hear the opera."

Krupikov sat, trying to watch the stage, but shame and worry overcame him. At the intermission, he repeated his apology. The general with irritation assured him it was forgotten. At home he told his wife, and repeated his embarrassment and concern. The next day he dressed his best, got in line with those being heard by the general, and repeated his apology.

"Drivel, sir, you're wasting my time. Next!" said the general.

"He won't talk about it. He must be angry," Krupikov concluded, and waited until the general had heard his last petitioner, then followed him from the room. There he protested

his deep repentance and his good intentions. "Are you trying to be funny?" the general snapped and turned away.

"Funny? Never. I'll write him a letter to explain." But after a sleepless night, the shame had grown unbearable. The next morning he went again in person to explain. His speech of apology was long, and abject.

"Clear out," bellowed the general, turning purple with rage.

"Wh . . . what?" Krupikov asked in a whisper, in terror.

"Clear out," he said again, stamping his foot.

Something snapped in his stomach; without seeing, hearing, thinking, he staggered off, entered his home mechanically, without taking off his uniform, lay down on the sofa and . . . died.

(Chekhov 1982, 11–14)

FOLKTALE
Yoruba Tribe, West Africa

In a town called Irandonwo (it is pleasant to watch) lived a man called Elenuobere, that is to say "sharp mouth," who had no shame.

One day, his shameless mouth got him into deep trouble. When the king's wife had been seduced, he went to the palace to explain the plan by which a man had stolen the heart of the queen. When they asked him how he knew, he took credit for devising the plan. (His family told him to be quiet, but it was like trying to pack corn on the back of a calabash. He said, "Nothing will happen to me; the person who has no maize will not put pepper on his vegetable.")

Instead, Elenuobere was taken to court and fined one pound. Since he could not pay, he looked like trouble had given him her child to rock. Then a kind farmer agreed to pay his debt if he would work for him one week. Did he not agree? Will the man who is about to inherit a beautiful widow provide medical care for her sick husband?

So Elenuobere followed the farmer as they set out for his yam fields. After working for the first day, they sat down to eat. As they were filling their bellies, the farmer sighed with satisfaction. "If I can tell you the meaning of your sigh, will you wager with me for two days' work?" asked clever-mouthed Elenuobere. "Of course," said the farmer, thinking, "I have caught this fellow for two more days, since I alone know my thoughts, how can he win?" He sighed, again in satisfaction.

"I will tell you the meaning of the second sigh for two more days' work."

The farmer laughed as he nodded again, thinking the jackal will always have a red coat, and this man will always have a stupid mouth. He lit his pipe and sighed a third time. Now Elenuobere claimed he knew the meaning of the third sigh without a doubt. They agreed on the threefold wager, for the six days of work, then argued over who should be the judge. At last they agreed it should be no one less than the king, who knew the thoughts of his people.

When they stood before the king, Elenuobere shamelessly requested that all the royal family be called. Then he said to the farmer: "The first thought that came to your mind was: May the Almighty God give long life to our king. The second: May this royal family rule long in our land. The third: May God grant that the king's heir will rule after him."

Immediately the king, his family, and all the court said, "Amen, amen."

And the poor old farmer was forced to put his lips together and say, "Amen, amen, amen" as well, for how dare he anger the king, or shame himself before the royal court?

The mouth that commits an offense must talk itself out of punishment, but it is always easier, even for the shameless, to talk yourself into trouble than to talk yourself out of it.

(Gbadamosi and Beier 1968, 5–7, abridged)

Kalauna tribe, Goodenough Island, New Guinea. On a dark night, an accuser delivers a public harangue from a housetop. The village is compact enough for most of it to be in clear earshot of a single shouting or chanting voice. The long list of charges, the public delicts, is assimilated in absolute silence. The particular individual being accused would be found sitting inside his darkened house with head bowed under the imagined stares of the entire shaming community (M. Young 1971, 125).

•

Caribou Eskimo tribe, Canadian Arctic. A foster father had grown angry at his foster son's unwillingness to work or hunt, so he sang a public song of derision. The malicious words with which it ended are:

> I wish you were dead!
> You are not worth
> the food that you eat.

The power of the shaming and the loss of face for the young man were so great that he said in retort,

> I hear your words.
> I know your hate.
> I will never eat again.

To make his starvation suffering as brief as possible, he lay down on the ice that night, stark naked, and was frozen to death (Rasmussen 1927, 96).

•

Merina peoples, Madagascar. A theft has been discovered in the community, but the identity of the thief is unknown. The public shaming process is carried out as a part of normal conversations. People, sitting in the meeting place or market place, speak ruefully and pointedly of the evils of stealing in general, and of the recent event in particular, expressing their sadness at what has happened and their hope that it will not occur again. As this continues, persistently from day to day, the impact becomes too intense for the wrongdoer to face and he desists from the disapproved behavior. "As an old woman is uneasy when dry bones are mentioned, a thief is uncomfortable when stealing is condemned" (Roberts 1979, 62).

•

Mbuti tribe, East Africa. A skilled and powerful hunter, who can retaliate dangerously against anyone who opposes him, has taken cattle from a "weaker man" with less repute and power. Although he would tolerate no criticism from any man in the village, he is powerless before the village mime who acts for the community in shaming him in public meetings. His misbehavior is mimicked in an absurd and exaggerated way, which brings the community's disapproval home to the wrongdoer and leaves everyone with no doubt as to whom the display is fingering even though he is not named.

Mime, among the Mbuti, is one of the few forms of specialization encouraged. Those particularly gifted develop into acknowledged clowns and buffoons who habitually take the edge off disputes by miming the disputants and pouring scorn on any person whose conduct threatens to disturb the harmony and security of the group (Roberts 1979, 89).

•

The Daribi, New Guinea. In an angry conflict between two parties, the person attacked may choose a shaming strategy. When approached by an antagonist who is "beside himself " with rage, and usually swinging a length of cane, a person will frequently adopt the role of "righteous victim." As the protagonist lays into him, lashing, screaming, and sometimes kicking, the righteous victim retains his composure, stands his ground without striking back, and "encourages" his opponent, saying "go ahead, hit me again (we can all see what kind of person you are)." This of course makes the protagonist even more furious (and thus morally defenseless); he redoubles his efforts (and hence his shame), trying harder and harder to land the blow that will convince everyone of the seriousness of his anger. Should he succeed, a wise "victim" will make himself even more "righteous" by collapsing and feigning death or serious injury, attempting to show everyone that the protagonist's anger was, in reality, all too serious (Wagner 1981, 96).

•

Belfast, Ireland. The tradition of the hunger strike in Ireland dates to medieval times, when it had a place in the civil code, the Senchus Mor, as a way to right a perceived injustice. The aggrieved person would fast on the doorstep of the offender. If he died, the householder was held responsible and had to pay compensation to the dead man's family. Terence MacSwiney, the lord mayor of Cork, who died in 1920 on a hunger strike after being imprisoned by the British, said, "It is not those who can inflict the most, but those that can suffer the most who will conquer" (Beresford 1989). In the 1981 Irish hunger strike, ten men died in the prison just outside Belfast that the English call the Maze, the Irish, Long Kesh. The prisoners, demanding treatment as prisoners of war in the struggle for Irish control of Northern Ireland, staged and sustained a protest they referred to as being "on the blanket" (that is, refusing to wear the uniform of common criminals and thus wearing no clothes) and a determined fast to death. The resolution to conquer through suffering led these men, among them Bobby Sands and Brendan McFarlane, to stand by their demands with unconditional commitment until death by starvation. The appeal to the consciences of their captors, the attempt to call forth shame and thereby elicit justice as they perceived it, was unsuccessful before the British insistence on defining the situation in narrow terms of guilt.

•

Maori tribe, New Zealand. In a large meeting house named for a famous ancestor, a Maori was addressing fellow tribes people from all over New Zealand. His speech had turned vitriolic; he was making scathing comments about the political positions of persons both present and absent; and he was interlarding his comments with English swear words. A woman went up to him, laying her hand on his arm and speaking softly. He shook her off and continued. The crowd now moved back from him as far as possible, and as if by general agreement the listeners dropped their gaze to their toes until all he could see was the tops of their heads. The speaker slowed, faltered, was reduced to silence, and then sat down. Immediately the hum of conversation began again. The speaker, ignored and isolated, fidgeted and hurried to greet a relative who made no mention of his speech; then he left the hall, and by breakfast had left the *marae*. The experience of this man — being shamed, ignored, silenced, turned to stone, only there in body, carved in wood, petrified — resulted from his community's rejection of his unacceptable behavior and ended in his own silence, withdrawal, and flight (Metge 1986, 16, 27, abridged).

•

Caribou Eskimo tribe, Canadian Arctic. A song of derision may be sung before the whole community to shame someone guilty of wrongdoing. These satires, with merciless personal attack, hold the other up to public ridicule.

Utahania's song of impeachment against Kanaijuaq reports on his quarrel with his wife and his attempt at deserting her out in the wilds. It honors her for standing up to injustice, taking her son, and making a new life for herself.

Something was whispered
Of man and wife
Who could not agree.
And what was it all about?
A wife who in rightful anger
Tore her husband's furs across,
Took their canoe
And rowed away with her son.
Ay — ay, all who listen,
What do you think of him,
Poor sort of man?
Is he to be envied,
Who is great in his anger
But faint in strength,
Blubbering helplessly,
Properly chastised?
Though it was he
who foolishly proud
Started the quarrel
with stupid words.

The power of shaming, one woman speaking for her sister woman, justifies her action in resisting injustice (Rasmussen 1927, 95–96).

Shaming behavior, as a means of either conflict suppression or escalation, may be a complex series of social cues — the maintaining or loss of face — or a climactic public event. The preceding vignettes offer a variety of scenarios for the latter, and only hint at the power and pervasiveness of the former.

In this chapter, we will examine shame and guilt as social controls that inhibit or permit conflict, and we will then explore the dynamics of conflict and face, conflict and harmony, conflict and honor, and conflict and dignity as parallel processes in traditional and modern cultures.

Shame is an intensely painful social experience. "Nothing is so costly as that which costs shame," the Portuguese proverb observes. The world of observers, critics, and judges surrounds the shamed person. "Shame has watchmen," the Bantu say. The awareness of disapproval or rejection by the social context of significant peers can shape behavior, control choices, silence differences, and conceal conflicts.

CONFLICT: SHAME AND GUILT

Guilt is an equally painful internal experience. The self-punitive judgment of conscience that condemns the person for violating moral, social, familial, or existential rules and values can be a merciless voice demanding the internalization of all conflicts.

Anxiety, shame, and guilt are the normal and sequential control processes that emerge in the first, second, and third years of a child's development in every culture. Each culture has its own balance and its own integrative hierarchy of these internal controls that are contextually congruent. Individualistic cultures seek to minimize anxiety and shame while socializing the child to function predominantly by guilt direction. Socio-centric cultures develop shame functions to levels of mature, sensitive, interpersonal moral relationships (Augsburger 1986, 126).

Guilt and shame are two significantly different processes, however. One can lead to the other; one can conceal the other; each can exaggerate or distort the other. Developmentally, there are immature and mature stages of each: The guilt of a child with its cosmic thought patterns and narcissistic omnipotence gradually changes to a concrete guilt with exacting reciprocity and later to a more formal guilt grounded in principles and values. Similarly, the cosmic and narcissistically omnipotent shame structures of early experience should mature to more limited, concrete processes with reciprocal referents in the ideals held by both person and community and later to a value orientation that prizes congruence with the context and solidarity with significant others. However, individualistic societies repress shame experience, inhibit its resolution, and arrest development at the earliest stage with guilt being overdeveloped as a cover and as the major psychic administrator of internal control. When shame is felt, it is in primitive and infantile rage and self-immolation, as the face burns. In more collective cultures, the maturation of both shame and guilt may be fostered, and the internal controls function conjointly and cooperatively.

Shame arises from tension between the ego and the ideal. In low-context cultures that foster internalization of all controls to facilitate individualism as the goal of personhood, the shame is felt as tension between ego and ego ideal. Shame warns that a goal, internalized as an ideal value, is not being reached; the "shortcoming" is experienced with inner embarrassment and regret. Guilt, in contrast, is anxiety accompanying transgression; shame is anxiety before failure; guilt is commission; shame is omission.

In high-context cultures fostering the development of a collective personality, with a socio-centric sense of identity, the tension of shame is felt less between the ego and the ego ideal and much more between the ego and the social ideal as represented by and actualized in the group or familial ideal. Since the child, in development, was socialized by a larger number of parenting figures, and by processes that model and form controls along patterns of external responsibility to external ideals held by the community, the experience of shame has clear external referents. Honor, face, and the maintaining of accounts of respect given and received become significant to the sense of commonality that defines the collectively experienced selfhood.

When guilt and the law of retaliation function, there has been an act of commission, a transgression that requires repayment, retribution, or revenge. When shame and the law of honor function, there has been a failure that cannot be repaid or requited, an omission that is a shortcoming, an inadequacy or inferiority in the self and in self-presentation. Thus shame is a more total self-valuation, and the emotion cannot be attached to an act that can be rectified; it is associated with a way of being that leads to an embarrassed sense of loss and emptiness, a failing of the ideal.

In individualism, the personality differentiates the control functions into internalized images of the good parent (with loving, valued ideals) and the bad parent (with punitive, punishing demands) with the former becoming the ego ideal, the latter the superego. In violation of rules (guilt), one fears the punitive wrath and the annihilation or mutilation of punishment administered by the internal whip of the superego. In falling short (shame), one fears contempt, abandonment, disgust, and emotional starvation (Piers and Singer 1953, 16).

Guilt, as a form of self-aggression, is interlocked with an allocentric worry that one may have hurt another person; shame, in contrast, is more egocentric (Lebra 1984, 51). In a cross-cultural sentence-completion study, Takie Lebra found striking differences in response to the item, "If you do not know manners and etiquette . . . " The majority of all cultural groups responded egocentrically ("You will be ashamed") or didactically ("You should correct yourself"); but the Japanese demonstrated a higher incidence of guilt ("You will cause discomfort in the people around you," or "Your parents will be criticized") than the other groups studied. Thirty-three percent of the Japanese demonstrated guilt, while only 8 percent of the Koreans and 6 percent of the Chinese gave answers that showed guilt.

Various new religions in Japan and the secular Naikan therapy utilize guilt for revitalization. They induce and intensify guilt as a means of dissipating anger and blame toward others and turn them toward reversal in love and bonding with the other. Yoshimoto, the founder of Naikan, says, "Before you jump, you must squat. As long as you remain standing, you cannot jump up." Squatting in guilt empowers the leap in revitalization.

CONFLICT AND FACEWORK

"Do not remove a fly from your neighbor's face with a hatchet," the Chinese proverb poignantly advises. Face must be honored, respected, preserved, and enhanced in all human relationships. In Western cultures the loss of face is rarely reckoned in conflict strategies or identified as a factor in disruptive encounters, but it is an element in any alienation. More often it is identified as a loss of self-esteem, a threat to self-regard, sense of competence, or pride. In the East and throughout the Southern Hemisphere, the concept of face covers both self-esteem and the esteem of the other, affirmed and reflected regard, felt and recognized worth, and pride and social significance.

A Western couple in South East Asia discovers that valuables are disappearing. They set repeated test situations by leaving money where only the maid has access, and narrow their suspicions to her. To fire her with public accusations and evidence would create a loss of face for her family and a loss of social acceptance for themselves. They consult with a wise older colleague of the host culture. He notes that the Western woman is pregnant and suggests, "Your maid is young and has not been through childbirth. Tell her that you need an older maid to support you and allay your fears, a mother who understands." This statement allowed for a change of personnel without loss of face for either party, even though both sides may have known the primary reason for the action.

A Western administrator in an Asian hospital discovers that the laboratory technician is not on duty to run tests of a patient going into surgery. She sends a servant to the ill man's house demanding the keys to the lab. The technician refuses to give them. She then goes to his home and requests the keys. He surrenders them; she enters the lab and does the necessary tests. In the following weeks she senses a distance in their former good relationship, so she calls him in and asks if something is obstructing their working understandings. He denies that there is anything wrong, but the relationship worsens sharply. At last she consults with a colleague from the culture and recognizes the three levels of attack on his social face implicit in her peremptory actions. The resolution is, of course, by silent third party. The compatriot mentions casually to the man that she is deeply embarrassed by her actions, that she realizes she acted in a European way that was inappropriate and ill advised. In compassion for her loss of face, he responds to her with acceptance, and his own face is restored.

Facework is a universal human experience, a ubiquitous concept that occurs in all cultures.

Face is a psychological image that can be granted and lost and fought for and presented as a gift; it is the public self-image that every member of a society wants to claim for himself or herself; it is a projected image of one's self in a relational context. Face is an identity defined conjointly by the participants in a setting.

Stella Ting-Toomey argues that in some cultures, such as individualistic Australia, Germany, and the United States, maintaining consistency between the private self-image and a public self-image is of paramount importance. The public self-presentation of "face" should correspond to an invariant "core-self" within the person. In other cultures, such as collectivistic China, Korea, and Japan, the self is a situationally and relationally based concept (Gudykunst and Ting-Toomey 1988, 85).

The self in most collectivistic cultures is maintained and defined through active negotiation of facework; in contrast, in Western societies the self is grounded intrapsychically in self-love, self-definition, and self-direction. In the solidarity of a collectivistic setting, the self is not free; it is bound by mutual role obligations and duties as it is structured and nurtured in an ongoing process of give-and-take in facework negotiations. In the West, there must be high consistency between public face and private self-image; in the East, the self is not an individual but a relational construct (see fig. 10).

> "Face" in high-context cultures is a psychological-affective construct that is tied closely with other concepts such as "honor," "shame," and "obligation." In low-context cultures, "face" exists only in the immediate time-space that involves the two conflict parties, while "face" in high-context cultures involves the multiple faces of relatives, friends, and family members that are closely linked to the interactants. "Face" is a relatively "free" concept in low-context cultures, but "face" is an obligatory concept in high-context cultures that reflects one's status hierarchy, role position, and power resource. The more power one has, the more one knows how to bestow, maintain, honor, and destroy face. For members of low-context cultures, directly dealing with "face" in a conflict situation signifies an honest, up-front way of handling a problematic situation. For members of high-context cultures, the indirect, subtle dealing with "face" in a conflict situation reflects good taste and tactfulness.
>
> (Gudykunst and Ting-Toomey 1988, 159)

Figure 10
Facework: Shame and Guilt

Face is a psychological image that can be granted and lost, fought for and presented as a gift. It is the public self-image that every member of every society wants to claim for himself or herself in relationships.

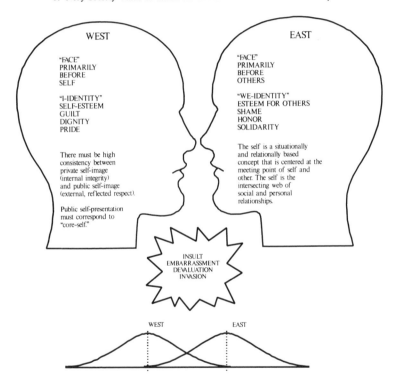

WEST

"FACE"
PRIMARILY
BEFORE
SELF

"I-IDENTITY"
SELF-ESTEEM
GUILT
DIGNITY
PRIDE

There must be high
consistency between
private self-image
(internal integrity)
and public self-image
(external, reflected respect).

Public self-presentation
must correspond to
"core-self."

EAST

"FACE"
PRIMARILY
BEFORE
OTHERS

"WE-IDENTITY"
ESTEEM FOR OTHERS
SHAME
HONOR
SOLIDARITY

The self is a situationally
and relationally based
concept that is centered at the
meeting point of self and
other. The self is the
intersecting web of
social and personal
relationships.

INSULT
EMBARRASSMENT
DEVALUATION
INVASION

WEST   EAST

Honoring another's face — politeness — is an elaborate process in some cultures, a minimal transaction in others, but is universal nevertheless. A theory of politeness offers significant dimensions to our understanding of facework. All members of a society have (and see each other having) "face" — the public self-image that each person wants to claim for herself or himself. The "face," like Janus, has two aspects: Positive face is the desire to be ratified, understood, liked, included, and approved; negative face is the desire to not have one's actions impeded, to be free from imposition, and to feel respect for one's autonomy, territory, resources, and rights. We may refer to these as "face" and "space."

This distinction between positive politeness and negative politeness, according to P. Brown and S. Levinson, distinguishes the ways cultures deal with distance, power, and the rating of an imposition on another person. Positive-politeness cultures can be characterized as having few serious face-threatening acts; impositions are regarded as small; a relaxed and level social distance permits easygoing interactions. These are friendly, "back-slapping" cultures, such as that in the rural and western United States, that among certain New Guinea groups, and that among the Mbuti pygmies. The negative-politeness cultures place high value on never imposing on, coercing, or inconveniencing another; people in these cultures avoid imposing on others by always acting or speaking indirectly, by hedging so the other has an option not to respond. These negative-politeness cultures include those of the British, Japanese, Malagasy, and the Brahmans of India (Brown and Levinson 1978, 250).

Both negative and positive facework are present in all cultures, but the value orientations of a culture will influence the members' preference for a particular set of facework in a conflict situation. The ability to use face-honoring, face-compensating, or face-neutral strategies in threatened relationships is a mark of interpersonal competence.

Figure 11 offers a model of facework constructed by Ting-Toomey. The basic assumptions of her theory of the facework-negotiation process are: (1) members of all cultures negotiate over the concept of face; (2) the concept of face is especially problematic in situations of uncertainty (for example, request situations, complaint situations, embarrassment situations, and conflict situations) when the situated identities of the interactants are called into question; (3) all face negotiation entails multiple-goal orientations (self-concern and other-concern, negative face and positive face); (4) all negotiators express a concern for self-face protection or other-face support (or both) in problematic situa-

Figure 11
Implicit Dimensions in All Facework

ONE: CONCERN FOR FACE: Care for one's own face, for the other's face or both
TWO: NEED FOR FACE: Need for inclusion or for distance

POSITIVE-FACE NEED
(ASSOCIATION AND INCLUSION)

SELF-POSITIVE FACE (SPF) maintained by the use of certain communication strategies to defend and protect one's need for inclusion and association.	OTHER-POSITIVE FACE (OPF) maintained by use of certain communication strategies to defend and support the other person's need for inclusion and association.
SELF-FACE	OTHER-FACE
MUTUAL	FACE
CONCERN	CONCERN
SELF-NEGATIVE FACE (SNF) maintenance means the use of certain interaction strategies to give oneself freedom and space, to protect self from the other's infringement on one's autonomy.	OTHER-NEGATIVE FACE (ONF) maintenance means the use of certain interaction strategies to signal respect for the other person's need for freedom, space, and dissociation.

NEGATIVE-FACE NEED
(DISSOCIATION AND AUTONOMY)

In conflict, low-context, individualistic cultures tend to use SPF and SNF strategies to defend and protect the self and autonomy (one's own face and space).

In conflict, high-context, collectivistic cultures tend to use OPF and ONF strategies in supporting and signaling respect for the other's face and space and in maintaining mutuality.

tions; (5) all negotiators express a need for dissociation (negative face) and/or a need for association (positive face) in problematic situations; (6) the self/other orientation dimension and the association/dissociation dimension are influenced by the relational variables (such as low/high familiarity level and low/high intimacy level) and the situational variables (such as informal/formal level and public/private level) of the context, and the salience (such as topic magnitude and topic commitment) of the problematic issue;

(7) the self/other dimension and the positive-face and negative-face need dimension are influenced by the cultural interpretation and the cultural expectation levels of the context; and (8) while the four sets of suprastrategy — SPF, OPF, SNF, and ONF (see fig. 11) — are present in all negotiation settings in all cultures, certain sets of suprastrategies are preferred by members of a culture more often than others (Gudykunst and Ting-Toomey 1988, 86).

All cultures have some concept of "face" — a public image that each person claims for herself or himself — but its function is significantly different in low-context or high-context cultures.

The low-context members hold to an "I-identity" in their facework with others; the high-context persons project a "we-identity." The I-identity makes facework a competitive process; the we-identity turns facework negotiation into a collaborative process.

The usefulness of this diagram (fig. 11) in illuminating the differing functions of facework in each context is worked out in propositional form in a careful analysis by Ting-Toomey, who developed the following series of hypotheses:

Proposition 1: Members of individualistic, low-context cultures express a greater degree of self-face maintenance than members of collectivistic, high-context cultures.

Proposition 2: Members of collectivistic, high-context cultures express a greater degree of mutual-face or other-face maintenance than members of individualistic, low-context cultures.

Proposition 3: Members of individualistic, low-context cultures use more autonomy-preserving strategies (negative-face need) than members of collectivistic, high-context cultures.

Proposition 4: Members of collectivistic, high-context cultures use more approval-seeking strategies (positive-face need) than members of individualistic, low-context cultures.

Proposition 5: Members of individualistic, low-context cultures use more self-positive-face (SPF) and self-negative-face (SNF) suprastrategies than members of collectivistic, high-context cultures.

Proposition 6: Members of collectivistic, high-context cultures use more other-positive-face (OPF) and other-negative-face (ONF) suprastrategies than members of individualistic, low-context cultures.

Proposition 7: Members of individualistic, low-context cultures use a greater degree of direct face-negotiation strategies than members of collectivistic, high-context cultures.

Proposition 8: Members of collectivistic, high-context cultures use a greater degree of indirect face-negotiation strategies than members of individualistic, low-context cultures.

Proposition 9: Members of individualistic, low-context cultures use more dominating or controlling strategies to manage conflict than members of collectivistic, high-context cultures.

Proposition 10: Members of collectivistic, high-context cultures use more obliging or smoothing strategies to manage conflict than members of individualistic, low-context cultures.

Proposition 11: Members of individualistic, low-context cultures use a greater degree of solution-oriented conflict style than members of collectivistic, high-context cultures.

Proposition 12: Members of collectivistic, high-context cultures use a greater degree of avoidance-oriented conflict style than members of individualistic, low-context cultures.

(Gudykunst and Ting-Toomey 1988, 159)

One culture's belief system is another's disbelief system.

Members of low-context cultures view the indirect way of handling conflict as a weak, cowardly, or evasive act while members of high-context cultures view the direct way of handling conflict as lacking in politeness, or good taste.

Low-context cultures prefer to separate the conflict issue from the person, but high-context cultures view the problem issue and the problem person as interrelated. So while the one perspective seeks to manage the conflict from an instrumental, solution-oriented, impersonal stance, the other sees the affective, relational, personal issues as indivisible, so open conflict is best avoided at all costs. Thus the low-context cultures tend to view the world in analytic, linear, logical terms that allow them to be hard on problems but soft on people, focused on instrumental outcomes but easy on affective issues; while high-context cultures perceive the world in synthetic, spiral logic that links the conflict event and its impact, issue, actors, content, and context.

Table 5
Summary of Low-context and High-context
Face-negotiation Processes

Key Constructs of "Face"	Individualistic, Low-context Cultures	Collectivistic, High-context Cultures
Identity	emphasis on "I-identity"	emphasis on "we-identity"
Concern	self-face concern	other-face concern
Need	autonomy, dissociation, negative-face need	inclusion, association, positive-face need
Suprastrategy	self-concern and positive face; self-concern and negative face	other-concern and positive face; other-concern and negative face
Mode	direct mode	indirect mode
Style	control or confrontational style, and solution-oriented style	obliging or avoidance style, and affective-oriented style
Strategy	distributive or competitive strategies	integrative or collaborative strategies
Speech Act	direct speech acts	indirect speech acts
Nonverbal Act	individualistic, nonverbal acts; direct emotional expressions	contextualistic (role-oriented), nonverbal acts; indirect emotional expressions

(Gudykunst and Ting-Toomey 1988, 93)

Privacy and autonomy are the trademarks of individualistic, low-context cultures just as interdependence and inclusion are the trademarks of collectivistic, high-context cultures. So in conflict, the individualist finds the greatest threat to face comes from an attack on the need for autonomy and the loss of control over self and others. Since the low-context culture offers little support or security, the threat to the person's face makes him or her look dependent (considered childish) or incompetent. When a conflict breaks out for a person in a more collectivistic setting, the threat

Table 6
Summary of Characteristics of Conflict
in Low- and High-context Cultures

Key Questions	Low-context Cultures	High-context Cultures

Why?	analytic, linear logic
	instrumental-oriented
	dichotomy between conflict
	  and conflict parties
		synthetic, spiral logic
		expressive-oriented
		integration of conflict
		  and conflict parties

When?	individual-oriented
	low-collective normative
	  expectations
	violations of individual
	  expectations create
	  conflict potentials
		group-oriented
		high-collective normative
		  expectations
		violations of collective
		  expectations create
		  conflict potentials

What?	revealment
	direct, confrontational
	  attitude
		concealment
		indirect, noncon-
		  frontational attitude

How?	action- and solution-oriented
	
	explicit communication
	  codes
	line-logic style
	rational, factual
	  rhetoric
	open, direct strategies
		face- and relationship-
		  oriented
		implicit communication
		  codes
		point-logic style
		intuitive, affective
		  rhetoric
		ambiguous, indirect
		  strategies

(Gudykunst and Ting-Toomey 1988, 158)

to face comes from the possible loss of inclusion, approval, and association by others. The perfect illustration is from the contrast of Japanese and American mothers' threats to their children. "I'll make you stay in if you don't obey," the American warns (a threat to independence, autonomy, and self-face). "I'll make you stay out if you don't behave," the Japanese mother threatens (a threat to inclusion, approval, and other-face).

A conflict between an Englishman and an American illustrates the difference between the level of high- or low-context influence. The Englishman, expressing the high-cultural demand and high-cultural restraint characteristics of his more hierarchical setting, plays out the conflict by cultural scripts mastered long before. His responses are quite cerebral, and focus on how the other is either not understanding or not playing by the rules that should prevail in this circumstance. There are specific, collective, normative ways to handle interpersonal altercations. The Englishman might say something like: "Something or someone has slipped up, but it's all right, though it's bloody embarrassing."

The American, demonstrating the low-context patterns of a culture with no collective consensus on manners or style of conflict resolution, plays by idiosyncratic rules and busily improvises coordination on the spot. Since the American improvises as the conflict unfolds, the probability of making an error in the interaction is much higher, and the likelihood of making a bad situation worse by insisting on processing feelings, spilling out anxieties, and disclosing uncertainties is so much the greater. He might say something like: "Let's be frank, get it all out on the table, clear the matter up once and for all, and end up as better friends because we ran the risk of spilling our deepest fears."

The high-context culture is more prone to misunderstandings and conflicts when the culturally normative expectations of appropriate behavior are violated. In response the Englishman thus says: "I say, we rarely see that sort of thing done around here." In the low-context culture the situation turns volatile when individual expectations are violated: "Hold on, I can overlook a lot, but this is too much."

HIGH CONTEXT, HARMONY, AND AVOIDANCE

High-context cultures tend to place a higher value on harmony, public conformity, and therefore the avoidance of conflict. In his analysis of conflict patterns in traditional Chinese culture, David Y. J. Ho observes:

The importance of extending due regard for the face of others can hardly be overemphasized in Chinese social intercourse. To be careful about not hurting someone's face is not simply a matter of being kind or considerate; it functions to avoid conflict, or, more precisely, to avoid confrontation or bringing conflict out into the open. This conflict avoidance is a basic orientation in Chinese social processes rooted in the Confucian model of society based on the maintenance of harmony in interpersonal relations. Thus the exercise of caution to prevent hurting people's face is regarded as a hallmark of social skill and experience which presumably mellow with advancing age. (Ho 1974, 248)

The traditional Chinese model of conflict resolution is based on saving face for both parties in dispute. Secret negotiations are utilized not only to save face before each other, but they are also precisely calculated to bypass difficulties arising from the fear of losing face by either party before other watching groups who are not directly involved in the conflict. Disputes are often settled on publicly announced terms in which neither party appears to have suffered a loss, when in reality one did gain an advantage over the other.

Special care is taken to not take advantage of one already in a defenseless position, to not cause a complete loss of face. It is dangerous to push people to the limit where there is nothing left to lose. There are a number of Chinese proverbs that express the wisdom that one dare not press another until such a desperate position is reached that the other has no alternative but to counterattack.

A particular danger inherent in the mode of dealing with conflicts based on face-saving, however, is that it can lead to confrontation avoidance, but not a genuine resolution of these conflicts. That is, face-saving has taken precedence over problem solving, rather than providing a more favorable climate in which conflicts can be resolved. When this happens, conflicts are likely to assume a violent form when they do erupt into the open. (Ho 1974, 249)

In ambiguous conflict situations, the fear that a social error of behavior or speech will cause a loss of face leads both parties to use withdrawal, silence, and indirect communication. The more potentially conflictual the situation, the more subtle will be the sender, and the more sensitive must be the receiver. Two Malaysian families offer an example of subtle communication. A daughter of a higher-class family and a son from a lower-class family fell in love. The son requested permission from his parents to marry the girl. His mother offered to approach the girl's family to see if the marriage were acceptable. She made an appointment, went to the home, was greeted by the mother, and was shown to the sitting room. Refreshments were served consisting of tea and bananas. The two mothers talked of the weather and village life but never mentioned their children. After a time, the guest thanked the hostess and left. At home she told her son the marriage was unacceptable. As inappropriate as bananas and tea, the two children did not belong together. This subtle cue avoided direct discussion that would have led to loss of face for both persons since face is a mutual reciprocal process in human relations (Shon and Ja 1982, 216).

CONFLICT AND HARMONY

Harmony and conflict are often pictured as mutually exclusive; many people believe that acceptance of the conflict model of society requires the rejection of the harmony model. This is an oversimplified, either-or, Western-style dichotomy.

The more harmony-oriented that a group is, the more conflict-sensitive the group will be; the more committed the group to practicing the cultural value of harmony, the more intensely conflict will be internalized: "Competition within a group which is in theory harmoniously united tends to become fiercer and more emotionally involved than in one where competition is accepted as normal. As such it leaves scars after the event in the resentful humiliation of the defeated" (Dore 1959, 343).

Conflict is inherent in harmony; at the very least, it interlocks with it, is bipolarly related to it, and is the emergence of inner vitality within harmonic structures.

The Japanese were described by Ruth Benedict with contradictory adjectives: polite but insolent, rigid but innovative, submissive but not amenable to control, loyal but treacherous, disciplined but insubordinate (Benedict 1946, 3).

These bipolarities make much more sense if one follows Lebra's suggestion and replaces the "buts" with "therefores" (Lebra 1984, 57). (And we might add that we should read the pairs of adjectives both ways since each is a cause, and each is an effect: polite and therefore insolent; insolent and therefore polite; and so on.)

In comparing harmonious and competitive societies, we do not discover that the former has no conflict and the latter much conflict, but merely different patterns of conflict. The one group may experience more conflict arising from goal competition or contrasting perceptions; the other group may experience more conflict from the felt need for more joint decision making, for greater inclusion in process and consequences. The greater the interdependence, the greater the potential for conflict; the greater the concern for inclusion in joint decision making, the more tension generated by the drive for harmony.

Japanese consciousness produces a tendency to resolve conflicts by use of patience, forbearance, and the passage of time, by "letting the dispute flow to the ocean." This concept of amicable, mutual understanding is based on trust in each other's good will. If this trust breaks down, a mutually trusted third party is involved. The third party is respected, or is said to "have face" with both. Conciliation, the goal of which is to protect the face of both parties, actually takes the form of an attempt to "save the face" of the influential person who now is entrusted with the dispute. The mediator does not use reason, a universal standard on rights, or a decision on who is right or wrong. The objective is to settle the dispute in such a way as to restore friendly relations, to regain a sense of harmony. The parties may not be satisfied with the solution but they go along to save the face of the third party (Hanami 1984, 116).

In the Chinese family, with its closed system based on harmony and the maintaining of social face, conflict is avoided by many ingenious means, and suppressed when these fail. In a fight between brothers, in spite of the different status levels of older and younger, both are blamed. The older is blamed for not giving in to the younger, while the younger is scolded for not respecting the older. Both brothers will be punished for their aggressive behavior (Tseng and Hsu 1971, 7).

Harmony, for classic Chinese thought, is the goal of human society. In personal virtue, marriage, family, village, and nation, harmony is the keynote of all thinking. Confucius plainly prefers social harmony to a just resolution of actual conflicts. *The Book of Changes* contains a hexagram called *sung*, meaning litigation, contention, and controversy. The interpretation of it, in summary, is: "If one is entangled in conflict, the only salvation lies in being so clear-headed and inwardly strong that he is always ready to come to terms by meeting the opponent halfway. To carry the conflict to the bitter end has evil effects even when one is in the right, because the enmity is then perpetuated" (Wu 1967, 227).

Lao Tzu summarizes this wisdom of harmony by saying, "The man of virtue attends to his duties; while a man of no virtue attends to his rights."

In reflection on the Chinese cultural value of harmony, John Wu concludes:

> Fatalism is our besetting sin. We are inclined to think too exclusively in terms of concord or a succession of concords. Whenever there is a discord, our harmony is disrupted. In other words, we seldom if ever think of a discord as an opportunity for rising to a new concord. The West is more adept in the art of resolution of discord, thus continuing the harmony through the discordant interval. When confronted with such a discordant interval, the Chinese too often feel utterly at a loss as to what to do except to wait patiently for the turning of the tide, and, when patience is exhausted, to burst out in uncontrollable passion and emotion. We have much to learn from the West in the way of resolution of discord. On the other hand, the West should remember that the discordant intervals are, after all, not the norm and that we cannot rest in restlessness. (Wu 1967, 233)

East Asian cultures share a broad heritage strongly influenced by the Buddhist, Taoist, Confucian, and Shinto traditions, which collectively stress the importance of social harmony. As Ahn Toupin suggests, the conflict norms throughout East Asian cultures share a common tendency toward the following: (1) deference to others, (2) verbal devaluation of self and family, (3) absence of verbal aggression, (4) absence of direct expression of feelings, (5) avoidance of confrontation, and (6) lack of assertiveness (Toupin 1980, 76–86).

To understand the value placed on community solidarity, it is helpful to examine the traditional Javanese perspective on harmony.

The Javanese value of harmony is rooted in a view of the universe as interrelated and interdependent in a balanced unity that includes all things in an assigned and necessary place. Thus unity, balance, and harmony are to be constantly maintained in the hierarchical structure of reality, so a neither-nor approach is the characteristic means of resolving all conflicts. All things are neither totally accepted nor totally rejected.

An either-or approach assumes that both claims cannot be equally true. One must be true, the other false; thus one must choose the one most true on the basis of certain objective and absolute criteria of truth. The decision is not seen as THE TRUTH, but is measured by it, and must conform to it.

A both-and approach presumes that both claims possess some truth. Absolute criteria are beyond our capacity to conceptualize, so there are no clear-cut, totally right choices. Both sides always possess elements of the truth that must be embraced wherever found, conserved whenever possible, and synthesized since life is a totality and all has value.

A neither-nor approach sees both claims as mixed, with both truth and falsehood. Life is a mystery; appearances are always deceiving; and harmony, unity, and balance are the essential things, not truth, perfection, and absolutism. One must be flexible, adaptive, absorbent, pragmatic, and gradualistic. Wisdom lies in discovering the agreements that are possible, the covenants that can be achieved no matter that they are partial and heuristic. Wisdom is the ability to achieve workable compromise that neither alienates one side nor excludes the other.

> A wise neither-nor decision is formulated in such a way that nobody will feel totally rejected, although nobody will feel that his/her idea is fully accepted either. But that is good enough to get a unanimous consensus. The wiser the leader, the more his/her decision will be characterized by the "neither-nor" approach, which seeks what is "suitable" for the immediate situation or condition. Not what is objectively good or right, but what is contextually or situationally or subjectively fitting. (Darmaputera 1982, 357–58)

> Life in society is characterized by harmonious unity, quiet peaceful helping each other, soothing over the differences, cooperation and mutual acceptance. In relation to superiors and supernature, one should be respectful, polite, obedient, and distant. To family one should be close with a feeling of belonging. (Mulder 1978, 39)

In community decision making, every member of the group is allowed to speak and is attended to by the others. After prolonged give-and-take and the weighing of all known pros and cons, a decision — at minimum a compromise, at maximum a new solution — is reached. The leader, as social head of the familial group process, is a father to the community, not an authoritarian power figure. The process is sometimes called "consultation in order to reach a unanimous consent led by the spirit of wisdom" (Darmaputera 1982, 70).

A characteristically Amerindian form of communal harmony is the model of equilibrium observed in the Mexican village of Tzintzuntzán. This system of maintaining "a balanced world" is based on a worldview of "an image of limited good." The Tzintzuntzanos see their social, economic, and natural universes as possessing almost all the desired things in life — land, money, health, love, friendship, honor, respect, power, influence, security, safety, and even *machismo* in absolute, given quantities sufficient to fill at least the minimal needs of villagers. Not only are they strictly limited, there is no way to increase available supplies. It is a closed world with a closed system: An individual or family can improve its position only at the expense of others. Change or growth is a threat; cooperation is undesirable; life is a constant struggle; and the equilibrium of shared poverty is the key to a healthy society.

In Tzintzuntzán, the basic principle of conflict resolution reflects these principles of limited good and necessary equilibrium. The concept of justice hardly exists; conflict resolution consists in restoring the status quo. Regardless of where blame may lie, the goal is to put things back into the previously existing situation. Conflict is dyadic. There is no familial or friendly cooperation. Since chance and luck explain character, behavior, and their consequences, vengeance is rarely pursued. Because balance is the final good desired, simple repayment, not damages, brief imprisonment, not punitive sentencing, the return of what was taken or damaged, not an abstract ruling of retributive justice are prized (Foster 1967, 180–83).

In concluding their excellent study *Conflict in Japan*, the editors, Krauss, Rohlen, and Steinhoff, offer a general contrast between Western and Japanese approaches to conflict:

> In the West, the preferred, the most frequent, and probably the most effective conflict management techniques are impersonal and formal, . . . shifting the problem to some impersonal authority, . . . to general principles that can be applied to all situations. Thus the most frequent, legitimate, and effective conflict management mechanisms are . . . law, contract, arbitration, unilateral decision by the highest authority, and majority rule voting (even within small groups).
>
> Contrast this case to Japan, where the most legitimate, effective, and frequent conflict management mechanisms are the informal and personal ones of small-group discussion, personal communication, and the use of go-betweens. These techniques keep the conflict localized and centered on the original parties. Wherever the norms of harmony are still strong, conflict can best be handled by personalizing it by bringing together the leaders of conflict groups and invoking

the norms of interpersonal relations. (Krauss, Rohlen, and Steinhoff 1984, 388–89)

CONFLICT AND HONOR

Honor is one's value in one's own eyes, but also in the eyes of one's society. It is an estimation of one's worth, one's claim to pride, and it is also the acknowledgment of that claim, one's right to pride, and one's ascribed excellence or prestige. Honor is the nexus between the ideals of society and their reproduction in the person who aspires to achieve them. The right to pride is the right to status, the right to a recognized social identity.

One makes a claim to honor, and the society or group validates that claim or ridicules it. Because honor is a hierarchical concept, it is universally associated with the head, dishonor with the feet. The head is bowed, touched, uncovered, covered, crowned, and adorned when honor is being shown; one dishonors others by kicking them, treading on them, or showing them the sole of one's foot.

In conflict, one person may intend an insult, the other turn a blind eye and refuse to recognize it. Once the insult is realized, the person is dishonored. An insult given in jest may be dismissed with laughter; given in attack, it demands reply.

In hierarchy, one with the right of authority does not affront an inferior in exercising that right. It is honorable to be protected by an authority, humiliating to be protected by an inferior since this acknowledges superiority. One may overlook an insult from an inferior — it is from beneath — but not from a peer. One may accept an insult from superiors — it is their right — but not from an equal.

Self-regard is molested where one is insulted or defamed, or believes oneself to have been so treated. If one acts toward another in such a way that suggests the other is not worthy of consideration or recognition, this molests self-regard. The core of social personality is touched; manliness/womanliness and personal power are questioned. If this humiliation has been observed by others, the reputation for honor is at stake. If it is private, the ego ideal has been insulted, and the story can be told to the social world of judges.

In Mediterranean groups such as the Montenegrins of the Balkans, honor is fiercely defended by response in kind to any insult. The sullied group is required to retain its "honor," which is really a symbolic screen for its power. This honor-shame syndrome, so widely noted in the Mediterranean cultures, is directly linked to intergroup competition, the groups' ratios of recognized power, and their proud possession of limited resources.

> Honor can be thought of as the ideology of a property holding group which struggles to define, enlarge, and protect its patrimony in a competitive arena. As a political phenomenon, honor can attach to any human group from the nuclear family to the nation state. The problem of honor becomes salient when the group is threatened with competition from equivalent groups — especially when small, particularistic groups such as families, clans, or gangs are the principle units of power, sovereign or nearly so over the territories they control. (Schneider 1971, 2)

The two codes — honor and shame — are reciprocal forces that serve to unite groups, police the boundaries, define who is included or excluded, and enforce conformity. In the absence of state controls and macrocosmic stability and security, microcosmic groups develop and maintain their own means of social control — the codes of honor and shame — that are adapted to the intense conflicts that external pressures create within and between groups. A social order is generated that protects nuclear family solidarity, lineage solidarity, or communal solidarity.

The vulnerability of family boundaries to a violation of honor convinces others to exercise caution and restraint, and legitimates limited aggression in retaliating to restore the sanctity of that boundary. Social boundaries, turf lines, and especially sexual norms become the foci of honor and shame maintenance. Particularly among pastoral societies, which place a premium on large families, women become the repository of family and lineage honor, the focus of common interest among the men of the family who are committed to protect or avenge their virtue. Women become currency to be hoarded, protected, isolated, and shamed into virtue. Referring to certain areas of the European side of the Mediterranean, Jane Schneider writes:

> Women present a defensive front to the world, ... warding off aggression through posture alone. Their message, couched in the ideology of shame, and in the behavior of lowered eyes and conservative clothing, if not of total seclusion, is thus: "I would not conceive of violating the sanctity of this household, or defying the honor of its head, and you had better not either." (Schneider 1971, 20)

Virginity before and chastity after marriage are central to the code. Among various North African pastoralists, an unmarried girl's loss of virginity brings unbearable shame on her family, who, if they are to recover their honor, must kill the girl and then her lover. This is the traditional norm although the forms of retaliation vary widely in practice within and between groups (Peristiany 1965, 179).

> Honor is the ethic appropriate to an individual who always sees himself through the eyes of others, who has need of others to exist, because his self image is inseparable from the image of himself that he receives back from others. Respectability ... is essentially defined by its social dimension, and so must be won and defended in the face of everyone. (Bourdieu 1979, 113)

Many disputes can be quantified (*A* demands four pigs from *B*; *B* offers three pigs as settlement), but the crucial factor may be qualitative, that is, the issue of honor. In negotiation, the size of one party's demands — quantity — may be motivated by and measured against an indefinable quality — the honor sought.

Cultural values and standards specify what constitutes honor. Where equality among peers is prized, a person gains honor by refusing to take too great an advantage from negotiations — too much wealth or honor — and is prudently content with less goods

Figure 12
Honor and Esteem

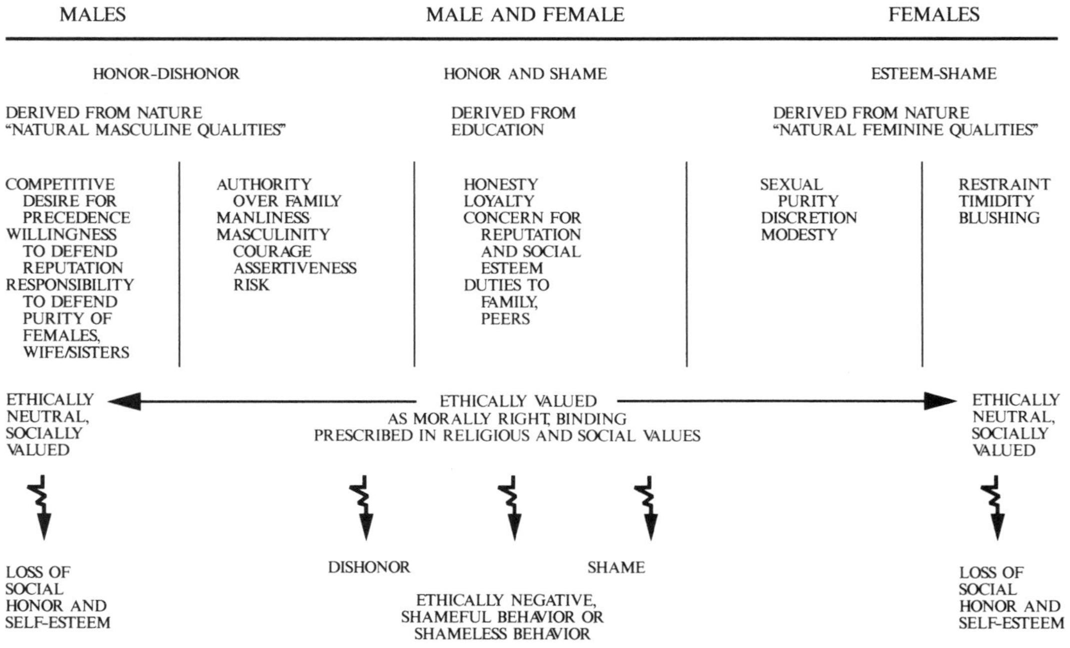

MALES		MALE AND FEMALE		FEMALES	
HONOR–DISHONOR		**HONOR AND SHAME**		**ESTEEM-SHAME**	
DERIVED FROM NATURE "NATURAL MASCULINE QUALITIES"		DERIVED FROM EDUCATION		DERIVED FROM NATURE "NATURAL FEMININE QUALITIES"	
COMPETITIVE DESIRE FOR PRECEDENCE WILLINGNESS TO DEFEND REPUTATION RESPONSIBILITY TO DEFEND PURITY OF FEMALES, WIFE/SISTERS	AUTHORITY OVER FAMILY MANLINESS MASCULINITY COURAGE ASSERTIVENESS RISK	HONESTY LOYALTY CONCERN FOR REPUTATION AND SOCIAL ESTEEM DUTIES TO FAMILY, PEERS		SEXUAL PURITY DISCRETION MODESTY	RESTRAINT TIMIDITY BLUSHING

ETHICALLY VALUED
AS MORALLY RIGHT, BINDING
PRESCRIBED IN RELIGIOUS AND SOCIAL VALUES

ETHICALLY NEUTRAL, SOCIALLY VALUED

ETHICALLY NEUTRAL, SOCIALLY VALUED

ETHICALLY NEGATIVE, SHAMEFUL BEHAVIOR OR SHAMELESS BEHAVIOR

DISHONOR

SHAME

LOSS OF SOCIAL HONOR AND SELF-ESTEEM

LOSS OF SOCIAL HONOR AND SELF-ESTEEM

Table 7
Issues of Honor

A demands complete vindication and restoration of honor (prestige or face). Thus, *A* demands:

1. Complete admission by *B* of responsibility for injury.
2. A public apology to all concerned.
3. Ritual performance.
4. Heavy compensation.
5. Promise of future good behavior.

B denies all responsibility for any loss to *A*'s honor. *B* (1) denies such loss occurred, or (2) refuses to accept any responsibility. *B* may concede the following steps:

1. Admit partial responsibility for injury to *A*'s reputation.
2. Admit total responsibility while acting under stress of intense provocation by *A*.
3. Admit total responsibility with no claim of provocation by *A*.
4. Take step 2 or 3, plus make a tacit apology to *A*.
5. Take step 2 or 3, plus make a formal (public) apology to *A*.
6. Take step 2, 3, or 5, plus make a public ritual (and accept its expenses) to promote restoration of *A*'s reputation.
7. Take step 2, 3, 5, or 6, plus pay compensation to *A* of a nominal amount.
8. Take step 7, except make the compensation substantial.

(Gulliver 1979, 163)

in order to gain the honored good. So sufficiency is chosen rather than claiming a competitive advantage. Where competitive victory is valued highly, the gain for oneself may be ignored; the crucial concern is the victory of denying advantage or satisfaction to the opponent. The attempt to cause harm, inflict punishment, and even old scores may rise not as much from resentment and hatred as from the social need to deprive the opponent of honor, reputation, and political status in the community.

Honor may be visualized in quantifiable terms in some cultures where it is prized as a central value. In a dispute between two kinship groups in a Jordanian Arab village, the issues were all defined as matters of honor between the families. The relative honor was expressed and compared in terms of the formal slaughter of sheep by each lineage. "Honor, an abstract concept, is symbolized by material goods whose exchange serves as some sort of balance sheet for calculating the relative quantity of intangible resources (honor) held by each side in the dispute" (Antoun 1972, 101).

CONFLICT AND DIGNITY

Honor, as a concept of self-definition, is absolute, an ideological leftover. It has been replaced in modern thought by the concept of dignity, argues Peter Berger. In the rest of this section I will summarize Berger's thought on this matter (see Berger 1970, 339–47).

That honor is obsolete is revealed by the inability of most contemporaries to understand insult as an assault on honor. Motives of defending honor have no standing in Western law. Those who claim to have lost it are objects of amusement rather than sympathy. The decline of honor in the West at the beginning of the modern era was paralleled by the rise of a morality with unprecedented concern for the dignity and rights of the individual. What is honor? What is dignity? Why this change?

Honor is associated with a hierarchical order of society, the codes of chivalry, the structures of feudalism, and the surviving guilds such as the military, the law, and medicine. Obligations of honor dictate standards of relationship to inferiors, but the full code applies to those of like elite status. In contemporary honor-based societies, such as rural Mediterranean societies, the community exists within an all-embracing system of honor with particular obligations according to status and gender. Honor is the possession of idealized norms and a legitimization of defending those norms in retaliation. Dishonor is a loss of face in the community, a loss of self before the ideal of being human. Honor is one's persona, one's social mask, and the mask is what is valued, what is real.

Dignity, as distinct from honor, always refers to the intrinsic humanity apart from socially imposed roles or norms. The solitary self — the person alone — is the bearer of dignity and in-alienable human rights. This is not a new thought. It is found in the confrontation of Nathan and David, in Sophocles's clash be-tween Antigone and Oreon, in Mencius's parable of the criminal stopping a child from falling down a well. But, as Berger notes, what is peculiarly modern is the manner in which the reality of this intrinsic humanity is related to the realities of society. Mod-ern anthropology, sociology, and political theory locate the real self as over or above race, color, gender, creed, age, and physical status: "The concept of honor implies that identity is essentially, or at least importantly, linked to institutional roles. The modern concept of dignity, by contrast, implies that identity is essentially independent of institutional roles" (Berger 1970, 343).

In the world of honor, the individual is the persona, the pub-lic reputation, the knight in full regalia, not the naked man in bed. In the world of dignity, the regalia and armor are disguises that hide the true self. It is the naked person, specifically in his or her most intimate sexuality, that is more truthful than the pub-lic façade. Self-discovery is reversed. Where the honor-oriented person discovers true identity in roles and turns away to false con-sciousness in introspection, the dignity-defined person finds true identity by disposing of socially defined roles that are illusions, masks, alienating expressions of bad faith. In the one view, identity is an extension of history reiterated in performance of prototypical acts; in the other, history is a succession of mystifications that must be laid aside to attain authenticity.

This change has been aptly characterized by the terms *de-institutionalization* and *subjectivization* to summarize technology and industrialization, urbanization and population growth, the communication explosion between all groups, social mobility, the pluralization of social worlds, and the profound changes in the social contexts of childhood development. The institutional fab-ric has been fragmented, its plausibility lost, so the individual is thrown back on subjective experience to create a foothold in reality, to dredge up the meaning and stability we require to exist.

Honor was lodged in the world of intact, stable institutions, and their disintegration makes it an increasingly meaningless no-tion. Institutions and roles are no longer a "home" for the self.

Identity is no longer an objectively certified, subjectively received fact, a given; instead it is the goal of a devious and difficult quest. The demise of honor is costly, since humans have a fundamental need for order as well as freedom. It has made possible the fuller discovery of the autonomous person with intrinsic dignity derived from one's very being over and above all and any social identifications.

We have both gained and lost dignity in losing sight of the stability and security of honor. "A rediscovery of honor in the future development of modern society is both empirically plausible and morally desirable," concludes Berger, since the fundamental constitution of humans requires us to construct an ordered reality through institutions. The crucial ethical test is whether they can succeed in embodying and stabilizing the discoveries of human dignity to transform and direct the sense of honor that returns, *ipso facto*, with any return to institutions in social life.

This synopsis of Berger's argument has been pursued with depth because it is central to any evaluation of the functions of honor and shame, dignity and guilt, and respect and disrespect for face in the interfaces of human conflict.

NONCONFRONTATIONAL CONFLICT MANAGEMENT

Confrontation — a direct challenge — may be very undesirable in a culture where harmony, or at least the appearance of harmony, is highly valued. In such settings, for example Japan, nonconfrontational strategies are first attempted and exhausted before a direct process is initiated. Takie Sugiyama Lebra has gathered seven such strategies from Japanese experience, although, as she notes, they are not unique to Japan (Lebra 1984, 42–55).

1. Anticipatory management. A conflict can be anticipated, defused, and managed in a preventative way before it is generated. Foreseeing one's inability to reciprocate, one may refuse to accept a favor that would demand a return gift. Or a farmer who is a good mechanic may not do his own tractor repair because it would open him to his neighbor's request.

2. Negative communication. Silence, avoidance, evasion, and absence may show disagreement or even anger without confrontation. "I did not answer" may mean "I objected." Silence, which may have many meanings from social reserve to sulking, can communicate what the person intends without the threat of invasion, and its negative implications can be denied if it is challenged.

3. Situational friendliness. This "code switching," as Lebra calls it, allows persons who avoid each other to assume friendliness when necessary at town meetings, in the presence of important guests, or in an emergency such as observance of a death. This happens commonly when people may discuss frustrations over a drink and then return to formal conversation or avoidance.

4. Triadic mediation. The conflict between A and B may be reduced or managed indirectly by go-between C. The mediator may use her or his power or prestige to negotiate a breakthrough. "Save my face," the mediator will say, threatening to take offense if the conflict continues in spite of her or his third-party efforts. The third party's taking vicarious responsibility is institutionalized in many societies; in Japan, a superior may accept accountability for failure by staff members and resign to both resolve the situation and retain personal honor while being publicly dishonored.

5. Displacement. Anger or disapproval of one party is conveyed to another who is more vulnerable or whose retaliation is less threatening. A contractor who took over his father-in-law's business scolds his employees or his son when his real hostility is toward his predecessor. When asking a neighbor to stop playing the piano at night, a woman might say it is "because my husband can't sleep." Emotions may be discharged in gossip to a neutral friend, in prayer at the household shrine (with the other present), or in possession rituals in spirit-possession cults.

6. Self-aggression. One party may express a grievance by exaggerated compliance, "remonstrative compliance." An apology by a victim may be rebellion through obedience. It may go as far as self-destruction in "sacrifice" for one's superiors, or in atonement for failing one's obligation, company, or peer group. It may take the form of self-accusation as interiorization employed for the purpose of conflict management, or self-aggression as a final form of conflict resolution.

7. Acceptance. A conflict situation can be accepted with equanimity. Instead of rejecting or correcting an undesirable state of affairs, the person accepts it as destiny, absorbs it in resignation. Seeing an event as inevitable can impersonalize a highly emotional experience. The subjective anger, resentment, will, and reasoning dissolve into an acceptance of nature. Equanimity is reached by achieving an "empty" or "thoughtless" state of mind through meditation or an art form.

These are all forms of nonconfrontational conflict management, Lebra concludes, not of conflict resolution. The very same cultural values of guilt consciousness and avoidance may both intensify conflict and be used for its management, and what is ultimately aimed at is an empty, egoless, joyful, and thus conflict-free self (Lebra 1984, 56).

CASE: A SPOILED FEAST
Magar Tribe, Nepal

The following story has been related by John Williamson:

The Magars show appreciation to friends by giving a feast that encourages eating and drinking beyond one's capacity.

Our development staff was invited to a feast thrown by the headman of a nearby village on a beautiful winter day. Although the headman was not at home to welcome us on our arrival, we were shown to a house where food was spread and invited to begin with the fried pork, fried bread, and milk.

We understood the reason for our presence. Two years previous the village had begun building an irrigation canal, starting digging from both upper and lower ends. We had given them surveying advice and funding. The project stalled when they struck a ridge of hard rock in the center. The following year the villagers raised R20,000 ($2000) from their own resources to finish the canal. After months of hard work, they found that the upper end was lower in elevation than the village. Another R5000 was needed but all resources were drained. Because our survey advice had not been followed, it was a loss of face for them to ask us for further aid.

An hour after the beginning of the feast, the headman made

his appearance in shabby clothes, appearing to be very drunk, and shouting incoherently at me. I was tense and afraid, preparing to run away if attacked. I recalled the words of an old Magar man: "When we have a conflict with an outsider, and no one to go between, we drink a little *rakshi* (alcohol) and then act very drunk. We go to the person with whom we are angry and fight them. Everyone will blame the alcohol, not us for what was done."

When the headman was seated on the ground, and still vehemently abusing me, my colleague went to his friends and said this was no way to resolve the problem of the canal. They should take him away. As everyone became extremely embarrassed at their headman's behavior, they soon talked him into returning to his house to sober up.

We visitors rose, declining to eat anymore, and telling the headman's brother that we were very hurt by our host's behavior.

He replied that his brother was not at fault, not angry at us, he was only made drunk by his father-in-law. It was during festival time and he was obligated to drink as much *rakshi* as served to him by a family elder.

I then asked about the canal. "My brother has lost face with all the villagers because after all their work and all their money, the project which you planned for him was a failure."

I told him we would be ready to help and scheduled a meeting for the following morning. I repeated that I too had lost face at the feast and was very hurt.

The following morning, the headman and another villager appeared early. He reported no memory of the evening before, and expressed his hope that I was not too upset. He blamed it all on his father-in-law. He made him drink.

I replied, "What to do? When I visit my mother-in-law I must eat and drink until the table is bare."

We both laughed, tension subsided, and we worked out a mutually satisfactory settlement of the canal question.

(Williamson 1983, 9–11, abridged)

Chapter Four

Conflict: Anger, Anxiety, and Aggression

Anger punishes itself.
— Chinese proverb

UNIVERSAL INSIGHT
(The Bottom Line)

Anger is a judicial emotion, the assertion of an ought, the expression of a demand, the exercise of forcefulness, and the threat of retaliation.

FOLKTALE: ANGER, NOT AGGRESSION
India

In the tall grass and bushes surrounding an ancient Indian temple, there lived a king cobra with a temper terrible and explosive. Many pilgrims who passed innocently by his den ventured too close and were fatally struck.

One day, the priest of that temple, learning of still another tragic snakebite, sought out the great snake. "Have you been striking my people as they come to the temple to do puja?*"*

The snake closed his proud hood, bowed his head in shame, and shook it in the sideways nod that means "yes" in the Indian subcontinent.

"You shall never strike another human being, as long as you live. You shall not act in rash anger no matter what the provocation may be," the priest commanded. The snake's head moved sideways again in assent.

A year later, the priest happened on the cobra once more. The great king now was beaten and scarred. His once proud hood was stripped of scales; a fang was missing.

"What has happened to you, my friend?" asked the priest.

"Oh, it iss a ssorry life ssince I can no longer sstrike. Everyone ssteps on me. Children sswing me by my tail. I am sslapped, sstomped, ssmitten until I am ssore and sscarred. It is a ssorry life ssince I have given up all anger," said the snake.

"But you must not give up anger," said the priest. "I told you that you dare not strike, but I did not say that you cannot hiss."

FOLKTALE: EMPTINESS OF REVENGE
Yoruba Tribe, West Africa

Once there was a beautiful woman named Folake, who was married to a wealthy trader. He loved money more than beauty and made love to his gold, but not to her.

And Folake said to herself, "The farmer who has a hoe but does not till the ground has only himself to blame if others trespass on his land." So she took two lovers, Ojo and Kunle, with whom she enjoyed herself alternately. The two became jealous, angry, and hated each other, but could do nothing lest Folake tell their secret to their wives.

One day Folake was playing with Kunle, and as they were about to forget the world together, they heard the voice of her husband. Folake quickly hid Kunle in a large pot. As the trader, oblivious to her excitement, sat down to eat his yams, Ojo appeared. Quicker than a hawk pouncing on a chicken, Folake said, "This is the pot you have come to collect. Please give my greetings to my mother."

The husband, slower than a tortoise walking uphill, helped Ojo put the pot on his head. When Ojo realized what he had, he did not release Kunle; he planned how he could eliminate him from his lover's life forever. He took the pot to Kunle's own wife and said, "I deliver greetings from your good friend Folake. She sends you this pot as a present." Then he quickly left.

When Kunle was discovered naked and with a shining rod, she threw hot porridge on him and called in the neighbors. He was ashamed before all, and looked ridiculous with a blistered face.

Now Ojo had Folake to himself, until Kunle had healed. When he reappeared, she was so pleased to see him, her wrapper was off before he could say, "I greet you for the other day. . . . " Suddenly the voice of her husband was heard again, so the naked Folake jumped into a large pot, leaving Kunle to explain himself.

"I met your wife in the market," he explained, "and she sold me this pot, so I have come to claim it." So the husband helped him put the pot on his head.

As he walked away, he wondered, "Why did she save herself this time and leave me in danger?" So he decided to punish her. He carried the jar to Ojo's house and said, "Folake's husband has asked me to bring you this present." Then he quickly left.

When the naked woman came from the pot, there was fighting and screaming, as fifty cocks quarreling over one hen. Then they fell on Ojo and scratched and beat him.

So Kunle got revenge, but hatred is like rain in the desert, it is of no use to anybody. He lost Folake because the husband was at last wise, like the man looking for his trousers and finding he is wearing them.

Thus Ojo was like a man who relieves himself on the road, and then curses the flies on his return. But Kunle was like the palm wine tapper, who cuts his own rope in order to punish the palm tree.

(Gbadamosi and Beier 1968, 8–10, adapted)

Are humans not only conflict-prone, but also intrinsically violent?

The crucial, irreducible focal point of debate over the roots of conflict lies in one's theory and definition of aggression. Are those roots primarily universal (i.e., biological and constitutive), cultural (i.e., social and environmental), or individual (i.e., personal and developmental)?

Is aggression an instinct or drive? Are people naturally aggressive? Are men more aggressive than women? Is human aggression the root cause of all social conflict, all violence, all warfare?

Western biology, psychology, sociology, and anthropology have been strongly influenced by doctrines of intrinsic and essential aggression at the core of human nature: the myths of the wild and unbridled horse we ride (Plato, Augustine, Freud), of the beast within (Darwin, Lorenz), of the reptilian brain stem (Maclean), of the selfish genes (Wilson, Dawkins), and so on. These are myths that (1) cannot be demonstrated to be true and (2) are metaphors for common cultural understandings of human conflicts and contradictions. The assumptions on which universal biological explanations of behavior have been built are misleading and mistaken. The three basic assumptions underlying the myth of the beast within are:

> First, that human behavior is a combination of the separate contributions of human nature and human culture; secondly, that human nature is necessarity (i.e., it could not be other than it is), whereas human culture is contingent (i.e., it could be other than it is); and, thirdly, that human nature is fundamentally competitive and combative, whereas human culture may favor greater or lesser amounts of concord and cooperation, depending on the circumstances. (Klama 1988, 33)

These assumptions are basic because all three are necessary to give coherence to the biological arguments for the essential nature of human aggressiveness, yet none of these is supported by contemporary biological studies. Parceling out behavior — some pieces to nature, some to culture — produces controversy but not productive inquiry. Both humans and their culture are dynamic,

developing, changing, and changeable processes. There is no conclusive evidence supporting a biological base for human behavior.
From the basic biological capabilities, the culture selects, designs,
labels, and harmonizes elements into elaborate relational patterns
of behavior that express its basic values.

AGGRESSION: INTRINSIC OR LEARNED?

Among ethologists and paleontologists of various persuasions,
there are those who argue from the evidence of the bones that
we are all children of "killer apes," that the earliest fossil, a hominid bone, gives clear indications of prehistoric homicide. "This
is completely unfounded," argues Richard Leakey. "It is one of
the most dangerously persuasive myths of our time." This myth
may well be, as several women paleoanthropologists have suggested, the product of a systematic and distorting male bias in
the literature that seeks to excuse the obsession with warfare in
Western civilization. There is more evidence to support the theory
that cooperative relationships among women and children rather
than competitive relationships among men were central to prehistoric life (Tanner and Zihlman 1976; Tanner 1981). As Leakey
concludes, "The fossil record is more compatible with a peaceable
than with a violent scenario of early hominid emergence" (Leaky
1977, 197).

The data on peacefulness and bellicosity, when surveyed across
societies, are a study of stark contrasts. On the violent end
is the well-known case of the Yanomamo, the so-called fierce
people, rudimentary hunters and agriculturists of the Brazilian-
Venezuelan border, among whom violent combat is at such a
level that 24 percent of adult males meet death by violent means
(Chagnon 1977). At the peaceful end there are peoples such as the
Eskimos of the North American Arctic, the Pygmies of central Africa, and the bushmen of the Kalahari, who are frequently termed
harmless people (Thomas 1969). All three groups, it is believed,
reject violence of all kinds, although all of these have shown themselves rapidly able to learn violence when drawn into relationships
with a more violent context.

In 1942, Quincy Wright published an often-cited study of primitive warfare, seeking to analyze the relation between bellicosity and other characteristics of what were then called "primitive peoples." Six hundred and fifty-two societies were defined as primitive groups. These were divided by region of the world (54 regions); by character of warfare, this being categorized under four types: defensive war, social war, economic war, and political war; by climate (cold, temperate, hot); by habitat; by climatic energy; by race; by culture (hunting, pastoral, agricultural); by subculture; by political organization; by social organization; and, finally, by intercultural relations.

Of the 652 societies, 4 percent (27) showed only defensive warfare; they were not seen as initiators of any kind of warfare, and appeared extremely pacific. Fifty-three percent (347) engaged in social warfare: war as a social ritual with expressive functions but no instrumental goal and relatively limited bloodshed. Twenty-six percent (168) engaged in economic war. Seven percent (43) engaged in political war with clear power connotations. Thus 33 percent engaged in war that would fall within our present definitions of warfare. (For 67 societies, 10 percent of the total, the patterns of warfare were not ascertained.) (Wright 1942).

In later analysis of Wright's data, Galtung used more incisive forms of statistical inference to compare groupings, and noted two matters: First, people become more belligerent as they "progress" from primitivity to more developed forms of society. Second, there is a correlation between degree of contact between peoples and the likelihood of a civilization producing belligerence. As culturation increases, so does bellicosity. Formation of states leads to a high degree of belligerence (Galtung 1975–80, 2:34).

Recognizing that the "causes" of violence or war are multiple, complex, and at times indecipherable, we still must state that there is no cumulative evidence to contradict the judgment of Margaret Mead that war is a social invention lacking a specific biological base, and that a violent approach to solving problems is learned behavior that can be unlearned (Mead 1968, 213).

ANGER: UNIVERSALLY COMMON
OR CULTURALLY UNIQUE?

Is anger a universally similar human experience? Irritability and arousal are biologically human capacities, but anger — the compound of arousal, appraisal, and resulting affect — appears in cross-cultural comparisons to be a learned, conditioned, contextualized experience.

Although the wisdom of proverbs from various cultures at first glance seems universally applicable, the deeper meanings reveal the local and situational complexities of the anger experience. Compare:

"Anger beats the shoulders with its own rod until they bleed; love tints the face with its own rouge." (Finland)

"When the pot boils over, it cools itself." (Germany)

"A live coal burns the one who stirs it up." (Bantu tribe)

"Anger expressed dissipates, anger contained grows." (California)

"It is better to spend the night in anger than in regret over having taken revenge." (Tamashek tribe)

"If a cock ruffles his feathers, it is easy to pluck him." (Burma)

"The more intimate the friendship, the more deadly the enmity." (Yoruba tribe)

"A broken thread can be tied together, a broken chalk is forever." (Malaya Peninsula)

"The better heart eats its owner." (Bantu tribe)

It is common in anthropological literature to find references to the various emotions that suggest that the emotions are a universal coinage of human experience. The closer we are to physical processes, of course, the more universal our definitions and labels will be. Thus anxiety, sadness, joy, surprise, and disgust, often called primary emotions, are more nearly similar in different cultures.

Figure 13 is a presumedly objective exercise in charting emotions and differentiating emotional states. Such an exercise demonstrates that in Western psychological experience the emotions are extremely intertwined, interrelated, and interactive.

Western emotions, clearly defined in Western culture by Western traditional values, may be quite different from Japanese emotions using the same names but holding different contents, meanings, or dynamics. Dependent affection, acceptable for children or the temporarily ill in Western societies, is the life-long norm of parent-child and husband-wife relationships in the Japanese family (Doi 1973, 15). *Ikari*, the commonplace word for anger in Japanese, possesses far more delicate connotations than we assume in our usages (Yeda 1962, 341).

Colors spread across the graduated band of the spectrum are broken into red, orange, yellow, green, blue, and violet when seen by eyes trained to perceive and identify these particular hues. However, there are cultures that do not differentiate between green and blue. The light waves received are the same as in a culture that sees two different colors; the labeling — or contexting — is done according to each culture's instructions. Similarly, among the Kaingang Indians of Brazil, the emotion of *tonu* is described as "fear-anger, one emotion with two facets." Where Western anger always implies an accusation of wrongdoing, *tonu* contains no accusation but includes a component of direct threat (Henry 1936, 254–56).

The compound emotions, charted in figure 13, are composed of multiple affects permitted and prescribed by Western values. Anger — the compound of intense disapproval of another's blameworthy action plus displeasure and distress about this undesirable event — appears in some cultures to be more similar to hate; in others it is more similar to resentment; in still others it may be composed of elements of shame, distress, and reproach.

"If you strike me, why should I be angry?" a psychiatrist in Bangalore, India, asked me. "It was your destiny (karma) to strike someone, and mine to be smitten. How economical of nature to bring us together at the perfect moment for each of our lives. I may feel pain, or sadness, but not anger." He feels the distress, but not the reproach, so grief emerges when he is attacked, but not anger.

Figure 13
Chart of Emotions and Emotional States

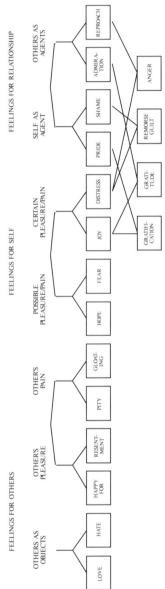

COMPOUND EMOTIONS:

Gratification: approving of one's own praiseworthy action plus being pleased about this desirable event.
Gratitude: approving of someone else's praiseworthy action plus being pleased about this desirable event.
Remorse: disapproving of one's own blameworthy action plus being displeased about this undesirable event.
Anger: disapproving of another's blameworthy action plus being displeased about this undesirable event.

FUNDAMENTAL OR BASIC EMOTIONS

The spectrum of human emotional states can be broken down to its essential components.
A culture may use less than ten or more than seven hundred words to describe emotional states.

We do not feel the same things, in the same way, though we may speak the same words.

Emotion-talk differs greatly from culture to culture. Some cultures appear to have a very limited lexicon of words to describe inner mood states. The Chewong of central Malaysia utilize only eight words (Howell 1981, 134). In contrast, neighboring Malays use some 230 words referring to emotional states (Boucher 1969, 170). The Taiwanese have a richer lexicon, 750 words, than we English-speaking people, who have only 400 words to describe emotions or emotional states (Davitz 1969, 10).

A cross-cultural study comparing Ugandan and American adolescents found significantly different boundaries dividing emotional states. Among the Ugandans (half the Ugandan sample spoke English), the meaning ascribed to anger in either language included tears and crying. Among Americans, these were clearly identified not with anger but with sadness. We classify our emotional experiences by cultural values — some languages may conflate anger and sadness as in a number of African languages, or worry, tension, and anxiety as in several Chinese languages (Heelas 1986, 250).

Secondary emotions, such as anger, gratitude, and remorse, are a threefold compound of bodily arousal, mind appraisal, and moral-cultural approval (fig. 14). Anger is composed of the biochemical arousal, cognitive evaluations, and moral directions that create the resultant emotional experience we label as feelings. The bodily arousal is a part of basic human experience in any and every cultural context, but the context offers contrasting cognitive appraisals and approvals. We define what is threatening, how it will affect us, what responses one appropriates, and which are acceptable in the given situation according to the cultural program and our individual developmental pilgrimage. The perceptions and expectations (cultural definitions of "feelings") determine what part of the process is symbolized into awareness and *how* it will be labeled. We inherit and inhabit linguistic vocabularies and emotive categories that tell us what we are experiencing (fig. 14).

There may be as many ways of feeling as there are of thinking and talking. Most likely, we may safely infer, there are more varieties of feeling than there are verbal patterns or cognitive

Figure 14
A Three-component Theory of Emotions:
Arousal, Appraisal, and Approval

PERCEPTIONS FOR DISCERNING

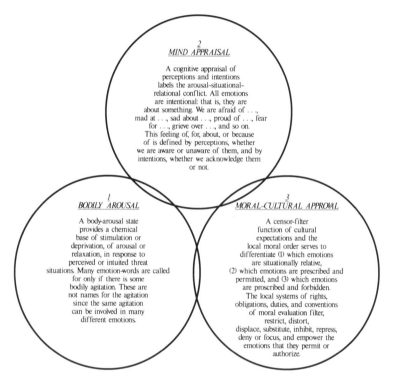

MIND APPRAISAL

A cognitive appraisal of
perceptions and intentions
labels the arousal-situational-
relational conflict. All emotions
are intentional: that is, they are
about something. We are afraid of . . .,
mad at . . ., sad about . . ., proud of . . ., fear
for . . ., grieve over . . ., and so on.
This feeling of, for, about, or because
of is defined by perceptions, whether
we are aware or unaware of them, and by
intentions, whether we acknowledge them
or not.

BODILY AROUSAL

A body-arousal state
provides a chemical
base of stimulation or
deprivation, of arousal or
relaxation, in response to
perceived or intuited threat
situations. Many emotion-words are called
for only if there is some
bodily agitation. These are
not names for the agitation
since the same agitation
can be involved in many
different emotions.

MORAL-CULTURAL APPROVAL

A censor-filter
function of cultural
expectations and the
local moral order serves to
differentiate (1) which emotions
are situationally relative,
(2) which emotions are prescribed and
permitted, and (3) which emotions
are proscribed and forbidden.
The local systems of rights,
obligations, duties, and conventions
of moral evaluation filter,
restrict, distort,
displace, substitute, inhibit, repress,
deny or focus, and empower the
emotions that they permit or
authorize.

ENERGY FOR EXPERIENCING   PROTOCOLS FOR DEFINING

definitions available within any culture. So why should we be surprised at contrasts between groups? The ethnography of emotions has not been sufficiently studied for us to accurately map the differences that exist in defining an emotion such as anger, and it is clear that we dare not risk any assumptions about equivalent affective experiences simply because the words for the particular feeling may be translated in synonymous or parallel phrases.

Anger is always experienced within a moral context. Thus we hear such statements as: "You should limit your anger in most situations, express it acceptably in public altercations, and allow it to flame out of control only in extreme provocation." As an example for contrast or comparison with other cultures, the rules and norms for morally approved anger in Western culture are charted in the accompanying outline. Many of these values direct us from unconscious levels we call habitual learnings. Each culture trains its members from infancy to adulthood on the appropriate ways to express anger in a particular age group, social group, social setting, and so on.

Mind appraisal of a threatening situation interacts with the bodily arousal activated and flows down channels permitted or prescribed by the moral approval patterns structured within and sanctioned from without. Culture affects all three elements in shaping the degree of expectations that trigger arousal, in charting the cognitive map that frames appraisal, and in setting boundaries of proscription and prescription that channel the actions and expressions. Anger is a three-dimensional depth-expression of cultural programing.

Anger, in an American context, tends to be expressed assertively, expressively, and with a significant degree of ventilation allowed. In Mediterranean contexts, anger may be even more volatile, but less calculated and sinister, more explosive, but less durable.

On the opposite end of the continuum of expressiveness, there are cultures, and subgroups or classes within cultures, in which open altercation would be uncouth, or perhaps even unthinkable. In these, the other is not directly accused of injustice; rather one seeks to make clear one's own status as victim and victimized. (An example is the ritualized clamor of Australian Aborigines.) Or the anger may emerge in accusations of being bewitched by the other (Tiv, Nyakyusa, Azande), in histrionic suicide (Trobriander), or in chilly silence (upper-class British, Japanese). Or the "offender" may be treated with an intensified "respectfulness" expressed by an increased formality

Rules and Norms of Moral Approval and Anger
(Western Values Controlling the Experience
and Expression of Anger)

1. *Instigation/Irritation*
   a. You have the right to become angry at intentional wrongdoing — any injury to your honor, freedom, property, etc.
   b. You have the right to become angry at unintentional misdeeds — negligence, carelessness, oversight, or irresponsibility.
   c. You are foolish to become angry at events beyond your influence or control, or to be angry when the situation could be remedied by some rational choice.

2. *Object/Target*
   a. You should direct anger at persons or institutions that can be held responsible for their actions.
   b. You may more appropriately direct anger at a peer or a subordinate than a superior; at someone familiar more than a stranger; at men more than women.
   c. You are unwise to direct anger at persons who cannot be held responsible (e.g., because of age, illness, ignorance) or cannot profit from it (because of infirmity or insanity).

3. *Aim/Behavior*
   a. Your objective in anger should be to correct a bad situation, to restore equality, to prevent repetition.
   b. Your goal in anger should not be to inflict injury or cause pain for the object.
   c. Your aim should not be a selfish, unilateral, or exploitive end.

4. *Actions/Behavior*
   a. Your anger-response should be proportional to the irritation, directed to its cause, and directed to the issue so the target knows who is angry and at what cause.
   b. Your anger-response should be within community standards of appropriateness for that particular target and issue.
   c. Your response should not exceed what is necessary to correct the situation, prevent its recurrence, and regain equity, and it should not unfairly humiliate or injure the object.

5. *Duration/Content*
   a. Your anger should be immediate, spontaneous, and authentic, not calculated, deliberate, or delayed.
   b. You should first express the harm done and the demand for change felt, and only if that fails move to threat or action.
   c. Your anger should terminate when the target apologizes, makes amends, or promises an end to the instigation.
   d. Your anger should not last more than a few hours. An unresolved situation may still be negotiated, but it should not be out of open anger.

6. *Responsibility/Clarity*
   a. You should be able to demonstrate a causal connection between the offender, the offense, and your response.
   b. You should place the anger on the offender not on an innocent third party.
   c. Your anger may be, in objectionable circumstances, interpreted as a passion rather than a decision or action.
   d. You do not need to be held completely responsible for the tone or intensity of passionate anger-behavior.
   e. You are responsible to direct all anger at the target only for the instigation in focus, to deal with one irritation at a time, and to not include reasons beyond the immediate instigation.

(Harré 1987, 324–25, adapted)

of vocabulary and information (Korean) (Warner 1986, 142). Or the offended person may experience the frustration as feeling "clogged up" and may withdraw until able to be open again (Utku Eskimo).

What is common to all of these is that the angry person's offended stance and accusations are being communicated by conventional and ritual conduct.

We may come to some basic conclusions about emotional experience across cultures (adapted from Harré 1987, 10–11):

1. There is an inversion of standards or values. Bravery in the Northern Hemisphere may become foolishness in the Southern. Cowardice that is shameful in Western societies is commended by the Ifaluk of Micronesia or the Tonga along the Zambezi.

2. One culture encourages what another suppresses. The Japanese prize the "sweet dependence" of *amae* (the positive, supportive dependency of an intimate relationship, such as that between mother and child), but Western cultures consider it a regressive attachment of childhood dependence. What Indian therapists refer to as appropriate interdependence, in the West would be weak dependence.

3. Strong forms of emotion in one culture exist only in weak forms in another. Spaniards feel an acute emotional outrage when seeing another behaving badly. It rises out of an Iberian cultural complex of personal dignity. These elements exist weakly in other Western groups.

4. There are historical changes in emotional repertoires of a continuous national culture. The long discussions in European literature of the Middle Ages of *accidie* as an emotion of religious gloom and joylessness in fulfilling religious duties have largely disappeared with the rise of Protestantism and the change in attitudes toward duty, guilt, and shame.

5. There are quasi-emotions that are culturally distinctive psychological phenomena related to the conditions of life, health, climate, and atmosphere. Examples are the coziness of a winter evening's fireside in North America, the *gezellige* state of Dutch togetherness in warmth, the *Gemutlichkeit* of German fellowship, and the *Kodikas* of a Finnish homelike atmosphere.

ANGER: AN URGE FOR DOMINANCE OR JUSTICE?

Anger may be defined as a conflictive emotion that, on the biological level, is related to aggressive systems and, even more important, to the capacities for cooperative social living, symbolization, and reflective self-awareness; that, on the psychological level, is aimed at the correction of some appraised wrong; and that, on the sociocultural level, functions to uphold accepted standards of conduct (Averill 1982, 317).

Anger is a socially constructed response that helps regulate interpersonal retaliation through the threat of retaliation for perceived wrongdoing, and that is interpreted as an impulsive passion rather than a deliberate action so as not to violate the general cultural proscription against deliberately harming another person. The general cultural directive, in virtually all cultures, might be summarized as Averill suggests:

> You should avoid becoming angry.
> However, under certain circumstances, for example, A, B, or
>   C, a reasonable person cannot help but be angry.
> If under such conditions you respond in manner X, Y, or Z,
>   then your behavior will be interpreted as passion, and you
>   will not be held responsible. (Averill 1982, 321)

In most societies, conflicting norms simultaneously discourage and encourage angry behavior as well as prescribing a means for resolving the conflict by interpreting the response as a passion. So A, B, and C in Averill's code stand for adequate provocations, and X, Y, and Z represent acceptable responses. These variables change in cultural mores, according to sex, age, social status of actors, setting (barroom or courtroom), alternate means of dispute resolution, and so on.

Anger has evolved and is maintained in culture because it serves to uphold accepted standards of conduct; it regulates interpersonal relationships; and it encourages recipients to conform to accepted cultural standards of conduct. Wherever it is up to individuals to see that their personal or group rights are respected and their justice protected, anger serves as an immediately available judge, police, and enforcer.

Whenever official law is cumbersome, inappropriate, or unavailable, anger provides an immediate, informal, and economical court of appeal. In the absence of a formal judiciary, anger operates as a personal one.

People in every culture get angry, and the anger is in service of, obedience to, and defense of their culture's rules. Anger is a sign that the web of oughts, the culture's mores, has been broken. Anger asserts an ought. By power of censure, threat of rejection, and warning of retaliation, anger seeks to regulate infractions, quarrels, disputes, or disagreements. In the absence of a legal representative, anger operates as a personal policing power.

Whenever the members of a tribe must struggle to survive and cooperate to nourish each other — whether in the arid deserts of Africa, the frozen tundra of Alaska, or the parched bush of Australia — the clan has created ways of regulating distribution through a unique dance of anger and negotiation, accusations and disputes, bickering and laughter. But the anger is kept within bounds, and inappropriate anger is kept in check by ridicule, gossip, shaming, miming, group discussions, or ostracism. Without rules for limiting and channeling anger, in any society, it can slip into emotional anarchy, lasting longer than its function requires, spreading farther than its purpose justifies, or exhausting persons beyond the limits of sympathy and compassion.

The amount of anger stored up in a culture varies widely. The level of irritability, the tendency toward anger expression, may be quite low, as in Tahiti, or volatile and explosive as in America. In the gentle, forgiving environment of Tahiti, people relinquish control, relax, and accept the bounty of nature in passive optimism.

In the harsh deserts of the Middle East, the Jews demanded dominion, striving, and work. That combination produced active pessimists who saw nature as an enemy to be conquered.

The individualism of the American way of life, to our glory and despair, creates anger and encourages its release; when everything is possible, limitations are irksome. When the desires of the self come first, the needs of others are annoying. When we think we deserve it all, reaping only a portion can enrage (Tavris 1982, 65).

ANGER, VIOLENCE, AND CONFLICT

Anger can erupt into violence — if so, it seeks to violate the other's integrity, safety, and security. Or anger may escalate into conflict — in which case it seeks to challenge the structures of control. The former seeks to eliminate the other party, the latter to limit or negotiate limitations to the other's influence.

> Violence differs from conflict in that violence is about structures of integrity while conflict is about structures of control. The two are related in that violence may be a tactic in conflict, and in that control itself may violate the integrity of those controlled. Though the two may occur separately they are often found together. (Corbin 1986, 31)

Violence, viewed cross-culturally as a social/antisocial behavior, has four key properties, which can be asserted as universally valid (Riches 1986, 8–11):

1. Any act of violence is inherently liable to be contested on the question of legitimacy. In every culture, sanctions are imposed on the type, intensity, expression, motivation, and authorization of violence, and an act of violence never fails to be one of contested legitimacy. The points of the violent triangle — performer, victim, witness — are rarely, if ever, in complete agreement on the legitimacy of violence. Societies arrange compromises, norms, limitations, and means of contesting actions taken. There are, universally, limits imposed on violence. For example, among the Nuer, spears are permitted for intervillage conflict, but intravillage conflict is restricted to the use of clubs (Evans-Pritchard 1940, 121).

2. There is a universal consensus among those involved as to what constitutes a violent act. Everyone implicated in violence is very likely to recognize it as such.

3. All the senses keenly perceive the act of violence. There may be debate about what is playful and what is intended as threat, but the sensory data — the sight, sound, hurt, and injury — are recognizable in any culture.

4. Violence is, in essential nature, an act of unskilled labor, possible for untrained hands, thus available to all humans.

These four cultural universals — its questionable legitimacy, recognizability, perceptibility, and accessibility — make violence highly appropriate for practical (instrumental) and for symbolic (expressive) purposes. So it is used to change the social environment or key social ideas or values.

There are laws within violence that prevent violence from having positive results. This argument on the self-defeating, indeed self-destructive, essential nature of violence has been made by the French sociologist Jacques Ellul (1969, 92–105). These essential laws are:

1. There is a continuity in violence in the sense that one act leads inexorably to another, so that violence begets violence.

2. There is a sameness about violence, so that however high its goal all practitioners are reduced to the same level.

3. There is a desperation in violence, so that one who uses it will go to any length, even someone's death, to justify both it and oneself.

4. There is a close link between violence and hatred. Thus violence leads toward death or toward physical or psychological harm. Violence is the antithesis of peace, of life.

We could resort to violence with a clear conscience only if we were surgically certain that we were excising a cancer that would never grow again. In seeking to erase it, we infect ourselves; in removing a part, we double the growth in the future.

In Albert Camus's play *Les Justes*, the character Kaliayer says: "We are killing to build a world in which no one will ever kill. We accept criminality for ourselves in order that the earth may at last be full of innocent people."

But the final message of *Les Justes* is that violence is justified only if those who inflict it lay down their own lives (Camus 1950).

ANGER AND AFFILIATION: THE GEBUSI

The tension in a society between affiliation and anger is expressed intriguingly by the Gebusi of lowland New Guinea. The ethos is structured between the desire for solidarity in friendship, camaraderie, and good company, on the one hand, and the reality of anger, accusation, and violence, on the other hand. Key elements or cultural orientations of Gebusi society are good company, anger, fear, and reciprocity.

Good company means togetherness, communality, friendship, and collective activity. The Gebusi live in communal long houses, prefer to act as a large group, fear being alone, and are reluctant to do anything individually. "To wander off alone can indicate only that the lone individual has gone crazy. It is inconceivable to Gebusi why someone, unless they are very angry, would want to be aloof from others or have privacy" (Knauft 1985, 64). The vehicle for community is talk. Secrecy is rare. Collective enjoyment is the ideal of life.

Fear is the force that maintains equanimity in good company. Individuals express fear by being uneasy, afraid, anxious, and embarrassed, but the primary form of expression is anxiety, not shame. Confrontation and the use of even individual names to "call out" others as separate persons are seen as disruptive of solidarity. Direct confrontations are avoided, disagreement brushed aside, and anger ignored.

Anger is the greatest fear, and every effort is made to placate a person who becomes angry. Complaints may be heard, but a strong attempt is made to create an atmosphere of nonantagonistic reconciliation. The person may become aloof, and go with wife and family to the garden for a period of cooling off. Anger is downplayed. Hostile parties stay clear of each other. If it erupts into violence, there is a stunning lack of condemnation or escalating retribution. Anger and violence are simply accepted without blame, as a de facto reality. The goal is simply to separate the angry parties and give them time to defuse their anger. Good company must be restored as quickly as possible, even if superficially or through avoidance (Knauft 1985, 75).

Reciprocity is not a public demand, but a private hope, since communal give-and-take is supremely valued. An exact exchange of hurts, penalties, and punishments is avoided as coercive. The give-and-take of sharing, of mutuality, is emphasized. The customs of good company and reciprocity, Knauft reports, "do not strike the field worker as repressive, superficial, or forced; they seem genuine, relaxed, warm, and pervasive." The ideals of good company are not just lids on the expression of inevitable discontents; they are a viable and rich cultural alternative to the discontents themselves, and they "function very effectively in this capacity most of the time" (Knauft 1985, 80). This comment, interestingly enough, comes after Knauft attempts to apply Western hydraulic theories of overcontrolled hostility in explanation of Gebusi anger eruptions. He cites the embarrassingly disproved studies by Edwin Megargee, one of which made inference from a group of ten imprisoned pacifists who were Jehovah's Witnesses to pacifists in general (Megargee 1966; see Augsburger 1974). Knauft then returns from Western theory to direct observation.

ANGER AND SOLIDARITY: THE UTKU

Entering the Utku Eskimos' emotional world, the world of the *Utkuhikhalingmiut*, we discover a very different way of construing anger, frustration, depression, and aggression.

Anthropologist Jean Briggs writes of living within the emotional field of this tight-knit nomadic band of twenty-five to thirty-five people who occupy 35,000 square miles in the Canadian Northwest Territories. The band lives in igloos in the winter, tents in the summer, and follows the availability of prey by moving across a vast region of tundra and ice.

The Utku are generally peaceable and nonviolent. They value love and nurturance above all else, and condemn what we would label as angry feelings or aggressive behavior. They do not deny frustration or aggression.

The Utku have no noun equivalent to our word *anger*, only verbs describing angry feeling, thinking, and acting. Their word *qiquq*, which translates as "being clogged up," suggests our notion of pent-up anger: "*Qiquq* in its physical sense is applied to objects such as iglu ventilators, fishing holes, and primus nipples, which get, quite literally, clogged up and have to be cleaned out. In its emotional sense, the behavior most often labelled *qiquq* was sulky, silent withdrawal" (Briggs 1970, 333).

Qiquq is associated with childishness, with being immature and not fully developed. The normal adult develops an equable temperament naturally, and one who expresses too much *qiquq* is expected simply to grow up. It is important to observe that *qiquq* is quite different from our notions of frustration or anger; it is a form of behavior rather than an internal feeling state; it carries no implications of explosive violence; it is mostly passive, including withdrawal from the group, refusal to share, and depressive silence. The cure for *qiquq* is not catharsis, but the development of greater reason and maturity (*ilhuma*). Angry children are reasoned with, encouraged; angry adults are ignored, teased, or ostracized.

The grammar and vocabulary of Utku emotion, the common-sense understandings of relationship and growth, and the successful process of stabilization and "therapy" reveal a different cultural construction of the emotions of anger and aggression; the Utkus' knowledge and beliefs about frustration within and between persons deal with frustration, arousal, and tension, but with very different processes.

Jean Briggs experienced Utku anger sanctions the hard way. After losing her temper ("very mildly as we ourselves view it") at several Caucasian fishermen who damaged an Eskimo canoe, she found herself shunned and ignored. Even though her anger had been on behalf of the Utku and directed toward her own group's injustice, the Utku saw the anger as a sign of untrustworthiness, regardless of its logical motivation. "As a result of my unseemly and frightening wrath at the fishermen, I was ostracized, very subtly, for about three months" (Briggs 1970, 285).

Parallel anthropological studies of emotional experience indicate "feelings" develop within specific cultural contexts and with varying cultural content, just as knowledge, beliefs, values, and perceptions are known to do. The "orchestrations of anger" used as declarations of intention, perception, and motivation among the Kaluli people of Papua New Guinea reveal culturally distinct ways of feeling (Schieffelin 1983, 183–84). The experience of passion and knowledge (heavy feelings that burden the heart versus passionate feelings that well up in oratory) among the Ilongot of the Philippine Luzon provides still another emotive field (Rosaldo 1980, 188). The point here is not to record all the variants but to demonstrate that cultural components of how emotions are labeled, then defined, then experienced follow each culture's common sense, not any universal common experience.

ANGER AND REASONABLENESS: THE TONGA

"If pursuing vengeance is defined as manly, seeking reconciliation with one's foes must be unmanly," writes Victor Turner in analysis of the Icelandic saga of Njal (Turner 1971, 373). Wherever honor is displayed in heroism, courage is measured by martyrdom, and dignity is defined by willingness to retaliate, then men see their manliness as requiring desperate action in times of extremity, and women feel their integrity demands sacrifice of self or repayment from others.

For two thousand years and more, Western writers have glorified valiant deeds and given adulation to the hero and martyr. To demonstrate exalted courage or boldness and to voluntarily accept death or great suffering on behalf of any belief or cause are seen as supreme virtues. The nonhero, or antihero, is seen as evidence of cultural decay, of human decadence demonstrated in compromise, cowardice, and weakness.

Leonidas and the Spartans in the pass of Thermopylae, the Maccabees in revolt, the tragic heroes of Masada, Roland at Roncesvalles, and Peter who once denied his commitments but later chose the cross — all model unyielding action for a justifiable cause.

These are not the values of all cultures, and they are certainly not those of the Tonga, who live along the boundaries of Zambia and Zimbabwe. Neither heroes nor martyrs exist in their tradition, and valor is not a primary value. They find no virtue in the last-ditch defense and no shame in cowardice. They have no sense of falling short of a valiant ideal.

When the Tonga defied the colonial government in the 1958 confrontation over the Kariba hydroelectric dam and charged guards at the Zambezi River construction site, the Europeans opened fire. Eight Tonga were killed, many wounded. The Tonga view this confrontation as a miscalculation, a wrong estimate of the colonialists' response. Those who hid in the bushes, who were first to run and first to reach home, argue about the honor of the most clever escape.

Willingness to compromise in the face of overwhelming force or to surrender before inevitable defeat creates no internal conflicts. It is being "a reasonable man," choosing "a sensible solution," recognizing "a necessary direction."

The Tonga vocabulary for bravery, for fierceness, and for violence holds warnings of danger and destructiveness. In contrast, the coward is like the "hyena who is the one living longest." Their goal is neither submission nor confrontation, but peaceful negotiation, clever strategy, and reasonable behavior. Of the Tonga and other tribes it is said: "The Krange tribe submits, the Shukulumbwe fight, but the Tonga neither fight nor submit." They make their way between threat and danger with fortitude, with endurance, and with resolute strength.

In summarizing her study of Tonga ethics, Elizabeth Colson concludes:

> For what is one prepared to die? In the interests of the kin, but only as a last resort when one can no longer serve them in any other way.... Tonga ideas of courage are congruent with the loyalties required of them by their society. In life and in death they are expected to practice the quiet virtue of fortitude.... The fearless man is a danger to his fellows. (Colson 1971, 32–33)

Perhaps Samuel Johnson, English wit and lexicographer, was right when he quipped, "It is thus that mutual cowardice keeps us in peace. Were one-half of mankind brave and half cowards, the brave would be always beating the cowards. Were all brave, they would lead a very uneasy life; all would be continually fighting; but being all cowards, we go on very well." Unfortunately, we are, in most cultures, less reasonable and sensible than we might be, and more brave and courageous than we need be.

CASE: THE HIT-AND-RUN DRIVER

The following case offers a way of experiencing (1) contrasting emotional styles; (2) differing expressions of face, honor, and dignity; (3) opposite worldviews — fate versus personal responsibility; (4) differing moral views of negotiation versus bribery; (5) opposing views of friendship; (6) differing reasoning processes (i.e., rational-linear versus affective-intuitive); and (7) contrasting styles of anger, insult, and confrontation.

Mr. Smith, an expert working in a non-Western country, is hit (not seriously) by a car that he recognizes as that belonging to Mr. Isphahany, a high-status local official. Mr. Smith, upset that the driver did not stop after the event, seeks out Mr. Isphahany in an exclusive local club. Here is their conversation:

Mr. Smith: Ach! Mr. Isphahany? My name is Mr. Smith.

Mr. Isphahany: Mr. Smith? How are you?

Mr. Smith: I am fine, thank you. I might be a little bit better if it hadn't been for an unfortunate incident that happened just a little while ago.

Mr. Isphahany: What do you mean?

Mr. Smith: As I came into the club I saw a car parked outside. An orange car. Is that your car?

Mr. Isphahany: Of course, it is my car. A beautiful car. Twenty-five thousand dollars.

Mr. Smith: Well — uh — about a half an hour ago, Mr. Isphahany, I was downtown, walking along the street and I was practically run over by a car that looked very much like your car.

Mr. Isphahany: Yes?

Mr. Smith: And I think I saw you driving that car.

Mr. Isphahany: That was my car. You . . . you are the one who was standing in my path?

Mr. Smith: Yes, that was me.

Mr. Isphahany: What were you doing over there?

Mr. Smith: I was walking down the street and you practically ran over me with your car.

Mr. Isphahany: You're supposed to walk on the sidewalk here. That's what sidewalks are for.

Mr. Smith: Well . . .

Mr. Isphahany: The road is meant for beautiful cars like mine to drive on.

Mr. Smith: I was walking on the road because it was impossible to walk on the sidewalk because of the crowd.

Mr. Isphahany: You should still have walked on the sidewalk.

Mr. Smith: You should have been driving more carefully.

Mr. Isphahany: What do you mean, more carefully? You think I didn't drive my twenty-five-thousand-dollar car carefully?

Mr. Smith: You were not driving carefully half an hour ago, that's for sure.

Mr. Isphahany: You shouldn't have been there first of all, in my path; you should have been where the other people walked.

Mr. Smith: Listen, Mr. Isphahany, I'd like to sit down and have a rational discussion with you about this. Alright?

Mr. Isphahany: A rational discussion? What is there to discuss? You are Mr. Smith; I am Mr. Isphahany. Let's shake hands and you go.

Mr. Smith: I am not going. I have something to discuss with you. It is important, . . . and either the two of us discuss it right now or we discuss it at the police station!

Mr. Isphahany: You please sit down. Sit down; I'll discuss with you. You came to the right place to discuss. First of all, who allowed you to come into this exclusive club of ours? You are illegally here and I could arrest you. You know that? Do you have your membership card with you?

Mr. Smith: No, I don't have a membership card. I have been here before as a guest of other members of your club. They happen to be members of the same company I work for and they are members of your club.

Mr. Isphahany: Do you admit that you are here illegally?

Mr. Smith: Do you admit that you hit me with your car a half hour ago?

Mr. Isphahany: I don't remember hitting you.

Mr. Smith: Mr. Isphahany, I'd like to . . .

Mr. Isphahany: If I hit you, you must be hurt. Is that right?

Mr. Smith: Yes, I have a terrible bruise on my leg. . . .

Mr. Isphahany: If you have a bruise on your leg, how come that you are walking then?

Mr. Smith: You can walk with a bruise on your leg. . . .

Mr. Isphahany: You have not been hurt. Nothing has happened and you are just trying to extract some money from me, I know. You are an American, aren't you?

Mr. Smith: Yes, I am, but I didn't say anything about money.

Mr. Isphahany: No wonder. You want to claim all the money you can. . . .

Mr. Smith: I didn't say anything about money. I came here because I wanted to discuss with you something that had happened half an hour ago. I think your car was involved. You were driving your car at that time.

Mr. Isphahany: I was driving the car, sure. I also know that, yes, something happened to you and you fell down, yes, . . . but it is not my fault. If you were not present over there I wouldn't have hurt you. Right? So it is your fault, not mine.

Mr. Smith: Mr. Isphahany, I was not seriously hurt.

Mr. Isphahany: Yes, you should be very grateful! You see there is a good thing. . . .

Mr. Smith: I was not seriously hurt and it is not necessary for me to see a doctor because I don't need medical attention.

Mr. Isphahany: You want to see a doctor?

Mr. Smith: I don't want to see a doctor.

Mr. Isphahany: I'll tell you what, I have a very personal physician. I'll call him over here so that when you come tomorrow, he will see you.

Mr. Smith: In the meantime, this is what I want to talk with you about. I was walking along the street and I had to step off the sidewalk into the road because of the crowd on the sidewalk. At that moment, your car, I believe it was your car, was coming down the street very fast. . . .

Mr. Isphahany: Yes, yes, . . . I always drive very fast. . . .

Mr. Smith: It would have been possible for you to drive out of the way to avoid hitting me. Instead, I think you exercised very little care and practically ran over me. As it was, I jumped out of the way just in time and you bruised my leg. I was not seriously hurt. I don't need medical attention but I want to talk with you about this.

Mr. Isphahany: First of all, it is your fault. How come you were there in that bazaar at that time of the day? Aren't you supposed to be in your office?

Mr. Smith: Aren't you supposed to be in your office, too? Why were you there?

Mr. Isphahany: Well, I was going to my office after dinner. This is my office.

Mr. Smith: Well, I was on my way to my office at that time.

Mr. Isphahany: Well, it is not. . . . What kind of work do you do?

Mr. Smith: That's not the important thing. The important thing is someone has been hit by a car and the driver was not driving carefully. That's what I want to talk to you about.

Mr. Isphahany: You see, . . . you should realize first of all that it is your fault. You stepped aside from the sidewalk. You were in my path. That car is a very powerful car. Even if you put on the brakes it does not stop so easily. It is a machine. You cannot blame a machine. A machine is a machine. So you got hurt. But you were on the road; if you were on the sidewalk this wouldn't have happened. . . . Now, you say you were not very much hurt?

Mr. Smith: Yes.

Mr. Isphahany: You should be very grateful for that. This tells you something. You were not careful, and you might have gotten killed. Right? . . . And you should be happy because I did not kill you. So let's shake hands on that.

Mr. Smith: Before we shake hands, there are just a few things I would like to share with you.

Mr. Isphahany: Well . . .

Mr. Smith: I have been in your country for a week now and one of the things I have noticed is that people here drive their cars very fast.

Mr. Isphahany: Right.

Mr. Smith: They sometimes go through red lights. . . . They frequently bang into each other's cars. I have seen . . .

Mr. Isphahany: Red light is only a machine. . . .

Mr. Smith: Have you seen many cars damaging each other in

the process of parking? People drive very recklessly. Accidents are almost always happening. All day long.

Mr. Isphahany: Life is like that ... full of risks ... big adventures.

Mr. Smith: People do not drive like that where I come from and furthermore if someone gets hit by a car, in my country, a policeman is called.

Mr. Isphahany: This is not your country! Why are you telling me all this? This is not your country.

Mr. Smith: I know it is not my country but I am telling you what I think is reasonable. People don't drive their cars here the way they drive them in my country. I am still trying to adjust to the situation.

Mr. Isphahany: It does not matter what happened. The important thing is that you're not dead. Now you adjust. You're in an exclusive club and you are talking to the most powerful man in this club. I am the manager. Yes. You understand? I want to make you a member of my club. I am glad you came to me. I want to extend an invitation. . . .

Mr. Smith: You are inviting me to become a member of your club?

Mr. Isphahany: Yes, very simple, a two-thousand-dollar membership.

Mr. Smith: Two thousand dollars ...

Mr. Isphahany: Since you are my friend: one thousand dollars. . . . It is very simple. You see you are away from your country. There is no entertainment for you. Become a member of my club. It is a prestigious club. People of best qualities come over here.

Mr. Smith: May I ask you a question? If you had been walking along the street with your son and the same thing happened to you that happened to me half an hour ago ...

Mr. Isphahany: OK. Since you started bargaining ...

Mr. Smith: What? ... Let me make something clear: I am not here to join your club. . . .

Mr. Isphahany: No, no, you have to join; you are my friend. Why not? I am the manager. Why shouldn't you join the club? You see, fate has brought us together, you and me, even though it is in a strange way. You are here now so I am your friend. You are my friend. You don't believe me?

Mr. Smith: What I came here for this afternoon is to find out yes or no....

Mr. Isphahany: You don't believe me?...

Mr. Smith: Was that your car? Were you driving that car?

Mr. Isphahany: I was driving my car. Yes, I saw you. I hit you, but I didn't kill you. So, on that basis, let's become friends.

Mr. Smith: That is not the point. The point is: There was an accident that should be reported to the police.

Mr. Isphahany: You want to report to the police? I'll call him right now.

Mr. Smith: You will?

Mr. Isphahany: The chief of police is a personal friend of mine. ...Why don't you do this? This will satisfy you?

Mr. Smith: I think it should be done. Isn't it the custom? Isn't it necessary to call the police when there is an accident?

Mr. Isphahany: I'll tell you what. I will have the chief of police come over here and you can report to him in my presence. He will be happy to hear your story.... You see, fate has brought you here; we cannot let you go without becoming a member. Seven hundred and fifty dollars?...

Mr. Smith: Let's talk about joining your club another day. That's not what I came here for.

Mr. Isphahany: I want to be your friend. I want to have you as my friend. I speak from the bottom of my heart. You believe me or not?

Mr. Smith: Yes, I believe you, but it is not what I came here to talk about today. I want to call the chief of police, as you mentioned a few minutes ago, and I would like you to call the doctor, too, because I have some insurance forms that I have to send back to the States and I need some statements from a doctor.

Mr. Isphahany: Everything will be taken care of after you become a member first. That is the first step. I cannot let you go without becoming a member. Believe me. Don't you believe me?

Mr. Isphahany: Yes, certainly I believe you.

(Casse 1981, 107–11)

Chapter Five

Conflict: Triangular
in Origin and Resolution

When the first wife fights with the second, the husband gets
his nose cut off.

— Nepalese proverb

**UNIVERSAL INSIGHT
(The Bottom Line)**

The disputants are in the worst position to discover the solution
to their conflict.

FOLKTALE: KING FEARSOME THE JUST
African Highlands

In the western highlands of Africa there once lived a great king known as King Fearsome the Just. He prided himself on the exact fairness with which he heard all cases brought before him.

One night in the king's city a thief, named Asrat, was breaking into the home of a rich merchant by digging a hole through a wall when a brick fell from the top row and struck him on the head, leaving him with a great bruise for his night's work.

The next morning the angry Asrat appeared before the king. "What kind of city is this where a thief has to fear the houses falling down?" he asked.

The king was equally angry. "What has this country come to when a thief cannot break in without a wall falling down? Bring the merchant before me."

"Oh king," said the merchant, "it is true it was my house, but it is not my fault. The person to blame is the carpenter who built it for me."

"Let the carpenter be brought!"

"Oh king," said the carpenter, "it is true that I built the house, but the masonry was done by one of the finest brick-layers in the city. It is he who should be punished for shoddy work."

"Bring the bricklayer to answer charges!"

"O good king," said the bricklayer, "it is not I who should be punished. The one who prepared the mortar was Melek the Mudman. If the mortar had been good the brick would never have fallen."

"Summon the mudman."

Melek the Mudman was a huge oaf who had great strength but little wit. He could think of nothing to say in his defense, and King Fearsome, relieved at last to have found the guilty man, condemned him to be hanged at once.

The carpenters were commissioned to build the gallows, and Melek was led out to the stage. But due to his great height, when the rope was put in place, his feet reached the ground. When this was reported to the king, his anger grew. "How much longer shall the wrong done to the good thief, Asrat, go unpunished? Any man in this kingdom has the right to justice, even a thief. Find someone who will fit the gallows and hang him!"

So the guards went into the streets, and the first man they met was a little onion farmer who had just come to town to sell his crop. He was well known as a good man who had never harmed anyone, but he was small and from the countryside, so he fit both the gallows and the orders perfectly.

When he was brought before King Fearsome, the king said, "Yes, yes, do not bother me with details. He will do perfectly. Justice has waited long enough."

So justice was done.

(Davis and Ashabranner 1959, 112–15,
abridged and adapted)

FOLKTALE: THE SOUNDS OF JUSTICE
Swahili Tribe, East Africa

One morning a baker brought a beggar before the cadi — *the chief of the city — and made this complaint: "Every morning this man stands beside my shop, and smells the pleasant odors of my pastry baking without paying. I do all the work of baking these lovely breads, and he breathes their fragrance for nothing. I demand payment."*

The cadi *reflected for a long time, then gave his ruling:*

"You are right. The beggar has enjoyed the smell of your cakes and in doing so he has used the fruits of your labors. For that he owes you compensation. I shall set the payment at two golden dinurs.*"*

The eyes of the baker shone, but the poor beggar explained: "Great lord, I am a poor man. I have no money. Shake me and nothing will tinkle. Can you squeeze juice from a dried currant?"

The cadi *considered his predicament, then responded: "Since you are a poor man, I will pay the sum from my own pocket." Then of the baker he asked, "Did this man ever eat one of your cakes?"*

"Never."

"Did he even nibble at them?"

"Never."

"Did he harm them by breathing on them?"

"No, sir."

"So you still sold the cakes and made your profit?"

"Yes, sir."

"Then, in that case, since the poor man consumed nothing but the odor, you will be paid nothing but the sound. Open your ears and hear the ring of true gold."

And the judge, with the sounds of gold, repaid the baker for the scent of his goods.

(Knappert 1970, 209)

FOLKTALE: A RICH MAN AND A POOR MAN
Akamba Tribe, Kenya

Long ago in one of the villages of the Akamba, two men lived as neighbors. One was rich, the other poor, yet they were good friends. Then a famine came, and the rich man grew hardhearted. When the poor starving man came begging food, the rich man chased his old friend from the village.

One day, when the poor man had found some maize, he sat with his wife eating the flat stew without spices or salt. Then in the distance they smelled the savory food of the neighbor. So they took their dinner over to the wall where the smell was delicious, and breathed its fragrance while they ate their plain gruel.

A few days later, the poor man met the rich man, and he thanked him for the fragrance of his dinner that had made his maize porridge so appetizing. The rich man became furious. "So that is why my food was tasteless that day. You ate the good smell and taste and you must pay me for it. I will take you to the judge and file a case against you."

So they went to the judge, who heard the case, and ruled that the poor man must pay a goat to the rich man, but he had no goat, and no money to buy one. As he wept, on his way home, he met a lawyer who asked for his story.

"Come with me, I shall obtain justice for you," said the lawyer. And he gave him a goat to hold until the day of payment. On the appointed day, the poor man brought the goat. As he was about to pay, the lawyer stepped forward.

"What is happening here?" he asked.

The judge reported the judgment and penalty.

"May I offer a second opinion?" asked the lawyer. The judge agreed.

"If the poor man breathed only the smell, he must pay back only the smell."

"How can he do that?" asked the judge and the people.

The lawyer replied, "Watch and listen, and I will show you."

Then he picked up a stick to beat the goat. And as he beat it, he said to the rich man: "Come, take the sound of the goat bleating as payment for your neighbor's breathing the smell of your food cooking."

And everyone clapped in agreement.

So the poor man was saved from the oppression of the rich man.

(Carey 1970, 99–100)

The friend of my friend is my friend.
The enemy of my friend is my enemy.
The friend of my enemy is my enemy.
The enemy of my enemy is my friend.

Triangular relationships form rapidly in times of conflict, most often as a coalition of two against a third party, or a conflict of two that draws in a third party.

Conflict is inevitably, inherently triangular, as the following cases will show.

•

A driver in a West Bank, Palestinian, Arab village fatally injures a child who dashes in front of him from behind parked cars. Immediately the driver blends into the crowd, and hurries to the police where he is safe until all reports have been made. Now a conflict between the driver, his family, and the family of the child awaits resolution. First, representatives of the two families meet. It is important that the driver not appear or he may be attacked, beaten, even killed by angry kinfolk. Second, the two groups may meet for a number of times until the parents are convinced of the driver's regrets and his willingness to pay some compensation — in urban settings, money, or in the village, goats, sheep, and so on. Finally, a settlement is reached, payment is made, and the situation is seen by both as resolved. Only then can the offending driver meet the other persons incidentally or socially with acceptance. At no point does face-to-face conversation about the accident take place between the offender and the offended. Third parties are both necessary and more effective in the ventilation of the anger and the negotiation of the resolution.

•

A Jordanian man and woman are discovered having an affair. He is a bachelor, she married. Immediately he flees the village to avoid death. His family assists him in hiding in a distant city with a relative. If, however, the offender is discovered, he will be killed by the husband and relatives. After he is secure, representatives of his family — the oldest and wisest possible — approach the husband and his family representatives. If he no longer wishes to be married to the woman, he may divorce her, demand some payment to appease the anger, and repair the injury done. The young man will then be married to the woman by the family and the appropriate payments will be made. If the husband desires to keep his wife, the offending man will not be allowed to return until and if resolution can be made through the passing of time, the repeated meeting of family representatives to negotiate, and the achievement of an acceptable settlement. All resolution must be done by third-party representatives. The form is constant although the style of negotiation, the number of meetings required, and the size and type of payment expected vary from village to village within the same geographical area.

•

A young Indonesian driver — Christian and minority Chinese —
is moving slowly through an intersection when an old man —
Muslim and Javanese — loses control of his bicycle, is thrown
against the side of the car, and suffers serious injuries. An angry
crowd gathers; fortunately friends passing by encircle the young
man to protect him. Threats are made; tension builds. One friend
cycles quickly to the home of the pastor, who is respected in the
community as a mediator. He comes, inspects the old man lying
on a mat, and offers the family free hospital care at the Christian
Hospital, to which they agree. Two of his associates take the victim
and a family member by car to the hospital. Then the pastor and
Muslim family sit to discuss reparations. It is agreed that the bicycle will be repaired and a sum of money given — they ask for three
times the young man's annual earnings. And at last the crowd dis-
perses; the family returns home; and the young man — his life
spared — is free to leave.

•

Two drivers collide on a Cairo street. Both silently circle the cars,
examining the damage, until a crowd has gathered with supporters around each. When each has four to six strong people to hold
him back, the threats and invitations to fight begin with angry fist
waving and name calling. The more supporters to restrain him, the
more angry he is permitted to become. When the ventilation has
reached a peak, the supporters separate and lead the principals
away. Now family members can begin negotiations for settlement
without the drivers holding conversation. When a resolution has
been reached, the two may pass on the street, and eventually even
show recognition of each other.

•

Two upper-class Englishmen take umbrage at each other's behavior. A conflict grows between them in the escalating silence,
aloofness, and avoidance. When it at last surfaces, in English culture, it is a very cerebral process. The confrontation will be rightly
argued, with no evidence of emotion. The issue will be who is

playing by or disregarding the rules of institution, class, or club. The interchange will be brief, but the real impact will be hidden, delayed, and exacted when the appropriate time comes. The one with power will drop a criticism at a crucial meeting, "drag the feet" when a decision affecting the other is being made. "If you are going to risk a confrontation with an opponent, you must be absolutely certain he or she will never be in a position to influence your future," an Oxford don advised me.

•

A Japanese husband comes home. As he enters, he looks at the flowers in the alcove, arranged by his wife. There is something disorderly in the way the flowers are put together. The message is clear that something is upsetting his wife. As he greets her and their evening together unfolds, he tries to understand what has happened. If the arrangement is deliberately unbalanced, he will sense what is causing the unhappiness without her needing to tell him explicitly that there is disharmony with the mother-in-law. She is in no position to talk against his mother, yet she wants him to know of this trying experience. His sensitivity and kindness in response to her pain assist in overcoming an unspoken dilemma (Aida 1970).

•

In an Irish village, the families have been divided for a generation of silent co-existence. The two groups maintain an invisible wall prohibiting all communication with the other side. In crisis, a tragedy or a death, the silence is temporarily suspended. Everyone willingly gives aid; communication flows until after the wake; then the curtain falls again. What was learned about the other during the period of open exchanges may be used in even more hurtful gossip to confirm justifications for the cold war. Each side, maintained by networks of gossip, supported by neighboring villages, claims superiority over the other. Privately other villagers explain the conflict with: "Tuppence ha'penny looks down on tuppence" (two and a half pence looks down on two pence).

THE ETERNAL TRIANGLE

Triangulation, the use of a third party, is as old as human communication. In the Hebrew story of Adam and Eve, it is the first response to conflict.

In its most common folk-form, the telling of one's story to neighbor or friend, it is feared yet familiar, despised yet used, discounted yet trusted. The images and sounds of language related to this phenomenon of triangling, which is better known at the popular level as gossip, provide intriguing figures of speech. They might be considered the onomatopoeias of triangling. For example, the Garifuna have the word *shushushu* for gossip and talk behind the back. In Uganda, the word is *olugambo*, pronounced long and in leading tones: "Ohhh — lu — gaaaam — bo," which means that something goes way out, circles around, and comes back like a rope or boomerang. Nicaraguans use the word *bola* to signify rumor, meaning a ball that bounces all over the neighborhood. The English word *grapevine* offers an image of entanglement and connecting tendrils (Lederach 1989, personal note).

The most frequent pattern for resolution of property damage, accident, interpersonal offense, or injury to another's face is the use of a third person — mediator, elder, go-between, lawyer, relative, compromiser — to defuse the anger, carry the demands and counterdemands, and work out a mutually agreeable solution. The use of the third-party process is the most frequent methodology in the third world, while the Western, ex-Soviet, and Eastern European worlds tend to utilize direct confrontation and negotiation in resolving interpersonal differences.

However, even in cultures that prefer direct address, confrontational negotiation, and involvement of only the principal parties, conflict is still essentially triangular.

Conflict is triangular in structure, whatever the cultural forms may be. There are the two parties and the issue; then the first ally is drawn in; then the other party's ally becomes involved. By now there are a number of triangles, and the number rapidly increases as the conflict circle expands.

Love, trust, loyalty, and faithfulness are essentially dyadic; they are commitments between two persons. As these break down, one or both parties draw in a third to stabilize the threatening situation. The dyad is essentially unstable; the triad is the human way of gaining support, power, leverage, and stability.

Conflict is, intentionally and productively — or automatically and dysfunctionally — triangular. "When elephants fight, it's the grass that gets crushed," the Swahili proverb notes. When two parties fight, it is often the third — an innocent or powerless party — who suffers.

The two-person relationship, the dyad, is the primary human relationship. The dyad offers the deepest support, the fullest authenticity, and therefore the greatest risk and the most dangerous potential for hurt and alienation. The concentration of both persons' emotional needs into the smallest possible system makes the dyad the maximally threatening interaction that is inevitably unstable and essentially in need of a third pole to provide support and stability.

In stress, a third party is drawn in to release tension by providing support for either one party (a less functional step) or for both persons (a more constructive option). When the third party is allied with one member of a conflictual dyad, that recipient feels relief of tension, but the trouble in the relationship is unchanged or confirmed. When the third party refuses to form a coalition with either of the other two, a triad, not a triangle, is formed, in which a neutral third can assist both principals equally in moving toward a mutually satisfactory solution. In a functional triad, a dyad can double its power for change, but in a dysfunctional triad, here called a triangle, power is decreased, diffused, and deflected, and the result is destructive of the relationship.

Triangulation is the natural human way of handling and diffusing anxiety. In times of low stress, the triangulation process operates automatically in conversation, in gossip, in support-seeking, and in simple problem-solving attempts. These triangles are not problematic as long as they are transient, flexible, and constantly change their cast of characters. No one gets locked into an outside position, or becomes the focus of the other two persons' animosity; no one gets frozen into a role as counselor, rescuer, or peacemaker. Any one person may perform these functions at a point in time, and then be free to move into other, more equal relationships.

When triangles become intense, rigid, and indissoluble, all the relationships involved tend to deteriorate. Perceptions become distorted, then frozen into stereotypes; persons no longer respond; they react to each other in fixed reflexes; positive relationships become alliances, then collusions; problem-solving attempts become blaming, and negative conflict spirals escalate.

Triangles function in fairly predictable sequences. As tension mounts in a twosome, the person who becomes more emotionally uncomfortable brings in a third person. The former will tell the latter a story about the other person in order to relieve tension between the principals. As conflict rises, the preferred position is as the outsider. As conflict rises within one triangle, additional triangles are formed by the two parties drawing in an additional third. Conflicts in one triangle may be fought out in related triangles, or spread through an extended system of triangles in family, community, or other social networks. At times, family tensions, for example, may be fought out largely by outsiders — neighbors, relatives, school officials, police, staff at clinics, and others who participate in the family problem.

Detriangling, or reducing the emotional intensity of taking sides and connecting with only one person in a two-person conflict, is the way to growth and maturation. The more maturity a person achieves, the less he or she is caught up in different triangles and the more that person can respond genuinely, openly, and authentically to persons on both sides of a conflict. As one is no longer locked into old, frozen triangles, or paralyzed by the anxiety that moved triangularly through the system, the more effective she or he can be in relating in conflict or in calm.

In contrast to triangulation, clear triad formation is intentional, methodical, and purposive. The participants know that the triad is a temporary arrangement designed to clarify and strengthen the dyadic relationship through reconciliation of its difficulties so that a third party will be unnecessary and undesirable.

The third person of a triad is committed to neutrality, to availability to each person, to flexibility in offering interventions, and to equal justice for all concerned. Effective mediators, who can form triads without triangulation, are recognized by disputants in every culture. The wise person who can maintain a median position and mediate from that centered stance is prized, honored, and trusted, whether in Asia or Africa, Australia or the many cultures of Latin America.

TRIANGULAR CONFLICT

Conflict is inevitably triangular. At its simplest, it is party A, party B, and issue X. If this is not immediately resolved, the most anxious person will triangle C to gain an ally, so the configuration may be AC-B. Triangling principles are:

1. The sides of a relational triangle are never equilateral; there is always a coalition of two and an outside party. Two may sustain mutuality in dialogue for a significant length of time, but a third person either alternates between, colludes with, or remains distant from both.

2. The area of a relational triangle remains constant, but the sides will constantly vary in length as persons move toward and away from each other in associative or dissociative response to anxiety or excitement.

3. The triangle of A-B-X exists when person A is emotionally oriented to person B and to an issue, object, or value we will call X, and similarly perceives that B is co-oriented to herself or himself and to X. The situation is now balanced when A perceives that his or her attitude toward X is similar to that of B. However, when A perceives that B's attitude differs in either positive or negative feelings toward X, or varies in intensity, then A experiences a tension or a strain toward balancing the system. The coping responses to unbalanced situations are shared within a culture and transmitted in early socialization. In associative responses, A changes his or her own attitude toward X to become similar to B, not in a permanent attitude change, but in relieving the imbalance. Dissociative responses occur when A neutralizes the relationship with B (likes B less) or increases negative feelings (dislikes B) or maintains the discrepancy (disagrees with B) (Newcomb 1959, 392–93).

Triangular conflict is a human universal, but the intensity of the feelings involved, the nature of the network of triangular relationships, and the importance placed on each particular relationship are important variables.

NECESSITY OF THE THIRD PARTY

"Disputants are in the worst position to solve their dispute," argues Edward DeBono (1985, 92). It is natural to assume that the parties involved in a conflict should settle their own conflict; it is their business, their concern, their hassle. But they may be the least equipped to design a solution to the tensions of hostility, the loss of trust, the resulting suspicion, the impulse to secrecy, the biased communications, and the concretization of position taking; the repetition of patterns and explanations that have become habitual, familiar, and twisted can render the disputants impotent.

For two reasons a third party may be necessary if the conflict is to be carried forward:

1. Because the parties involved in the conflict are bogged down by tradition, training, and complacency in the argument mode of thinking. The parties involved rarely have the necessary skill or experience in lateral thinking and the design idiom.

2. Because even with the best will in the world, the parties involved in the conflict simply cannot carry out certain thinking operations because these would not be consistent with their positions in the conflict. The structure of the situation is such that these things simply cannot be done (DeBono 1985, 125).

The first of these reasons put forward by DeBono makes a third party a practical necessity; the second makes a third party a logical necessity.

The third party may offer information or introduce an intervention into the dispute (as indicated in fig. 15) to break a negative cycle. The model, from the intercultural work of P.H. Gulliver, shows the interplay between the intrapersonal — each person's perceptions, expectations, strategies, preferences, and tactical decisions — and the interpersonal information and behavior that comprise the visible conflict.

The third party may introduce information to either or both parties to break the cycle or turn it toward positive ends.

Figure 15
Cyclical Model of Negotiation

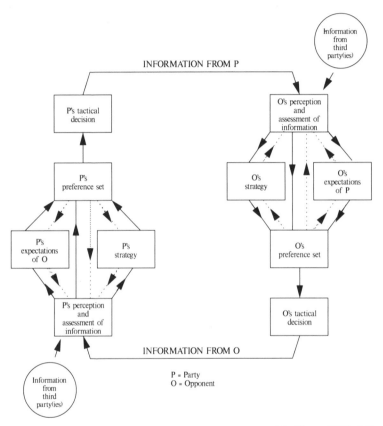

(Gulliver 1979, 84)

The third party, the mediator, performs a series of strategically important functions discussed below. These are adapted from Richard Walton's ground-breaking work (Walton 1969, 146–47).

First, the third party can assess whether the motivation to reduce conflict is mutual. Both sides must be self-motivated to enter the give-and-take of negotiation. If one side is not motivated, the third party can avoid the direct confrontation by continuing to act as a go-between, testing the waters, delaying the meeting by suggesting a later schedule or preliminary steps, and moderating the high-level of investment one party may be expressing. The goal is to achieve symmetry in motivation so that there is a mutual balance in initiating the conversation.

Second, a third party can seek to achieve a balance in the power situation of the two parties. Any power differential will undermine trust or inhibit dialogue. If one represents a larger organization, then the other may be permitted to involve more allies; if one possesses superior debating skills, the process may be designed to guarantee equality or favor the less articulate. The goal, again, is symmetry in situational power, a balance of strength and advantage.

Third, a third party can help achieve a balance in reciprocal confrontations between the two parties. If one moves to confrontation before the other is prepared to receive, the dialogue may abort; the behavior may be misinterpreted; and either party or both may feel rejected. Synchronizing the action on both sides helps both to interpret their process more accurately. Otherwise, a conciliatory move by one may be seen as weakness or yielding; the expression of negative feelings by the other may be seen as perpetuating the anger rather than a sign of new trust that is letting the person get old feelings finally off the chest and on the table. The goal is symmetry in process, in stages of negotiation, and in the sequence of movements toward eventual agreements.

Fourth, a third party can facilitate a mutual recognition of completion with each stage of the negotiation before moving into the next. Agreement by each with the problem definition, with satisfactory dialogue on differing perspectives, and with a clear statement of the range of issues for bargaining must be reached, expressed, and mutually recognized so that movement into the next stage can be balanced. The goal is symmetry in clear differentiation so that symmetrical moves toward integration may follow.

Fifth, a third party can assess the degree of openness occurring in the dialogue and introduce processes that may free the interaction to move forward with greater clarity and depth. For example, the third party may (1) challenge the social or organizational norms inhibiting clear expression of differences, (2) provide support while the parties express threatening feelings, and (3) introduce process exercises that draw out data needed for full negotiations. The goal is a symmetry of authenticity on both sides that is culturally congruent and socially and organizationally appropriate to the parties.

Sixth, a third party can facilitate communication to enable clear deciphering and interpreting of each other's messages. This can be done by restating messages in accurately interchangeable words, by interpreting statements until the intent of the sender and the impact on the receiver are nearly identical, by requiring responses that demonstrate that the listener has understood the speaker's meanings, and by contributing to the development of a common language. The goal is symmetry in communication so that there is a meeting of meanings in the exchange of statements.

Seventh, a third party can maintain an optimum level of tension in the negotiation process. Sometimes the tension level can be raised to create a sense of urgency, to increase information exchange, and to renew motivation; at other times reducing a higher than useful level of tension may decrease threat, rigidity, distortion, and defensiveness. The goal is to maintain a symmetry of energy and anxiety levels in each stage of the negotiation process.

In summary, the more symmetrical the motivation, power, progress through stages, authenticity, communication, and tension levels, the more successful will be the negotiation.

The goal: Be hard on process, soft on content. The third party has much power over setting boundaries for the negotiation, little power over the outcomes of the dialogue or the fate of the principals; much control over setting the steps and schedule, little control, in fact neutrality, over the final results of the principals' work together.

When the reverse of this is true, the mediator with power over the parties and their fate will find that this tends to inhibit candid interchanges, to induce approval-seeking behavior, to bias the preferences of strategies employed, and to gradually undermine trust in the mediator and in each other. Neutrality on content and outcome — the substantive issues under debate and the personal relationships between the principals — facilitates trust development, enables cooperation with the negotiation process, reduces threat and suspicion of interventions, and elicits open communication.

THIRD-PARTY SKILLS

The following skills for creative design focus on thought processes available to the third-party negotiator.

1. Search for solution rather than analyzing responsibility. The negotiator can refuse to allow a debate over assigning a ratio of responsibility (blaming). The third party might state: "The purpose of this discussion is to uncover possibilities, not to show who is wrong."

2. Set an agenda, plan stages. An agenda is best set by the third party. It should cut across the lines of argument rather than follow them. Identifying stages such as exploration, designing, narrowing options, evaluating outcomes, and defining agreements (and maintaining stage clarity) is an important discipline.

3. Recommend design exercises. Calling for specific exercises, experiences, and thought processes can move the parties from conflict thinking to creative design. An exercise should be carried out in its own right, completed, and let stand while another is explored.

4. Link and focus the principals. By doing that the third party can (1) hold persons to the agenda; (2) guarantee equal opportunity for expression; (3) make connections, link insights, and note possible reconciliation of positions; (4) cut off discussion on a crucial issue to hold ground gained; (5) introduce an exercise to break loose a stuck process; (6) renew the focus when discussion gets scattered; and (7) notice, harvest, and store ideas that grow out of each person's perceptions and contributions.

5. Contribute creative skills. Some of these might be identifying and offering a probe (a question, observation, proverb, quotation) or a provocation (a reversal, exaggeration, paradox, contradiction, polarity) or a picture (a metaphor, story, case, image) or a principle (a basic assumption the parties hold in common, a goal they now share, a value both have affirmed).

6. Pirate and promote ideas. A solution may be publicly or

Figure 16
Kinds of Role Relationships
between Third Parties and Principals

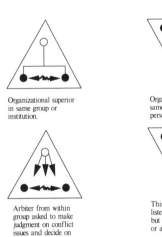

Organizational superior
in same group or
institution.

Organizational peer in
same group mediating
persons and issues.

Consultant from
within organization
addressing conflict
issues and process.

Arbiter from within
group asked to make
judgment on conflict
issues and decide on
winner and loser.

Third party asked to
listen, be a witness,
but offer no support
or advice.

Consultant from outside
organization or group
addressing conflict
issues and processes.

Marital affair with
the angry spouse in
the outside, devalued
position.

Marital conflict with
one partner having a
consultant, counselor,
or adviser.

Marital conflict with
partners communicating
through a child.

privately stated by one participant (but the competitive situation makes it necessary for it to be from a neutral party), so the mediator pirates the idea, paraphrases or redesigns it, and offers and promotes it as her or his own creation.

7. Review issues or concepts. At a central point in the negotiation process, it is important to review the issues on a more abstract level; giving an overview may help disputants to broaden their perspectives. This overview can be enriched by employing (a) theoretical perspectives; (b) functional descriptions; (c) historical flow charts; (d) force-field maps to show both drives and restraints, mo-

Table 8
Triangulation Checklist

TRIANGULATION

1. When your anxiety rises, do you wish for or look for a sympathetic third person who will understand your frustration and share your irritation at the opponent?

2. When anxious, do you have an immediate impulse to gossip to a friend with blaming and judging, to ventilate the intense feelings?

3. Do you have an ally who has been a support to you against a common enemy or competitor?

4. Can you be easily or loyally allied with a friend against an adversary who has mistreated him or her?

5. Do you find yourself anxious after your friend has shared frustrations? Do you feel a need to rescue, defend, and care for the other?

6. Are you tempted to think that others need your intervention, assistance, and management of their conflict?

7. When you are uncomfortable with a triangular relationship, do you cut off communication, avoid the other, and distance yourself?

8. Do you speak for the other by quoting her or his thought, carrying her or his message, directing her or his choices, and making her or his decisions?

TRIAD FORMATION

1. When your anxiety rises, do you suggest that you and your opponent could profit from conversation with a third person whom you might choose together with equal comfort?

2. When anxious, do you refuse to gossip and instead talk to the other party, write a message expressing your feelings, or wait until an agreed third person is available?

3. Do you have at least several neutral, trustworthy mediators or negotiators you can call on when needed?

4. Can you resist being allied with a friend, and seek to listen fairly, give feedback sensitively, and encourage using a mediator?

5. Can you think of the conflict between friends with caring but not be drawn into feeling responsible for the others' success?

6. Do you feel confident in others' ability to take care of their own needs and relationships?

7. When you feel demands to triangle, can you stay connected but still manage to distance yourself?

8. Do you speak for yourself, expressing your concern, sharing only your own observations, and taking your own position while respecting the other's positions?

tivations and blocks; and (e) pathways and progressive steps on both sides.

8. Modify, adapt, and adjust. The third party can present a solution design to each party separately, giving each time to modify and adjust it before a joint session. Multiple drafts can increase creativity and progressive design.

The variety of third-party roles is only suggested by the partial listing of such triads in figure 16. Each culture could supply a dictionary of possible triads, useful and unuseful.

In each facilitative triad, there are certain clear functions that are supplied by the more neutral person, who is able to see and perceive with a measure of creativity and objectivity.

Chapter Six

Conflict: Gender Differences and Conflict Styles

Even God is not ripe enough to catch a woman in love.
— Yoruban proverb

UNIVERSAL INSIGHT
(The Bottom Line)

Women possess many powers, but they are limited, channeled, suppressed, and denied by men's power. The more valuable, crucial, or brilliant the gifts of women, the more males and male-dominated structures are willing to exploit them or take the credit for them.

FOLKTALE: EVEN GOD CANNOT CATCH
A WOMAN IN LOVE
Yoruba Tribe, West Africa

Once there was a man who was too fond of watching his wife. Day and night he worried that she might see another man.

"Husband of my head, husband of my breast, husband of my front, husband of my back," she complained. "Why are you behaving thus? I am tired of this terrible war."

"What war is that?"

"The war of don't move, don't even have a movement. I cannot go to relieve myself but that you follow, expecting me to see a man."

"Is it not my right as a husband to be watching my wife?"

"Let me warn you then," she answered. "Even God is not ripe enough to watch me and catch me if I really want to love another man. What is wrong with it anyway? I was not born to hate people."

Now the man was frightened, so he built a second story and locked his wife upstairs every morning when he went to the farm.

One day the woman took a liking to a man passing by and invited him up. So she threw him a piece of soap with an impression of the key. The man made a key and daily came to dip his mouth in another man's soup. One day, he forgot to lock the door as he left, and the husband grew suspicious. He began such palaver that the wife said, "Come, let us go to the divine rock and settle this by ordeal." They both knew that a false oath would make the liar perspire, swell up, and die.

Now the woman's mind grappled with the problem like a leper's hand trying to pick up a needle. Then she called her lover and told him to dress as a beggar and feed his donkey along the road to the divine rock on the next day.

As the woman and her husband neared the donkey, she pretended to turn her foot. So the man hired the beggar to give her a ride. Then the woman drew her husband near and whispered, "A terrible thing has happened. As I was climbing on the donkey, my skirt blew up, and this beggar saw what he was not supposed to see."

"Never mind," said the husband. "The beggar may have set eyes on the dish, but it is I who alone may eat the food." So they hurried on to the mountain.

There the woman knelt by the rock, offered the kola nut sacrifice, and then sang:

> *Oh divine rock, I am praying to you today.*
> *Witness my words and punish me if I lie.*
> *I swear by your age and your divine power*
> *That no man has ever seen my nakedness*
> *Except only my husband*
> *and this ragged donkey man here.*
> *If I do not speak the truth*
> *let me swell up and die.*

She rose from her oath, and nothing happened to her. When they returned home, she kept both her husband and lover, and she proved the old proverb true: "Even God is not ripe enough to catch a woman in love."

(Gbadamosi and Beier 1968, 24–27)

FOLKTALE: THE GUILTY WOMAN
Basotho Tribe, Africa

This is a story of a man who was very rich, with many wives.

One day he went to hunt, but he was very unlucky. All he could find was a tortoise. He took it to his first wife and asked her to cook it for him, for hunger had caught him. But that big wife said: "H-ha, I do not cook such things as tortoises. Give that sort of work to one of your other wives."

The second, third, fourth, and all the others said the same thing. But the youngest one, the littlest one, said, "No, that will be good, father, I shall cook it for you."

Then she cooked it until it was tender and done. She dished it up in a little clay bowl, together with the gravy, and set it on a wall where it was safe, covered it with a grass mat to let it cool, and went for water.

When she returned, the husband said, "Little wife, where is the food? I was very hungry. Bring me meat so that I may eat."

"Here it is, big man," she said, giving him the covered dish. But when he lifted the mat, there was nothing left but the shell. He was cross. "You have eaten it!" he shouted.

"It was not I who ate it, Grandfather; I put it in a safe place, as you saw yourself."

He did not believe her. "I am going to the witch doctor right now. His magic bones will speak and tell me who ate my meat."

When they had agreed on a price, the witch doctor scattered his bones and stones in front of him, read their message, then told the man how to discover the thief.

He called his wives and all the people of the village to a deep pool in the river. There he stretched a strong rope of sinews across the water; then each wife in turn was asked to walk the tightrope while singing a song of prayer:

> Sinews of kudu break that I might fall.
> They say I ate the tortoise, if so let me fall.
> But I did not eat the tortoise or I would fall.

As each crossed the rope safely, the crowd acclaimed her innocence. First the little one crossed, then one wife after another until the first, the big one who first refused to cook the tortoise. When she came to the middle of the pool, the rope broke. Twaaah! And she disappeared, drowned in the waters.

Then everybody knew who was guilty. It is right, they said. You must stoop when you come to your own possessions, but when you come to others, stand up straight. Which means: Keep your hands off that which belongs to other people.

(Postma 1964, 53–57, abridged)

In *Lest Innocent Blood Be Shed* — Phillip Hallie's gripping account of Le Chambon, a small Huguenot community, and its courageous resistance to the Vichy regime in wartime France — the uniqueness of male and female responses to conflict is revealed. Hallie describes Le Chambon's heroic stand against Marshal Pétain's government; the resistance took the form of aiding and sheltering a stream of Jews fleeing the Nazis. Hallie terms this resistance a "kitchen struggle."

Although much of the book is focused on Pastor André Trocmé and the male resistance organization — on the courageous sermons, on the dangerous rounds made from house to house through deep snow by Pastor Trocmé, on his refusal to sign the oath of allegiance, and on his arrest and imprisonment — this is only the public face of the story.

The heart of the account is the "kitchen struggle," the courage of Mme. Magda Trocmé, who was confronted by the first Jewish refugee, took the stranger into her house, initiated the chain of activity, activated the networks of women, and carried on harboring the refugees while her husband was in detention camp. It was she who attempted to get papers for the refugees, and when refused, compromised her deeply held Protestant principles to counterfeit identity documents, and to painfully teach her children these deceptions and the higher moral law that she was obeying in saving human life. Her network of women in their safe houses continued to hide Jews in a silent domestic protest; in order to protect each other as well as their charges they had only a minimum of conversation (Hallie 1979).

Beyond the more institutional structures of the men's network, which did much in Le Chambon, there was the informal, more invisible, and silent network of women of faith and daily action. Two kinds of power, institutional power and relational power, are exemplified in this contrast of public and private conflict strategies.

WOMEN'S POWERS AND MEN'S POWER

This contrast between a public orientation among males (viewed as tending toward extradomestic affairs and matters of political and military import) and a domestic orientation among women (viewed as tending toward a lifestyle devoted to familial, communal, and relational concerns) was strongly made by Michelle Rosaldo in her 1974 "theoretical overview." As an outstanding East/West anthropologist, Rosaldo argued that this social dichotomy, which is commonly treated as a "natural" function of the physical differences between men and women, is, in reality, no more than a man-made device (Rosaldo and Lamphere 1974, 23).

In further clarification, Rosemary Ridd has put forward three important propositions. First, institutionalized power is for the most part controlled by men, and where women enter the public domain they generally do so within a male-ordered framework. Second, in any discussion of domestic and public orientations, it is more appropriate to think of *women's powers* and *men's power:* Women's powers being more diffuse and individualized outside the bureaucratic structures of society; men's power being more co-ordinated and structured within an institutionalized framework. Third, when a community is involved in open conflict with an ex-ternal threat, the social order will likely become more fluid, unless males take steps to conserve the old patterns by reinforcing the boundary between the domestic and the public spheres (Ridd and Callaway 1986, 2–4).

These propositions are exemplified by the position of women under Islamic law, as described by the Egyptian feminist novelist Nawal El Saadawi:

The men who dominate the judicial system in Egypt have been able to prevent women from becoming judges on the assumption that a woman, by her very nature, is unfit to shoulder the responsibilities related to a court of law. This assumption is built on the fact that Islam considers the tes-timony of one man equivalent to that of two women. The argument, therefore, is that testimony only consists in wit-nessing to something that has or has not happened, and if a woman cannot be trusted to the same degree as a man on such matters, how can she be considered the equal of man when required to give a decision on a point over which two parties are in disagreement? (Saadawi 1980, 186)

Although a woman may be appointed as minister in Egyptian government, with administration over thousands of male and fe-male employees, she is not allowed to mediate disputes even as a petty court judge or become a head of a village who will me-diate quarrels and conflicts. Male power is used to limit, channel, suppress, or deny women's powers.

Unequal power relationships, argues Jean Baker Miller, are le-gitimated and incorporated into a society's guiding concepts — its morality, philosophy, economics, law, and science. Because it is institutionalized, inequality becomes obscured and is regarded as natural and normal. Our institutions constantly reinforce the belief that the way things are is right and proper, not only for those possessing public power, but also for those in subordinate roles. With this institutionalization, it becomes self-evident to the society, though based on false premises, that these differences are due to sexual or racial or ethnic inferiority. Those in power doubt that the subordinated could perform the preferred roles, and still worse, those oppressed doubt their own capacities (Baker Miller 1976, 7–9).

MALE AND FEMALE POWER ROLES

The basic questions about male and female power have only tentative answers. Throughout history and across cultures, human beings have dealt with the relationship between the two sexes in an almost infinite variety of ways.

The basic questions include: Are male aggressiveness and domination of female adaptability and submission the products of nature or nurture? Why do women play a more prominent role in some societies than in others? Why do men — either as individuals or as a group — seek to dominate women? Why do some societies clothe sacred symbols of creative power in the guise of one sex and not the other (Sanday 1981, 1)?

The answers given are a blend of environmental, physical, emotional, religious, and political needs that are woven together in the web of life we call culture. These emerge in the sex-role scripts the culture creates to limit and direct, to pattern and guide behavior along predictable and therefore safer paths. These scripts or behavior plans shape development and growth of young women and men and pattern the institutions in which they will live out their lives.

These sex-role plans have served central functions including (1) division of labor; (2) defining relationships according to nature, symbolized in reproduction; (3) defining relationships according to the forces of the universe, symbolized in understandings of the universe and of God; (4) separation of the inner world of private life and the outer world of public existence; and (5) guiding the behavior of the sexes in everyday social, moral, economic, and political life. It is in this last dimension that the contrasting ways of handling disputes and resolving conflicts become a central issue.

Since sex-role scripts and plans are so foundational to a culture, they change very slowly. No matter the experimentation and exploration of alternatives, eventually the gravitational pull of history and the pull of culture are toward the patterns of past generations. In times of threat, in situations of conflict, we fall back upon what we have seen and known in the cultural milieu of our community of origins.

When we recognize that male dominance is cultural, not universal, that it is learned, not innately human, we find ourselves questioning its continuance when it contradicts other basic assumptions of human equality, human dignity, human worth, and the freedom to participate in shaping destiny that co-exist in many female-oppressive cultures. As we observe that female patterns of conflict management are in fact often superior to male styles, we may recognize that learning from both genders is not only necessary, but the survival of both may depend on men, at last, learning more human alternatives from women. As Peggy Sanday concludes:

> If a people can find alternatives within their cultural tradition enabling them to meet current exigencies, they are strengthened and so is their culture. Today's exigencies suggest that we may have taken the domination of nature too far.... The technology of male dominance has given us the wherewithal to destroy all life on earth. The ethic that sanctions control and dominion is now the problem, not the solution. Our hopes for social survival no longer rest on domination but on harmonizing competing forces. (Sanday 1981, 231)

THE POWER BEHIND THE "THRONE"

The rule that "you can either make peace or get the credit for it, but you cannot do both" is ironically most true between males and females. Women who make peace between conflicting parties often watch while males claim the credit.

Males often go through the visible motions of conflict resolutions, but the real work in reconciling was done by the invisible mediation of women working through networks, coalitions, and personal power relationships.

Public mediation processes may be *pro forma* transactions among male participants while the crucial consensus was reached and the resolution finalized by networks of women in both casual and structured conversations.

The case of insult and violence between two women in a Lebanese village reported by Cathie Witty reveals how the direct power and influence of the women carry the mediation from one stage to another while the males meet to publicly ratify the resolution (see fig. 17).

Case: Insult and Violence
Lebanon

Two young women, Muslim, met on the road from the village to the fields, and conflict erupted.

Fatuum, thirty years old and divorced, initiated the incident by shouting sexual insults at Saydi, who is twenty-six and unmarried. As the two approached each other, and Fatuum's insults grew more abusive, Saydi began hitting Fatuum with a large metal pan. In the physical struggle that followed, both women were bruised and bloodied in face and arms before they could be separated. After much shouting and screaming, the two were returned to the village.

Saydi, who had been en route to the field with food for her father and brothers, was considered by her family to be the injured party. The unspeakable insults by Fatuum had publicly shamed and dishonored both Saydi as a person as well as her entire family.

Fatuum's male relatives claimed she was the aggrieved party. She had been physically struck first when she had merely expressed her feelings about an unjust situation as she was bringing potatoes back from the field.

Each woman returned to her parental home and began, with

Figure 17
Diagram of Conflict Resolution
in a Lebanese Village

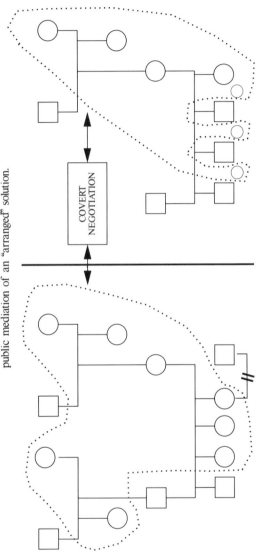

Male members meet for formal, public mediation of an "arranged" solution.

COVERT NEGOTIATION

Women achieve private consensus on appropriate resolution outcomes and communicate it to male family members.

shouting and tears, to give her account of the incident. The women drew them into the circle of feminine care and cleansed their injuries; the men clustered and began planning strategy.

Behind this eruption of violence lay the history of Fatuum's divorce. Her ex-husband and Saydi were the subject of village rumors, some accusing her of causing the breakup. The four children, economic hardships, and few prospects for remarriage intensified her hostility. Saydi's interests in marriage to the ex-husband deepened her feelings of investment and wounded honor.

Two separate and parallel negotiating processes now began. The women of the two families, many of whom were allied against a larger faction in the community, arrived at consensus on two arguments: (1) That the anger, pain, and injury being discussed were a common dilemma for women in general: "We all suffer these injustices and no man is worth it." (2) They agreed that they must stick together, work together, and be allied against their common opponent (the long-standing larger dispute with women of a third family). As all the women arrived at this consensus, the two principals began to cool off. They felt the support of their sisters and accepted, gradually, their definition and direction of the conflict.

Meanwhile, the fathers and brothers of the two women met and debated (1) who initiated the fight, (2) who was hurt most, and (3) who had the greater provocation. After two meetings with the mayor and three elders, they agreed that the insults and injuries were about even and that the two should apologize to each other. After six weeks of cooling-down time, a formal resolution was held, with the mayor present. Each woman, accompanied by her mother and maternal grandmother, apologized briefly; they then had coffee together and put the dispute behind them. They now avoid each other.

(Witty 1980, 70–73, abridged)

Reflections on the Case: The separate and complementary spheres of female and male power interact, interlock, and reinforce the impression that the men are in charge:

> The segregation of the sexes in Middle Eastern cultures does generate two dialectical forces. [The first force is] the per-

sonal and political frustration of being outside the culturally dominant political group, even though women compete and align successfully with other women. The second force is the closeness and solidarity that exist among women as a group or class of individuals. Women . . . value one another, understand something of the commonality of women's positions, and know it is often preferable to form strong alliances with other women, kin and non-kin. (Witty 1980, 73)

In the situation under consideration, the women explore the facts of the conflict in single-sex groups; they may be the key confidants who discover the truth when stories and reports conflict; they are consulted within the family, and the counsel of an older, respected woman may be the deciding factor in the family's position. But as mediation proceeds, men take the public role in the formalized proceedings and women, even though actively involved as parties and disputants, permit this division of labor according to gender.

In twenty interviews with the women involved, Witty reports that all were content to let men conduct public disputes. The three reasons uniformly given were: (1) Men argue strongly in public; women, though skilled, prefer not to argue in front of strangers. (2) Men take part in mediation more frequently and are thus more knowledgeable and skilled. (3) Mediation gives men something important to discuss and pursue in their leisure time (Witty 1980, 70).

The social and political power of women's networking is most often equal to and frequently superior to the relationships maintained by the males within and between families. Women compete and maneuver within political structures of their own and sustain factional alliances of their own that may be much different than the traditional boundaries of their families. These separate networks of influence can combine with, compete with, or frankly oppose the male political alliances. The external political ties a woman brings to marriage are as strong and broad as those of her husband. Her family's connections, her parents' and siblings' political networks, and their collective knowledge of political networking contribute as much to the family's standing in the community and savvy in influencing that community as does her partner's experience.

There are patterns, within every society, for conflicts between women as well as conflicts between men. But the regularities and irregularities are often unrecorded, and at times are hard to detect.

Jane Collier notes: "Whereas native informants usually explain conflicts between men in terms of culturally recognized rules, women's quarrels are often attributed to personal idiosyncrasies, or to particularistic circumstances" (Collier 1974, 89–90). She contrasts the limited data portraying women as passive participants with the emerging recognition of women as powerful agents. She writes that most anthropological approaches

> have limited utility, because they treat women as actors seeking to minimize unpleasantness instead of as actors trying to maximize gains; and, once unpleasantness has been minimized, there is no further basis for prediction. The active model of woman is not the affectionate daughter, hardworking wife, or loving mother who gets into trouble while trying to make the best of a difficult situation, but the cold, calculating female who uses all available resources to control the world around her, who seeks power: the capacity to determine her own and others' reactions. (Collier 1974, 90)

In most cultures, men function in political groups, women in domestic groupings. The former are defined in legal, contractual terms, the later in ethical language. Conflicts in the public arena are seen as political dramas; in the domestic world they are viewed as tragedies. This handicap is least powerful in groups where there is less separation between public and domestic spheres, greater where the division is more complete.

In some traditional societies, such as several African groups, parallel male and female socio-political processes for resolving disputes exist in women's associations and men's community organizations. Both function publicly, politically, and with binding legality.

Nancy Leis studied the functions of women's associations and their patterns of resolving conflict among the Ijaw in the Niger delta of West Africa. Within the network forming the associations, women serve as (1) informal mediators hearing cases between peers or between co-wives; (2) marital mediators negotiating between a husband and wife or wives; (3) binding arbiters on disputes over land boundaries between women or households; and (4) judges imposing damages against a woman who steals, defames someone's character, or insults or assaults another. These are separate judgments following public court hearings in which a woman is found guilty. She then must pay a fine to the court and to the women's association; if the court finds her innocent, the association may still think her guilty and demand the fine.

The sanctions employed to enforce decisions include shaming, ostracism, public protest, and virtual house arrest. Shaming may be done by dancing around the person, singing taunting songs, and afterward implementing complete exclusion. The group may confiscate an indispensable item, such as a cooking stand, and hold it until payment. A man who defaults on a loan from the association may find his house surrounded by women who hold him captive until he has arranged payment (Leis 1974, 236).

EVE AND MARY

In societies with patrilocal, extended households, men hold positions of overt prestige and authority, and women seeking power must do it through a man. Influence and persuasion with her husband and bonding, loyalty, and obligation with her sons become the coinage of power. As an outsider entering a patrilocal family, the woman finds her husband already tied to mother and family. So she must create her own power system: "Wives are the worms in the apple of a patrilocal domestic group. In a world where men gain political power from cohesive kin, young women gain power by breaking up domestic units. Men work to bind lineage mates together; women work to tear them apart" (Collier 1974, 92).

So wives are seen as threatening and challenging, mothers as uniting and self-sacrificing for their sons. Eve tempts men away from allegiance and obedience; Mary devotes herself to her sons. Every powerful woman must be both in her lifetime, but when young she is forced to be one; as she matures she becomes the other.

At marriage, the bride is a threatening stranger, at the bottom of the hierarchy. As she bears children she conspires to set up a separate household. She seeks to separate her husband from his mother and family while binding her sons to herself. Old matriarchs and young mothers are natural enemies. The competitive conflicts of the household are between generations as well as within, as sisters-in-law must struggle for scarce resources. Networking with other women who can cooperate helps balance out the lack of relationships with kin-women with whom she must compete. Household disputes become crucial power struggles; loyalties are defined; commitments are made; coalitions are struck; obligations are assumed; and political alignments are created.

Observing the domestic conflicts of Taiwanese families, Margery Wolf hypothesized that a woman builds a uterine family as a means of counteracting her isolation and of establishing security in her older age. This, of course, interferes with the uterine family of her mother-in-law. The wife must exercise influence over her husband to gain his loyalty, then through her social network with other women gain influence in the community through manipulation of opinion (the power of gaining or losing face for the family). These provide power as she moves from young-wife-outsider to become an eventual mother-in-law matriarch (Wolf 1972, 40).

After anthropological study of Navaho, Eskimo, Bushman, peasant, industrialized-urban, working-class, and lower-class families, Louise Lamphere concludes:

Women quarrel with or dominate other women when it is in their interest to do so; they share and exchange with other women when it suits their own goals. Cooperation and conflict among women in families or kin groups cannot be understood without reference to domestic power structure, to women's place within it, and to the factors that shape the relationship between the family and the larger society. (Lamphere 1974, 112)

Among the Hausa of West Africa, the subtleties of women's conflict patterns are described from the perplexed male viewpoint by the proverb:

> The wives of a woman are ninety and nine,
> Not even Satan has discovered the hundredth.

The codified, ritualized, and coerced patterns common among males offer a limited number of options; the mysteries of the courtyard and kitchen, the household and the market, cannot be easily deciphered or defined. The following case illustrates this point.

Case: Conflict and Reconciliation
Yoruba Tribe, West Africa

The preparation for a marriage feast has required cooking all night and morning. The groom and his extended family are soon to arrive for the evening rites when tempers begin to flare among the tired women. When a conflict arises among the women in the house, it is said that "someone has been careless with the salt; we now need water to cleanse things." The debate focuses between the bride's sister and the grandmother. The issues multiply — from cooking, to discipline of children, to husbands' behavior.

Finally one of the older women takes charge. She is trusted as a neutral person who never takes sides and ensures each will be equally heard. As the two begin to communicate about the matter and come to understand each other's feelings, the younger woman is asked to kneel and apologize for her behavior to initiate the resolution process. (This is customary, no matter who is recognized as the wrongdoer.)

Soon both women are in tears, and all the others join them in crying as they join in apology for past hurtful words or acts. The water has finally cleansed the salt. Bonding, cleansing, and healing have taken place.

(Asoera 1989, 7–8)

THEMES IN LIBERATION
FROM CONFLICT STRUCTURES

To be a woman is to be encumbered by the weight of generations of precedents, patterns, and practices of conflict suppression. Yet, it is also to be empowered by a consciousness that these repressive structures can no longer be suffered or tolerated. Psychiatrist Jean Baker Miller writes:

> We can think of conflict as a process between that which is beginning or new, and that which is old, or from which we are moving on. This conflict has been made difficult to perceive because we have been living within a structure which seeks to suppress all conflict in order to maintain a *status quo*. Such a structure has kept us from awareness of this most basic conflict, because it has to keep down all conflict. (Baker Miller 1983, 8)

For women, conflict always exists on two levels, the foreground conflict, whatever it is, and the background of conflict objectively built into male-dominated systems. Resistance to this historic, systemic, and social structure of injustice varies in degree, style, and character from one culture to another, but seven basic themes regarding liberation emerge from the women's movement that speaks from and for the "fourth world," the world of women.

1. The theme of a new consciousness: With the discovery of a new self-consciousness women are resisting the cultural domination permitted men as well as the discrimination favoring men.

2. The theme of new accountability: The responsibility of males for accepting advantageous cultural privileges or for actively imposing injustice, violence, and exploitation is being voiced and challenged.

3. The theme of rejecting violence: The past willingness of women to be intimidated, to cover for violent abuse, to tolerate sexual harassment, and to accept unequal justice concerning sexual violations is now confronted.

4. The theme of equal opportunity: Political, economic, athletic, ecclesiastical, and educational opportunities can no longer be retained by males without challenge.

5. The theme of progress: Although the degree of change on the above issues varies from culture to culture, and although movement in many settings is only beginning, the evidences of progress are visible and undeniable.

6. The theme of triumph: There is a celebration of battles won, of hope for an equality that exists now in dreams and aspirations, and of the confidence that a just society is and will be emerging.

7. The theme of solidarity: The capacity for networking with sisters both within and across cultures and the priority given to relationships and human connectedness make solidarity with other women in both the struggle and the celebration a natural theme for women's gender-awareness.

GENDER AND AGGRESSION

The relationship between gender, assertiveness, and aggression has many surprises to offer. Java offers a good case in point. Javanese women control household finances; they bargain tenaciously in the markets; men are embarrassed by such bargaining; they admit to being less capable in practical money management. The Javanese explain these gender-related traits by concluding that women's greater refinement enables them to be more assertive, more capable, and more dominant in the traditional arts of dance and the dying of batik cloth. Dances of strength and violence are characteristic of men; dances of assertiveness and refinement are characteristic of women. If we look for conflict in everyday life, women appear to stand out; if we look for rarer although more extraordinary bouts of violence, then it is the men who come to the fore. It is the women who are more continually assertive and aggressive (Klama 1988, 101).

R. P. Rohner examined the ethnographic records of 101 societies to trace universality of gender differences in human aggression. For fourteen societies it was possible to obtain separate ratings for boys and girls up to age six; for thirty-one societies it was possible to assess gender differences in adult aggression.

Among the boys and girls, ten societies (71 percent) rated boys more aggressive; the remaining four rated both sexes as equal. Although this indicates that young males are judged as more aggressive, the differences between the societies studied were much greater than the differences between the sexes in any given society. The statistical analysis indicated that cultural influences were more important than biological influences in determining the level of aggression in either sex.

Among the thirty-one societies studied in adult comparisons, the sexes were rated as equally aggressive in twenty, men as more aggressive in six, and women as more aggressive in five. Men become less aggressive as they mature; women increase in aggression; socialization seems to foster convergence between men and women (Rohner 1976, 57).

In 1911, Olive Schreiner characterized a callousness toward life and death as instinctual in men of certain cultures. "It is a fine day, let us go out and kill something" (Schreiner [1911] 1978, 176). One of the few irreducible differences between man and woman as such, Schreiner argued, is the differing angle from which each sex looks at and puts value on the giving and taking of human life, rooted in different sexual functions in reproduction: "To the male, the giving of life consists of a few moments of physical pleasure; to the female, blood, anguish and sometimes death" (Schreiner [1911] 1978, 175).

A woman, having given life, always knows what life costs and that it is easier to destroy it than to create it. Schreiner argued that this does not yield any general superior virtue, any greater mercy, or any lesser cruelty since a "woman will sacrifice as mercilessly, as cruelly, the life of a hated rival or an enemy, as any male, but she always knows what she is doing, and the value of the life she takes." Herein, she claimed, the knowledge of woman is

superior to man's, she knows the history of human flesh; she knows its cost; he does not. When woman's voice is fully, finally and clearly heard in the government of states, women would, because of their superior knowledge, because of their differing consciousness deriving from their different relation to human reproduction, eventually bring an end to war. (Schreiner [1911] 1978, 173)

Writing before the First World War, Schreiner argued passionately that women innately reject war. Many others have written equally compelling statements of the same position. Virginia Woolf in *Three Guineas* offered the most powerful feminist polemic against war.

Therefore if you insist on fighting to protect me, or "our country," let it be understood, soberly and rationally between us, that you are fighting to gratify a sex instinct which I cannot share; to procure benefit which I have not shared and probably will not share; but not to gratify my instincts, or to protect myself or my country. "For," the outsider will say, "in fact, as a woman, I have no country. As a woman I want no country. As a woman my country is the whole world." (Woolf 1938, 125)

In Woolf's view, women were not by nature opposed to war anymore than men were by nature warlike. The "fighting motivation" can be acquired by women with alarming rapidity in times of violent upheaval; pacifism can be learned by men out of recognition of the inhumanity of violence (Woolf 1938, 177–78).

But the structures of dominance and subordination, of manliness as aggression and womanliness as submission, of the infantile fixation of male militarism, and of the female mirroring of that vanity in service as admirers — all these must be dismantled (Woolf 1938, 35–36).

Women, as outsiders to much of the political process, have a valuable perspective to bring to interpreting war and peace, and a special contribution to offer to the deciphering of human conflicts. Are they, by nature or by socialization in ideology or experience, more pacific than men? Ruth Pierson answers this in concluding her review of feminist literature on women in war, peace, and revolution:

The recent historical record would appear inconclusive. Feminists have posited conflicting theories on women's relation to war and peace and women have, according to changing social historical circumstances, responded to warmongering and peace movements in a great variety of ways. The historic links between feminism and pacifism are counterbalanced by the instances when women have embraced revolution with hope and war with enthusiasm. There has not been a consistent women's response to war any more than there has been a uniform feminist position on women's relation to organized violence. (Pierson 1987, 225)

CONCLUSIONS ON THAT WHICH HAS NOT REACHED CONCLUSION

What transformation would occur if the conflict patterns of every culture were to be leavened by the more gentle, more human, and more relational processes used by over half of each culture — the women? In terms of conflict attitudes, changes are being initiated by women's movements with wide variation in values and strongly contrasting goals — from nonviolent social change to participation in armed resistance and revolution. Although such a spectrum of behaviors exists, the central tendencies indicate the following:

1. Women show a negative orientation toward the use of violent aggression in social, relational, or political matters. Violence is increasingly seen as symbolic of male domination and socially pathological.

2. Women show a positive orientation toward negotiation, verbal bargaining, and nonviolent demonstration rather than power, coercion, or violent solutions. Women hold the promise of being more comfortable at the bargaining table and more psychologically inclined toward assertiveness rather than aggression, toward horizontal control rather than vertical control structures.

3. In both Eastern and Western cultures, women show less inclination to be argumentative. (In some West African cultures, women practice the art of eloquent argumentation.) Western sex

differences in argumentativeness appear in a rich variety of studies. Women may view arguing aggressively and competitively as incompatible with their role expectations, or the tendency to cultivate less competitive relationships may be more pronounced because women network more effectively, affiliate more convincingly, and sustain open relationships with greater longevity. Perhaps the better conclusion to be drawn is that males are exaggeratedly argumentative, competitive, and irritable; females offer a more effective norm for productive relationships (Stewart and Ting-Toomey 1987, 19).

4. Women make stronger use of communication networks in community to rally moral, attitudinal, and social influence and effect nonviolent social change rather than resort as readily to coercion and violence as do males.

The socialization process of networking information, commonly called gossip, is a neutral, natural, and communal process of pooling data, equalizing power bases, and integrating people into the ebb and flow of life. The only thing worse than being gossiped about is not being gossiped about. That means you are a nonentity.

The more socially aware persons are, the better able to predict the power and functions of the gossip matrix in their community. They become discerning about what information will be shared with others, anticipating what will be used against themselves, intuiting what will come back garbled, and knowing that in the traditional societies the information may be there in the community for generations.

5. In the midst of conflict, women's core identities are more secure, less threatened, than are those of men. Males distance themselves via warrior images, macho styles, power postures, and rule limitations so conflict and control press them into more exaggerated either-or, win-lose oppositional stances. Women are more grounded in their female identity, more connected by biology and reality. They do not play out cultural acts with dreams of status and power, achievement and validation, to the same extent males are programed to do, so they are less fragile, less delicate in ego, and closer to actual interpersonal realities.

Chapter Seven

Mediation: The Necessity of a Go-between

The peacemaker gets two-thirds of the blows.
— Montenegrin proverb

**UNIVERSAL INSIGHT
(The Bottom Line)**

> The peacemaker is a bridge
> walked on by both sides.
>
> You can either make peace
> or get the credit for it.
> But you cannot do both.

STORY: THE MEDIATOR'S SACRIFICE
Taiwan

In the middle of the eighteenth century, a Chinese mandarin, Wu Fong, was assigned to pacify aboriginal tribes people in a mountain district of Taiwan.

These tribes, at every opportunity, took revenge on the Chinese from across the sea who had driven them out of the fertile lowlands into the high mountains. Their means of revenge was by the ancient practice of head-hunting.

Wu Fong befriended the head-hunters, slowly won their trust, and eventually succeeded in persuading them to discontinue their savage carnage. A period of peace followed, and Wu Fong became much loved by the aborigines as they came to enjoy a peaceful life.

Then a great drought struck the island. Week upon week and month upon month passed and yet not a drop of rain fell, and the harvest produced virtually nothing. Religious leaders declared that it was an omen of an angry god displeased with the aborigines' failure to offer the human heads in sacrifice that they had owed him as in generations before. Their agitation became so great that even Wu Fong could not dissuade them from returning to head-hunting in an attack on the Chinese. So he offered them an alternative. At such and such a time and in such and such a place they would see a Chinese man in red ride by on horseback. Him they could take. Wu Fong's prophecy came true; they saw the man and fell upon him and decapitated him in great jubilation and carried the head back to the village. But when they erected it on a stake, they all stared in amazement and dismay, for there was the head of their friend and mentor, Wu Fong. From that day forward, once and for all, the practice of head-hunting ended.

(Song 1979, 33, abridged)

FOLKTALE: HE-WHO-SEEKS-GOOD-ADVICE
Yoruba Tribe, West Africa

The tale was told by James Olá, chief arbiter in a village near Ibadan, Nigeria. He frequently utilizes parables to settle village disputes. This tale is an expanded form of the proverb: "To seek good advice is best; to try to solve problems by oneself is not good." The story is a statement about two philosophies of progress, tradition, and modern individualized education. One character relies only on his own wisdom and ingenuity; the other makes decisions collectively, thereby safeguarding harmony in the community and preserving continuity with the past.

Once there were two friends, Anikandagbon (or He-Who-Meets-Problems-Alone) and Aafogbonologbonsogbon (or He-Who-Seeks-Good-Advice). The first was well educated, literate, and widely read. The second was a man of the village, widely trusted, and much consulted.

When the old oba *died, the son who was next in line was looking for men to appoint as chiefs. Should he choose independent, educated men, or traditional men of the people?*

So he held a feast. He killed an ox, and had it roasted, except for the two hind-quarter legs. When the feast was ended, he called the two friends, and gave them each a leg of beef.

"Take this with you and bring it back in one week in perfect condition," he commanded.

When he got home, He-Who-Seeks-Good-Advice called all his people and presented them with his problem. They deliberated long, then arrived at a solution. The butcher was called, and the leg of beef given to him. He promised to return one week later with an identical fresh quarter.

He-Who-Faces-Problems-Alone discussed the matter with no one. He cut a tree, built a fire, placed the meat on a drying rack, and roasted it for a day. But meat must be cut in ribbons to dry, and he could not do that to the quarter. In a few days, flies had come, and the meat was full of maggots, and the bone kept slipping out of the spoiled mess.

When the day had come, the one man brought a fresh quarter carried by friends and family. The other carried his leg alone for the stench was so great no one would come near him.

The oba looked at each man, then demanded an explanation from the man with the putrid offering. "I attempted to roast it, to dry it, to preserve it the best I could, but it was impossible," he explained. The second man said, "I accepted the advice of my friends and the help of my community. Here is the beef."

The oba said, "This man shall be the chief, for he solves his problems collectively. The other man is a selfish person, an evil person, a blight, a scourge on the town," and they drove him from the village, for why should he be in the village if he is not of the village? To seek good advice is best; to try to solve problems by oneself is not good.

(Dorson 1975, 356–59, adapted)

"The peacemaker gets two-thirds of the blows," warn the Montenegrin people, who have been better known for retaliation than reconciliation.

"The hardest blow of the fight falls on the one who steps between," the Scottish proverb observes in cynical, yet clinical, accuracy.

A Spanish proverb counsels: "Between a hammer and a pliers do not stick your nose."

"The mediator is struck from both sides," the Kurdish proverb states.

The experience of mediation — a universal experience to be sure — is one of stepping between colliding forces, competing wills, and clashing temperaments.

Mediation is not only the ability to define and clarify, to separate and discern, to link and reconcile opposites; it is also the capacity to absorb tension, to suffer misunderstanding, to accept rejection, and to bear the pain of others' estrangement.

The position in-between is vulnerable yet vital; it is a precarious yet crucial and necessary human service.

"The chief is the tribe's garbage man," the Umbundu proverb from Angola concludes. Umbundu disputes that cannot be resolved immediately by the disputants are delegated to a mediator, and failing a satisfactory outcome are at last relegated to the chief's collection of community offal. As a mediator, he must sort the dispute out, sift truth from conjecture, and clean up the refuse.

Assumed as a communal necessity in traditional societies, the function of mediator has until recently become less and less available in Western society. As all societies grow more urban, more Western, and less personal and communal, the number of alternatives to formal law decreases. Rather than being a mark of social progress, the loss of avenues for dispute negotiation outside the court systems limits the opportunities for both relational and material justice.

Throughout virtually all traditional societies, mediation of conflicts by trusted persons or groups is the most frequently used

Figure 18
Contrast of Mediation Options
in Traditional and Urbanized Cultures

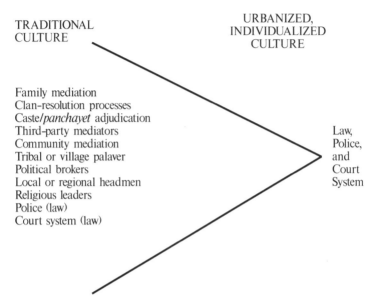

TRADITIONAL
CULTURE

URBANIZED,
INDIVIDUALIZED
CULTURE

Family mediation
Clan-resolution processes
Caste/*panchayet* adjudication
Third-party mediators
Community mediation
Tribal or village palaver
Political brokers
Local or regional headmen
Religious leaders
Police (law)
Court system (law)

Law,
Police,
and
Court
System

Law varies inversely with other social controls.
Where other social controls are weaker, law is stronger.
Where familial, tribal, and communal controls are strong, law is weak.

process of dispute settlement. Law as an abstract system of codified rules, collected cases, and established precedents may still be the dominant pattern of Western societies, but it is not, in human relational terms, the most effective or satisfactory pattern. In most societies a whole range of procedures and methods for resolving disputes and managing personal conflicts exists in addition to the use of court procedures.

In figure 18, the wide variety of mediation options in traditional cultures is contrasted with the narrow range of possibilities open to citizens of major urban centers around the world as well as throughout the West.

In her excellent study of Lebanese and American mediation practices, Cathie Witty writes:

> In the Middle East, mediation is a process of resolving and minimizing interpersonal conflict that is intimately connected to the social fabric of people's everyday lives. Mediation is a living, natural, and satisfying process in this setting. In comparison, many Americans no longer have available to them such indigenous, responsive methods of resolving disputes, and they must rely primarily on a bureaucratic court system that is impersonal, unresponsive, expensive, and personally unsatisfying. (Witty 1980, 6)

The involvement of the community and the intervention of community leaders give significance and meaning to the pain of alienation and offer inclusion as well as wisdom and support in the search for a solution to the conflict. In contrast, the police and court system are generally experienced as an alien intrusion into life, an alienating and estranging foray into a public forum that adjudicates but does not mediate, concludes but does not connect, and coerces but does not resolve the dispute or the pain of the disputants.

Direct negotiation and confrontation between disputants without a mediator allow the parties to retain their privacy and independence, but that method has serious liabilities. The confrontation of face-to-face, unmediated negotiation heightens power differentials and throws the decision-making process wholly upon the principals. Direct negotiations have a limited usefulness once the level of conflict has escalated in intensity. Hence, there are a number of reasons that argue for the necessity of a mediator: (1) If intense confrontation is possible, it is highly likely that one principal has sufficient power to coerce the other. (2) If a power-induced decision is reached, the likelihood of it being maintained is low, and the chances of a boomerang effect are high. (3) A compromise out of painful confrontation may be an escape from tension rather than a satisfactory resolution and may become the basis of future conflicts. (4) Direct negotiation tends to continue the fight, extend the coercion, support the manip-

Table 9
A Continuum of Mediator Roles

OBSERVER	CHAIRPERSON	ENUNCIATOR	PROMPTER	LEADER	ARBITER
The passive mediator's presence encourages positive communication and interaction. Deliberate passivity may be an effective strategy with two active and equal participants.	The mediator keeps order and tends to direct procedure, reiterate points of agreement, give priority or emphasis, set schedules, and curb interruptions or repetition.	The mediator enunciates rules, norms, and values. He or she directs and interprets the information and offers sign posts that point down traditional pathways.	The mediator contributes tentative and limited suggestions. This attempt to clarify information and encourage coordination uses restatement, reflection, summary, questioning, and focusing.	The mediator directly injects opinions, makes recommendations, evaluates preferences and demands of either party, and proposes solutions and their modifications.	The mediator acts as a go-between, messenger, interpreter, and persuader. Proposing solutions and making counterproposals can bring the two toward solution.

A mediator rarely takes a single role, and the strategy frequently changes in the sequence of stages. The early stages — establishing an arena, composing an agenda, and establishing limits — more frequently use the left three styles. The later stages — narrowing differences, bargaining, ritual affirmation, and execution of the agreement — more often utilize the three styles to the right. Leadership is needed in transitions between stages; within stages the mediator may lapse toward passivity. (Gulliver 1979, 219–27)

ulation, and merely transform the conflict from overt to covert modalities.

Mediation provides the disputants an external agent with alternative and additional information, experience, and expertise; mediation offers alternatives beyond those the parties themselves can generate; mediation keeps in focus the visible prejudices, values, stereotypes, fears, and needs of both parties and their communities in a way neither is able to do for herself or himself; mediation invites and often ensures full participation and full communication between the parties; mediation can equalize power differentials and provide maximum opportunities for both persons.

The mediator may serve a variety of needed functions or play one of many possible roles. The continuum in table 9 summarizes six of the key functions frequently supplied by mediators. Some mediators carry out a resolution process from one particular position; others may move from one role to another during a lengthy negotiation process.

Mediation, as described by Witty (1980, 7), performs six significant functions, wherever it is used, regardless of the cultural setting. Mediation allows disputants and their supporters to:

1. Talk with each other in a verbal style that is natural, comfortable, and mutually intelligible to all participants.

2. Ventilate anger and frustration in a free, appropriately open, and therapeutic fashion.

3. Receive an increased sense of power and personal worth from the attention of their neighbors who find these problems important.

4. Gain access to a readily available, quick, and inexpensive forum.

5. Equalize or realign status and interpersonal power struggles by promoting an egalitarian ethic.

6. Reestablish and realign the persons, place, and sense of belonging in the relevant social group, whether it be the family or the community.

The freedom for both parties to express and explain their sides of the dispute without limits on the style or content of the communication is not only therapeutic; it decreases confusion, cultural misunderstandings, and individual limitations to make the proceedings intelligible to all concerned.

MEDIATION STRENGTHS

Mediation aims to reduce largely psychological obstacles that prevent hostile parties coming together for constructive negotiation. When the channels are open, the protagonists are responsible to

Figure 19
Mediational Model

Each level rests on the foundation
of the previous agreements.

LEVEL THREE: CONTRACT

9 AN INVOLVEMENT IN REACHING
AGREEMENTS AND IN FINALIZING
COVENANTS WITH BINDING POWER.
Commitment springing from partici-
pation and personal involvement in
processes.

8 AN OPENNESS TO REVEAL PER-
SONAL NEEDS AND WANTS. The
ability to express feelings, define needs,
and share wants.

7 A WILLINGNESS TO SETTLE THE DIS-
PUTE IN A PRIVATE MEDIATION PRO-
CESS. Acceptance of a dispute resolution
procedure rather than resorting to flight,
force, or legal channels.

LEVEL TWO: PROCESS

6 A BALANCED POWER DIFFERENTIAL
DURING NEGOTIATIONS. Status and
power differentials equalized during the
process.

5 A BALANCED CONCERN FOR SAFETY
OF BOTH COMMUNITY AND PROP-
ERTY. Social respect — status and face —
valued as much as property, profit, and
goods.

4 A BALANCED CONCERN FOR RELA-
TIONSHIPS AND GOALS. Achieving
agreement as important as reaching individual goals.

LEVEL ONE: CONTEXT

3 A BASE OF CONTINUING RELA-
TIONSHIP. A commitment to ongoing
relationships with the other participants.

2 A BASE OF TRUST IN GOODWILL AND
NEGOTIABILITY. A confidence in the rationality and negotiability of the other
party.

1 A BASE OF PERSONAL INTERACTION
BETWEEN PARTICIPANTS. A context of
common culture, community, or social relationships.

move toward agreement through discussion bargaining or seeking an alternate option.

The mediator remains outside the conflict itself, refusing to slip into the role of judge, adviser, or advocate on content or policy issues. The mediator's role is not to negotiate, but to remove the psychological barriers and enable the principals to negotiate at a meaningful level. Figure 19 offers a mediational model for balanced processes.

The mediator maintains caring-neutrality. The commitment is not to a particular outcome, but to ending the suffering of both parties. The mistrust and suspicion are met with openness, with befriending of the protagonists, and with a suspension of personal anger and demands and a bracketing of values that would block commitment to facilitate both sides equally in their movement toward negotiations.

Mediators seek to progressively sharpen their basic skills of empathy, active listening, sensitivity to needs of parties, sense of timing, verbal and nonverbal communication skills, capacity to maintain neutrality while remaining in contact, and ability to understand the stages of negotiation and conflict resolution.

Mediators develop a sixth sense for timing. They recognize which side stands to gain from acceleration of the process and which will profit from postponement. (They recognize the crucial timing involved in face-saving time, adjusting to concession and change time, and coercive pressure tactics of controlling time. They know the best moment for negotiation is during a stalemate when both sides fear losing, and the worst moment is when one side feels that it is so close to winning that negotiation is unnecessary.) The accompanying "Guidelines for Mediators" from Folberg and Taylor offers eight propositions for effective negotiation.

Mediators recognize that their position is delicate, vulnerable, and at times physically dangerous. Persons who stand to profit from the continuation of the conflict may seek to have mediators removed. In larger communal, organizational, or national conflicts, threats, assassination attempts, or harm to family members may occur.

Effective mediation is *built on* a floor of basic commitments (context), *built by* a process of balanced concerns and understand-

Guidelines for Mediators

Proposition 1. People try to escape what they perceive as negative or destructive (pain) and go toward what they perceive as advantageous and positive (pleasure).

Proposition 2. People make more complete, and therefore better, decisions when they are consciously aware of feelings created by conflicts and deal effectively with those feelings. ("Dealing effectively" means integrating the feelings into decisions without allowing emotions to overwhelm rational concerns.)

Proposition 3. The participants in a personal dispute can generally make better decisions about their own lives than can an outside authority such as an arbitrator.

Proposition 4. The participants to an agreement are more likely to abide by its terms if they feel some responsibility for the outcome and develop a commitment to the process used to reach agreement.

Proposition 5. In mediation the past history of the participants is only important in relation to the present or as a basis for predicting future needs, intentions, abilities, and reactions to decisions.

Proposition 6. The more accurately a mediated agreement reflects the needs, intentions, and abilities of the participants, the more likely it is to last.

Proposition 7. Since the participants' needs, intentions, and abilities will probably change, the process should include a way of modifying the agreement in the future. Thus change is seen as a constructive and viable part of the agreement and must be considered in the mediation process.

Proposition 8. The mediation process is substantially the same for all participants and all situations, but techniques, scheduling, and tasks to be accomplished must vary to match the circumstances, the participants, and the uniqueness of the mediator.

(Folberg and Taylor 1984, 14)

ings (process), and *built through* personal involvement of the participants in making agreements (contract). See figure 19 for elaboration of these elements.

Mediation is built on a context with continuity. A base of personal interaction between the participants provides a floor of common connections. In traditional or tribal communities the participants are linked by a web of interactional patterns; in impersonal, urbanized settings such a relational context can be retribalized, cultural commonalities can be affirmed, and shared identities can be defined by the mediator. In traditional settings a shared belief system provides rules, obligations, and channels for disputes. Internal codes of ethics and norms of behavior are congruent with the external social order. In modern Western experience this shared base of norms must be defined, clarified, and agreed to by participants at the outset.

A base of trust in each other's goodwill, rationality, and negotiability creates an arena for the give-and-take of progressive mediation. In traditional societies, trust is evoked by the recognition of each other's solidarity with the surrounding community; in urbanized settings, every venture of trust is a risk; each risk both expresses and invites trust. The evolution of trust is a step by step sequence of risk and resulting trust, trust and ensuing risk.

A base of continual relationships between participants is desirable. The necessity to work through differences because of future interface and interaction offers a strong encouragement to finish difficult situations rather than leave them unresolved. In traditional societies each person's place in the social order will continue, so cut-off relationships are less common than in urban or Western societies where mobility facilitates flight and where continuities must be chosen, affirmed, and pursued intentionally.

Mediation is built by a process with balance and integrity. Mediation proceeds along pathways that balance relational as well as substantive goals. The mediator and the participants are effective only as they are concerned both with relational issues — status, face, honor, personal satisfactions — and the material goals being disputed. A balanced concern for the safety and security of the personal and communal relationships as well as for any values of money, materials, or land will be finally more productive than focusing on either to the minimizing of the other. In shared communal settings, social and moral relations are often more crucial and harmony receives greater attention; in more impersonal settings, monetary values and distributions may be used to compensate for personal values.

A balance of power differentials must be maintained in all stages of the negotiation. The mediator may be a sufficient filter to equalize many imbalances in verbal, personal, or interactional skills, or the process may require careful structuring to balance dynamics to ensure that both achieve equal need fulfillment.

Mediation is built through personal involvement in contract. People are more likely to adhere to agreements they have helped form than to those imposed by external authorities. People are more committed to agreements that emerged from a process that took their deeper feelings, needs, and wants into consideration. People are more committed to a process that they chose, entered willingly, and valued as personally satisfactory. In traditional societies, the resolution of personal matters within one's collective community affirms and strengthens one's place in the network of sustaining relationships. In less personal societies, the choice may rise from dissatisfaction with the court system and its costs, its impersonality, its slowness, its prejudice, and so on. Whatever the motivation, personal involvement in selection of the process, in participation in that process, and in personal self-expression through this process will deepen satisfaction and the ongoing impact of the attempted resolution.

MODERN VERSUS TRADITIONAL MEDIATION STYLES

"Entangled" in a conflict with Arnoldo, a fellow worker who has undercut Pablo's chance for advancement, Pablo is betrayed, angry, and overwhelmed by thoughts of revenge. In his Latin cultural context, Pablo is not alone with his conflict. He is surrounded by the members of his age-group network; they give him time to talk

(priority is given to people rather than tasks and time boundaries), provide security and continuity (friendships are not quickly developed or lightly ignored), and serve as go-betweens in facilitating discussion of problems (the initiative for change lies in the hands of the third party, not the first or second).

Pablo finds his sense of identity grounded in both the family and the social group that nurtured him (I belong, therefore I am), and his sense of status given him by the position he has received in family, group, and social networks (status is ascribed, not achieved). He trusts these networks to surround and support him in the entanglement that has occurred (his basis being *personalismo*, or "affective personal relationships," and effective personhood).

So Pablo trusts his friends to work at communication and clarification of the conflict (a mediator should be a trusted part of the community) and is patient for the problems to be resolved in time ("time is people"; time is the web of unfolding relationships that are lived out on many levels simultaneously) without a direct, face-to-face confrontation between himself and Arnoldo (go-betweens can serve as intermediary buffers, channels, and catalysts in resolution of differences) (see fig. 20).

In contrast, Paul, a North American real estate salesman, discovers he has been treated unfairly by another agent, who has not credited him with deserved listings. His anger is intense, but it is personal, private. In his individualistic context, his problem belongs to him alone (he covers himself by talking to no one until he can confront Jim, his opponent). He does not gossip to friends (friendships are made quickly, can be broken summarily, and are not to be "used" dependently). Besides, people are busy; they have their own schedules, conflicts, and agendas ("time is money"; responsibility is respected, boundaries honored, tasks and schedules have priority over personal issues).

Paul's identity is grounded in his ability to take control of his own personal situation, to be self-directing and self-actualized. He will wait for the appropriate time, situation, and setting, and then will confront Jim. (He will deal with the problem privately, interpersonally, and factually first to resolve it between the two of them if possible.) If there is no ensuing meeting of minds, a neutral,

Figure 20
Comparison of Mediation in Modern and Traditional Cultures

MODERN CULTURES   TRADITIONAL CULTURES

I
PERSONAL IDENTITY

Individualism: ego-centric,   1   2   3   4   5   Collective identity: familio-
self-reliant, self-directing, and   ◄─────────────►   centric or sociocentric reliance
autonomous.   on related and committed
                                                        autonomy.

II
SOCIAL STATUS AND
RANK

Status through accomplish-   1   2   3   4   5   Status from ascription: per-
ment: individual achievement   ◄─────────────►   sonal status received by posi-
and earned status.   tion, relationships, network.

III
PREFERRED
NEGOTIATION
PROCESS

Preferred process is rational   1   2   3   4   5   Preferred process is affective
and formal: business trans-   ◄─────────────►   and informal: understandings
actions and agreements sealed   and agreements reached by
by linear contracts. Structure is   social trust and assumptions.
crucial.   Relationship is central.

IV
SOCIAL ROLES

Leadership roles are special-   1   2   3   4   5   Leadership roles are holistic:
ized: technical expertise valued   ◄─────────────►   life experience and social posi-
as criteria for trust.   tion are criteria for trust.

V
MEDIATOR'S FUNCTION

Negotiator is impersonal, pro-   1   2   3   4   5   Negotiator is personal, rela-
fessional, from outside the   ◄─────────────►   tional, a part of community.
community.

VI
TIME FRAME

Linear time; bureaucratic time.   1   2   3   4   5   Cyclical time; tasks and sched-
"Time is money." Time is a   ◄─────────────►   ules are secondary. "Time is
commodity to be used effi-   people." Time is relationships
ciently. "One thing at a time"   to be explored and experi-
(monochronic).   enced. "Multiple relational
                                                        agendas" (polychronic).

anonymous outsider, a professional attorney or consultant, may be invited in (outsiders get in, get the business done as quickly as possible, and get out of the situation) or both parties' attorneys will talk as partisan negotiators.

The initiative for change lies with Paul; the process is completely owned by him; the mediation is employed as he can afford it; the goal is clear understandings, contracts, and boundaries. The desirable outcome is a better business relationship between colleagues who must cooperate from day to day. (Community is the smooth intermeshing of individual gears, each fulfilling a different task in the social machinery.)

Mediation arises from different cultural expectations, takes contrasting forms, yet may serve parallel functions in traditional and modern cultures. Clearly, as individualism increases, the preference for resolving conflicts by personal action in private interactions also rises. With the emphasis on personal achievement and status through accomplishment, any failure of understandings or breakdowns in relationship will be located in the self and negotiation will tend to be between individual selves. Immediacy, frank self-disclosure, clear statement of demands, respect for the importance of time, and use of accepted business or legal process are all valued.

Conversely, in a more collective context, the reverse of each of the above may be deemed both appropriate and tactically advisable. The models offered in table 10 summarize contrasts between the North American model of mediation and mediation processes in many of the third world's traditional cultures. The content varies widely with the diversity of cultural patterns and pathways for dealing with conflict, yet the communal, triangular, relational, and dynamic nature of trusted go-between processes is a constant across cultures.

Lederach's work in tracing the folk art of mediation in Central America and in doing conflict training in various cultures has offered a framework for looking at the contrasts in cultural expectations. The continuum of expectations adapted from his work (table 11) is helpful in tracing the implications of different self-other understandings throughout the stages of mediation from entry to final agreement.

Table 10
North American and Traditional Models of Mediation

NORTH AMERICAN MODEL	TRADITIONAL CULTURE MODEL
1. Mediation is a formal process with specialist roles. A crisp formal structure for discussing volatile issues provides a context of security and stability as well as channeling toward constructive goals and ends. Time and space (schedule and setting) are clearly defined.	1. Mediation is a communal process with involvement of trusted leadership. The normal structures for data flow and dispute management are trusted (contextualization). The pathways familiar to participants, the time frame preferred, and the settings of familiar social interaction will be utilized.
2. Direct confrontation and communication are desirable to both mediator and participants. The mediator's opening monologue establishes "the rules of speaking" that will govern the session; the ongoing facilitation controls and directs communication flow.	2. Indirect, triangular, third-party processes of a go-between are more desirable to save face, reduce threat, balance power differentials, and equalize verbal or argumentative abilities. So communication may be through others; demands may be carried by advocates; and agreements may be suggested by multiple participants.
3. Time is linear ("one thing at a time") (monochronic), is controlled in discrete "sessions," and is managed by rapid schedule of self-disclosure and statement of demands and counterdemands.	3. Time is relational (multiple relationships and issues are interwoven) (polychronic). Tasks and schedules are secondary to relationships, so self-disclosure follows social rituals, personal agendas, and communal concerns.
4. Process is structured, task-oriented, and goal-directed toward "reaching agreement on issues." The autonomy and individualism of disputants' choices, goals, and satisfactions are central.	4. Process is dynamic, rationally oriented, and directed toward resolving tension in network and community. The responsibility of the disputants to their wider context and the reconciliation of injured parties are central.
5. Mediator is presented as a technical specialist, with professional, anonymous, and impersonal relationship to the disputants. A written contract is facilitated and the mediator is out of their lives.	5. Mediators are recognized communal leaders or trusted go-betweens from the social context. They are personally embedded in the social networks and remain in relationship with parties in the dispute both during and after the resolution.

(Lederach 1986, 4–5, adapted)

Table 11
Continuum of Cultural Expectations

STAGES OF MEDIATION	(COMPONENTS) ELEMENTS	(MODERN) "PURE FORMAL"	(TRADITIONAL) "PURE INFORMAL"
1. ENTRY (CONTEXT SETTING AND GROUND RULES)	1.1 Setting	Public bureaucratic style	Private interpersonal style
	1.2 Mediator chosen	Professional, impersonal, anonymous	Known and trusted person, friend, or social leader; known and in network
	1.3 Expectations shared by third party and disputants	Restricted access to mediator's time	Unrestricted access to time and involvement
		Facilitate direct address	Provide surrogate, or go-between, for indirect communication
		Focus on issues and goals	All aspects of relationship may be involved
		Autonomous decisions made by each party	Appropriate groups will be involved in decisions
2. INTRODUCTION TO SESSION (MONOLOGUE BY MEDIATOR)	2.1 Process	Directive monologue	Nondirective introduction
	2.2 Structure	Formalized	Assumed in social customs
	2.3 Rules of talk	Directed by mediator	Familiar social process
	2.4 Priorities	Tasks confronted first	Relationships come first
	2.5 Roles	Formalized	Natural social roles of participants in community
3. STORY-TELLING	3.1 Interaction made	Face-to-face	Through third party(ies)
	3.2 Focus (topic)	Disputants' demands (I-topics) stated early	Disputants' demands (I-topics) stated later
	3.3 Sequence	Issues one-at-a-time	Multiple related issues
	3.4 Style	Analytical, linear causation	Relational, entwined stories
4. PROBLEM SOLVING	4.1 Time function	Linear (monochronic)	Cyclical-personal (polychronic)
	4.2 Purpose	Focus on issues	Reconcile relationships
	4.3 Person/context understanding	Issues must be resolved in isolation from the social network	Issues are embedded in the social network so both are interrelated
5. AGREEMENT	5.1 Form	Written and signed	Personal word given
	5.2 Continuing relationship to third party	No continuing relationship	Symbols of reconciliation exchanged; ongoing responsibility to parties and for implementation of agreement

(Lederach 1986, adapted)

CONTRASTS AND CONTINUITIES
ACROSS CULTURES

"Anglos are pushy; they want what they want immediately and start negotiating before they have built trust. They are too forward, too demanding, too socially insensitive."

"Hispanics are too slow; they beat around the bush; they don't get to the point until the negotiation is at an impasse."

This polarization of traits does not fall only between modern and traditional cultures. The Japanese see the Koreans as explosive and brash; the Koreans find the Japanese subtle and evasive; the contrasts between the overcontrolled German style and the expressive Italian style, or between the emotionality of adjoining African tribes such as the Hausa and the Yoruba, are equally great.

The ability to conceptualize the integrity of each culture's patterns of social interaction is necessary for any conflict participant, and must be second nature to a mediator or trainer.

"Deep within, all people yearn to be English," the colonial empire-builders once assumed. Today a Western assumption is: "Scratch any person on the globe, and underneath you'll find an American longing for freedom, democracy, individual rights, and Coca Cola." Perhaps every culture has such bizarre ethnocentricity secretly tipping its scales of justice. But its rightful place is in our humor, not our honor; in our history, not our present values.

Contrasts in expectations and continuities in human interactions separate and connect persons in every intercultural conflict. To illustrate, several key Western assumptions — conflict myths — are explored in the following paragraphs, and their inadequacies in intercultural settings are noted.

First, people and problems can be separated cleanly; interests and positions can be distinguished sharply. Negotiation can focus on problems and interests without becoming person- and people-oriented. However, in most cultures of the world, equal attention must be given to both person and problem, to relationship and goals, and to private interests as well as public positions if a creative resolution is to be reached. (See the list entitled "Western Values and Mediation Process: Getting to Yes" for a diagrammatic contrast of these polarities.)

Western Values and Mediation Process:
Getting to Yes

I. Focus on interests, not on positions.

All negotiating, mediating, bargaining should focus on the real interests, not on positions. Interests can be met in many ways; positions tend to freeze, block, limit. Push hard on interests while helping each soften positions.

II. Separate people from the problem.

The negotiator must be hard on the problem but soft on people. Those who are hard on both frustrate change; those who are soft on both accomplish little. The relationships and the substance must be separated and dealt with separately.

III. Invent options for mutual gain.

Looking for possible solutions should be separated from deciding which solution is best. Do not presuppose a "fixed pie" to divide. Create anew. Attack problems but support persons creatively.

IV. Insist on using objective criteria.

To simply take positions and then bargain from them on the strength of perceived power does not produce the best overall result. Seek a basis for objectivity grounded in equal treatment, fair outcomes for all, or other just and fair agreements that may serve as precedents.

(Fisher and Ury 1981, 56ff.)

Second, open self-disclosure is a positive value in negotiations. An open process of public data shared in candid style is assumed necessary for trust. "Open covenants, openly arrived at," Woodrow Wilson insisted, as did Harry Truman, were the basis for setting up the United Nations. However, when constituents can hear what is being sacrificed in reaching an agreement, then compromise becomes improbable and often impossible precisely because of that openness. The real negotiation is done in corridors or behind closed doors, and is announced publicly when agreements have been reached. Virtually nothing of any substance is agreed on in the official public UN debates.

Third, ownership is a crucial value in negotiations. A decision should be reached collectively, with responsibility for whatever decision is made shared equally with all who are involved or affected. In some cultures, only the person or persons at the top of the hierarchy make the decision. In negotiations, the decision can be best reached by persons delegated to act, trusted to decide, and empowered to close the process. In many traditional cultures, the larger community may participate in the process at various stages and be informed observers throughout the whole resolution process.

Fourth, immediacy, directness, decisiveness, and haste are preferred strategies in timing. The Western valuation that time is money can press the negotiator to come to terms prematurely. Many different cultures find that the best way to reach an agreement is to give the matter sufficient time to allow adjustments to be made, accommodations to emerge, and acceptance to evolve and emerge. Believing that "time is people," they are in less haste to reach closure.

Fifth, proportionate requests, negotiable terms, minimal expectations, and bottom-line positions should be offered as the starting point in negotiation (see the list entitled "Western Values and Mediation Process: Getting to Yes"). Some cultures are more visibly conflictual than others; they ask for much more than is expected as an opening gambit, assume the opponent has also inflated the requests, and accept compromise with a significant reduction of askings as normal process. Flexibility in negotiating styles and a willingness to respect and participate in each other's patterns of conflict resolution are necessary.

Sixth, language employed should be reasonable, rational, and responsible. In some cultures, deprecative language, extreme accusations, and vitriolic expressions are used as a negotiating power tactic. Admiral Joy, the senior UN delegate to the armistice talks at the end of the Korean War, has told of a note that was exchanged between North Korean delegates. In Korean characters large enough to be read by the noncommunist representatives, the note proclaimed: "These imperialist errand boys are lower than dogs in a morgue." Joy states that this was "the ultimate Korean insult." In a similar show of disregard for diplomatic courtesy, Huang Hua, the senior Chinese representative at Panmunjom (and subsequently Chinese ambassador to the United Nations), repeatedly referred to American Ambassador Arthur H. Dean as "a capitalist crook, rapist, thief, robber of widows, stealer of pennies from the eyes of the dead, [and] mongrel of uncertain origin" (Dean 1966, 54). At one point, after repeatedly charging South Korean President Rhee, President Eisenhower, and Secretary Dulles of the deliberate murder of Koreans and Chinese, Huang added that Dean "was a murderer lying in the gutter with filthy garbage, wallowing in the filth of a ram — that there was a saying in Chinese that a man was known by the company he keeps, and that... [Dean's] South Korean companions were execrable, filthy, bloody, etc." (Samuelson 1976, 41).

Seventh, no is no and yes is yes (an affirmation is absolute, a negation final). In some cultures, one does not say no to an offer; requests are not phrased to elicit negations; when an offer is affirmed, the real meanings are weighed and assessed carefully. Many negotiators have left a meeting with a perceived agreement only to find that the real position was more subtle, more concealed, and the reverse of their public expectations. A Mexican proverb advises, "There are a hundred ways of saying no, without saying it."

Eighth, when an agreement is reached, implementation will take care of itself as a logical consequence. The agreements negotiated may mean different things to parties in a reconciliation. Built-in processes, ongoing negotiations, open channels for resolving problems as they arise in ongoing interpretation, and circumstances that would warrant renegotiation are all useful elements for ensuring ongoing success.

GROUP AND COMMUNITY MEDIATION

At the risk of oversimplification of the range of possible ways of coping with conflict,... Italians are rather explosive and handle matters quickly one-to-one; English are more subtle and discreet; Americans tend to be confrontational and direct; it seems the most distinctive feature of conflict in the Kongo society is its *social* dimension. Strained relations between two persons quickly trigger a concern and involvement of all members of the group or groups to which the individuals belong. Disputes endanger the health of the social body. (Burke 1988)

So Joan Burke introduces her report on conflict among the Kongo people of Lower Zaire, where conflicts are experienced as a group crisis rather than simply as an individual or interpersonal issue. Although there are many varied interpersonal difficulties, disputes over land, compensation claims for crop damage by the neighbor's animals, dissatisfaction over dowry settlements, tensions between generations, division of inheritance, marital or in-law problems, injury from insults, and fear of witchcraft — *all* of these threaten the community and its solidarity. Thus the primary concern will not be revenge, redress, or justice, but the restoration of relationships and a return to functional cooperation.

In traditional Kongo society, social and economic relationships were leveled by the mutual dependence, cooperation, and sharing required by a subsistence economy. Individual ambition and advancement were inhibited by the recognition that personal success would be realized only at the expense of the group. With the change to a money economy with readily available consumer goods, comparison, competition, and envy become inevitable.

Insults, curses, and angry words are particular triggers for conflict in a culture where the word is seen as possessing effective, not just expressive, power. The impact of words is seen as proportional to the inner force of the person speaking them. Unilateral verbal attack, or a verbal duel, may tear the fabric of concord.

Horizontal conflicts — differences between persons within the same age group — are less complex and serious than vertical conflicts between members of differing age groups. Horizontal conflicts may be readily resolved by direct conversations after a cooling-off period following the initial eruption. This lapse of time is as important a part of the process as the later stages of negotiation and resolution. If the conflict is not resolved directly, either party may, in time, invite a mutually acceptable third party to serve as a mediator (not an arbitrator) to assist in reaching a resolution.

Vertical conflicts — between generations — face clear power differentials. The weight of respect owed by the younger to the elder makes direct address inappropriate. The younger is required to initiate the resolution process, no matter who has committed the socially recognized wrongdoing. A third party is usually necessary to facilitate the exchange of messages. The disputants, their sympathizers, and the mediator may first focus on the issues of who is right or wrong, but eventually the larger concern of all is the reestablishment of harmonious relationships.

If mediation in either horizontal or vertical conflicts fails to bring about resolution, the matter will be referred to the clan palaver, where the community as a body seeks to find a way to mend the broken relationship before it creates wider division. The palaver proceeds slowly toward consensus by well-practiced steps. The chief or his chosen representative acts as facilitator and postpones his own contribution until the time is ripe. The group formally assembles; there is ritual recognition of significant elders; then the two parties present their briefs; an open airing of views follows with all possessing an opinion expected to contribute it openly. Much time is allowed for group exploration of the conflict until finally the chief moves from being facilitator to articulator.

The chief sums up his judgment in eloquent proverbs and artful recommendations. "It is he who is as familiar with proverbs as he is with the matter at hand who usually arbitrates," say the Yoruba. This is equally true across West Africa, where the chief may make recommendations, assign blame, apply sanctions, assess payments, and define the final settlement.

The disputants usually ritualize the agreement with expressive actions, for example, by marking their foreheads with mud from palm wine poured into the dust; then all drink in ritual closure. If the decision ends with a clan division, a dish is broken and attached to a central tree; the palaver ends and people return to their daily chores (Burke 1988).

The palaver is an all-community hearing that is meant to ensure equal justice to all parties. As the Basa of Nigeria say, "The palaver drum is not beaten only on one side." It takes two hands, two complementary beats — that is, resolution requires ritual involvement of the two sides.

In his work among the Arusha of Tanzania, P. H. Gulliver records the dispute negotiation process of the moot (a community assembly in which complaints are heard). Conflicts between lineage members are heard before an internal moot. External moots — communitywide assemblies — assist the disputants and their counselors in interfamily conflicts. If a person is not heard within the clan he or she may take the case to the larger moot. The Arusha do not accept individual acts of retaliation and consider the use of violence to be tantamount to an admission of weakness in a man's argument and as an affront to the integrity and dignity of a person (Gulliver 1963, 220).

In his later work, among the Ndendeuli of southern Tanzania, Gulliver extended his discussion on the significance of the moot in communal dispute resolution. He observed that the moot (1) followed the mode of negotiation, not that of adjudication; (2) precluded violence and coercion since serious violence to gain one's ends destroyed the possibility of living together in a single community (the violent person was excluded and forced to move away); (3) reinforced and carried out the accepted norms of community justice; (4) tended to seek compromises between the conflicting claims; and (5) necessitated that neighbors take sides, make choices, and take positions on their own views of fairness.

> Moots are politico-jural institutions, the means of dealing with intracommunity disputes by processes of negotiation, the occasions for examining the development and readjustment of neighborly relations and expectations within the changing network, for expressing as well as fulfilling obligations, for acquiring entitlement to future claims for assistance, and for seeking further influence and prestige. (Gulliver 1971, 178–81)

S. Wilson has observed that among the Gitksan nation, in northwest British Columbia,

> conflict is a serious matter and is dealt with promptly. There is a feast at which one chief always begins by saying, "This is the way it is," putting the problem in the middle of the table (all in authority, the chiefs and the witnesses, offer their comments in a peaceful manner). [The people] have to walk around the problem, making suggestions until [they] come to a consensus which all can live with, not love, but live with. (Wilson 1988, 18)

The peaceful resolution process of the Gitksan is based on their belief in the continuous interrelationship of persons that makes isolation and individualistic solutions to conflicts unacceptable. Historically, among the Gitksan, the consequences of even murder were negotiated in such a consensus-oriented round table. Land would be transferred as compensation to help deal with the pain of the loss. The murderer might be required to give up his or her name and go nameless for a period to show respect for the life taken.

> Eventually, of course, all these surrendered things were returned. One of the phrases for that return was "the pain has passed." When the pain had decreased and time had taken care of the grief, land would be returned in a formal way because land was life. To give up a portion of your land was to give up some of the comfort of life for your people. (Wilson 1988, 19)

FAMILY-GROUP MEDIATION

Traditional conflict resolution in the Hawaiian extended family, called *ho'oponopono* (see fig. 21), is a gathering of the entire family for prayer (to the ancestor gods, originally, to the Christian God since Christianization) and for confession, forgiveness, and release. A Hawaiian named Pukui stated: "Every one of us

Figure 21
***Ho'oponopono* Flow Chart**

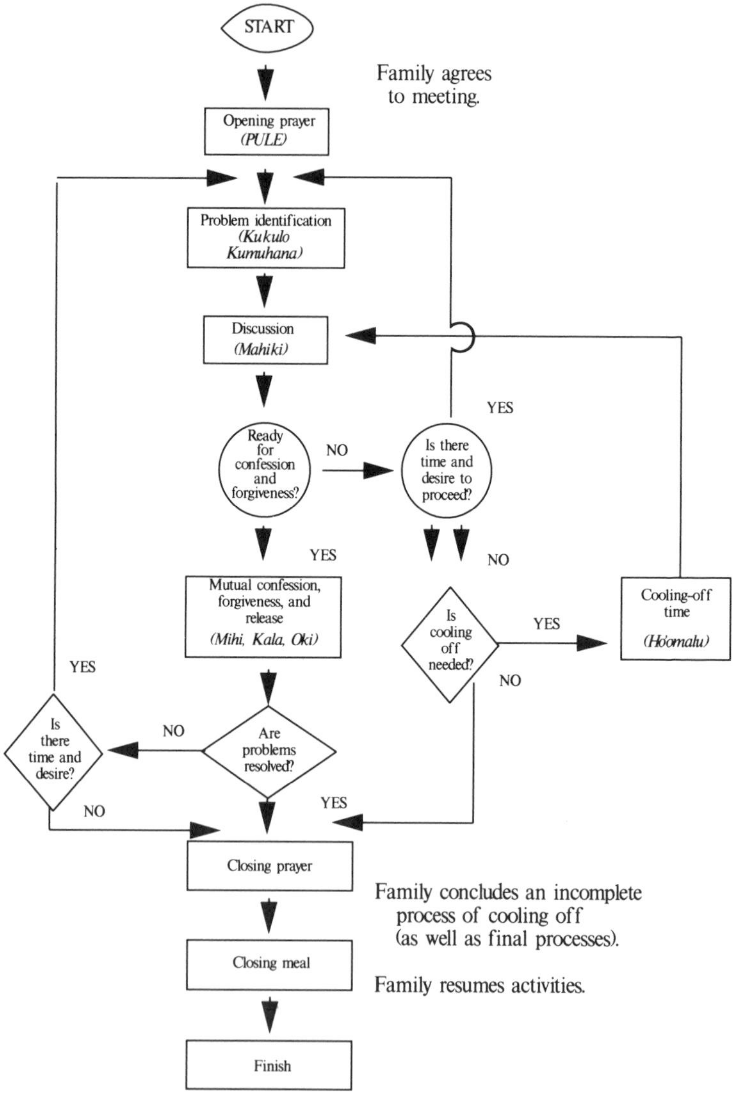

(Shook 1985, 89)

searched the heart for hard feelings against one another. Before God and with His help, we forgave and were forgiven, thrashing out every grudge, peeve, or resentment among us" (Shook 1985, 9).

Ho'oponopono literally means "setting to right, to restore and maintain good relationships among family, and family and supernatural powers." These are seen as interrelated, as a complex net of familial relationships in which anyone's part affects the whole. The process includes eight steps: (1) the family's agreement to gather for *ho'oponopono;* (2) an opening prayer for divine assistance in sincerity and truthfulness, led by the senior member; (3) problem identification that includes commitment of all to search themselves, identification of the particular conflict triggering the meeting, discussion of the layers of secondary hurts and conflicts that have accumulated, and cooling-off periods that may be called as tempers flare; (4) confessing-forgiving-restituting-releasing: sincere confession, willing forgiveness, appropriate restitution, and mutual release follow until conflicts and hurts have been released and "cut off" in a mutual, reciprocal agreement; (5) a closing phase — this may include a summary and a reaffirmation of the family's strengths and enduring bonds (the problem is declared closed, never to be brought up again); (6) a closing prayer; (7) sharing of a traditional meal to which all have contributed; and (8) the resumption of normal family life and activities. Multiple sessions may be required for resolution of some complex conflicts; cooling off may be necessary between sessions; each session ends with prayer and the agreement to maintain confidentiality and commitment to work again until all is thrashed out; a final session ends with the pledge to close the issues permanently (Shook 1985, 10–13).

In Africa, the group palaver is also used as a therapeutic process for individual psychiatric illnesses:

In many African societies, the group therapeutic palaver serves as the most important first step in diagnosis and treatment not only for the patient but for the immediate family members as well. Whenever a member of the clan is sick in the Kongo culture, the elder's role is to bring together members of the clan to attempt diagnosing the patient's illness in terms of broken relationships and then propose a plan of action for healing. (Mpolo and Kalu 1985, 6)

The healing process requires the establishment of hope, confidence, and the restoration of relationships between the patient and the clan. The healer plays the role of intermediary, offering suggestions, making connections, offering acceptance, and fostering a positive climate of loving reconciliation.

Makang ma Mbog tells of the *esye* ritual of the Ewondo of Cameroon. Zana, the diviner, had diagnosed social conflicts as the source of sickness, so a palaver was assembled, and the group was divided according to age and sex into small groups. Each member expressed feelings held against the patient and formulated wishes for the future. Then group leaders reported the feelings and wishes in a general meeting.

The speaker for the brothers' group reports: "Brothers are upset with the patient because he does not care for them; he steals from them. Four of the brothers want some restitution. Three brothers are asking for a share in the brideprice he holds for their married sisters while the fourth, more upset than the others, requests the restitution of his stolen four goats. Now our brother will not die."

The speaker for the children's group reports: "Elder, the unmarried sons are discontent with their father. They accuse him of being egotistic because, even though he is a well-to-do man, he does not want to help them get married while he himself has five wives. Thus they were unhappy and have willed him to die. But now, they wish him good health."

The speaker for the women's group tells of their anger and their wishes for his good health. Then the officiating brother declares: "My brother will live. Those who willed him to die are for his recovery. He will get better. But we have to offer sacrifices to the ancestors so that they return to us our brother they have already welcomed in their world."

At last Zana promises to give each member of the clan whatever his or her request was. (Mbog 1969, 325)

LEARNINGS FROM TRADITIONAL MEDIATION

In summary, we can draw the following conclusions from examination of the varied nondirective means used in the resolution of conflict in traditional societies. These characteristics show similarity to approaches emerging in noncoercive attempts at peacemaking in Western societies. The key factors in such peacemaking processes are that the process is:

1. initiated by a neutral or impartial third party. The mediator or go-between is not inclined to favor one party over the other, and is chosen because of this evident neutrality.

2. acceptable to both parties in the dispute, at least at the outset, although degrees of trust vary throughout the process.

3. noncoercive since the mediator does not possess the power or sanctions to compel the parties to follow a certain course; however, threats, costs, and consequences may be explored as interparty realities.

4. nonbinding, in the sense that the arbiter does not possess sanctions that may be used against the parties should they fail to reach agreement or to implement the contract; however, the community may consider the process binding once agreement is reached and exercise its sanctions in terminating the conflict and supporting distribution and implementation.

5. nonprescriptive, in that the primary goal of the mediator is to assist the parties in arriving at a mutually satisfactory agreement that they will fulfill because of mutual benefits.

6. nonthreatening; the go-between is responsible to, dependent on, and chosen by the parties of the dispute, and this reduces power differentials and aids the chances of success; this type of mediator is also less inclined to stimulate resistance by either party than an institutionalized mediator controlled or supported by an outside party or organization.

7. conclusive, in that it provides a setting for decision, distribution, and termination. The outcome is decided, the distri-

bution is administered, and the termination is effected. The mediation process contains mechanisms for all three of these essential functions.

CASES IN ETHNO-MEDIATION

To widen one's perceptions of the styles, uses, patterns, and rituals of mediation, one need only read through the literature of social anthropology and note cases of dispute resolution, conflict mediation, and community intervention. The following cases are selected as a basic introduction to mediation patterns in various traditional cultures.

It is helpful to read them as plots of human drama, as scenes of multilevel social interactions, and as stories of the most primary folk-art of resolving moral, legal, and social differences, not just as case histories of disputes and negotiations.

Case 1: Stolen Sheep
Lebanon

Early one morning, at the house of Abraham (a Maronite), it was discovered that a sheep was missing. After Abraham consulted with his brother next-door, the two decided to have breakfast while sending one of the children for the mayor, Elias.

The mayor arrived, heard the problem over coffee, and agreed to go investigating with them. At the next-door neighbor's, they sat for coffee, inquired if anything had been seen or heard, and discovered nothing. The next house was owned by Moussi, a Muslim who had heard nothing, but promised to see what he could find out on his own.

While the men were at the next house, that of Butros, another Maronite, the mayor's son came to tell the mayor that Subhi, a Muslim, was waiting to see him. The mayor returned home; he and Subhi discussed crops and fields; coffee was made; then Subhi reported that he knew of Abraham's search for a lost sheep, and might know something of the incident. Abraham was sent for.

The three men had coffee; then Subhi, who had been negotiating with Abraham for several days to buy 115–20 sheep, reported that he had met a young relative on the road at 5 A.M. that morning with a knife in his belt and blood on his clothes. He asked not to be named as an informant, but stressed how important it was for such matters between families to be cleared up. He described the boy as seventeen, irresponsible, lazy, and unwilling to work. Elias and Abraham thanked him for coming and agreed to visit Aziz, the boy's father, that evening.

At 7 P.M. Abraham and Elias called on Aziz. He was washing his feet. He rose, dried his hands, welcomed them, arranged pillows, passed out cigarettes, and invited them to stay for dinner. After ten minutes of social conversation, coffee was poured and enjoyed. Then Abraham told of his missing sheep, and said that he thought Aziz and his son could help them solve this problem. Elias told the report of the son's being seen that morning.

Aziz said he could not imagine why his son could help, but he would send for him. The conversation on farming resumed, and one-half hour later, Abdul arrived. The father questioned him, called in the mother as witness, then asked for the clothes the boy had been wearing that morning. The boy brought them and denied knowing what caused the stains. Aziz became angry, cuffed him on the ear, and sent him to wait in another room.

The men sat smoking for a few minutes. Then Aziz said he was not convinced the boy was guilty, but he would talk to him further and then speak to them again. Elias agreed that they should not intrude on family matters; they excused themselves and left.

Two weeks later, Aziz, his uncle, the Muslim mayor, and another Muslim elder made another visit. A boy was sent to call the Maronite mayor, who had already been informed of the visit. Coffee was served. Aziz's uncle said that they had discussed the missing sheep. The son had insisted he was not involved, but some other member of the family had taken the sheep. The Muslim mayor reported that the family would compensate for the loss and find out later who was involved, but for the family name they would settle now.

Abraham and Elias agreed, but added that they hoped this type of incident would not be repeated.

The group now went out to the sheepfold to come to agreement on the value of the sheep. After bargaining they agreed on an amount, and the money was produced. Abraham thanked them. They stood in silence. Then Elias said such incidents must be stopped for the good of all.

Coffee was brought; the guests were served first; they all drank, and, soon thereafter, the guests departed.

(Witty 1980, 49–52, condensed)

Reflections on the Case: Key dynamics for reflection on this case include: (1) the multilevel relationships within both kinship and religious groups; (2) the delicacy of the Muslim-Christian interface; (3) the networking within each group (i.e., Moussi to Subhi, to Aziz, etc.); (4) the functions of mayors as headmen mediators who speak on behalf of other parties, exert social pressure, temper violence, offer appropriate compensation, and express normative values; (5) the maintaining and saving of face for the victim, the family, the clan; (6) the willingness to wait weeks for a resolution in process; (7) placing higher priority on outcome and social harmony than on defining the "truth" or placing blame; (8) the recognition of the pattern of a present incident within the history of families and clans living alongside each other in community; (9) the confirmation of the weight, validity, and legitimacy of the resolution for the community by the presence of both mayors and elders; and (10) the necessity of strict observance of each other's social rules, customs, and symbols of hospitality and respect.

Case 2: The Never Leopardskin Chief
Sudan

A man reporting a stolen cow goes to the leopardskin chief, asks him to serve as mediator, and requests the return of the cow. The chief, along with several elders of the village, goes to the plaintiff's homestead. They are seated and given beer to drink. After conferring, a deputation is gathered from the village, and the group goes to the defendant's village. Here also the chief is presented with beer or a goat. The sanctity of the chief's presence reduces the likelihood of the deputation being injured. The visiting elders sit with the elders of the defendant's village. Each party presents his side of the case; then the chief and any other elder express an opinion. When everyone has had his say, the chief and elders withdraw and reach a decision. The disputants accept the verdict of the chief and elders. Later, the owner of the cow gives a calf or a sheep as a gift to the chief.

A dispute in the same village is also dealt with similarly. Both disputants go to the homestead of the leopardskin chief, and lay their spears on the ground by his house as a sign of respect. When both have stated their views, the chief and any elders present step outside to consider their decision, then announce their conclusion, couched in persuasive language rather than an authoritative judgment. Both parties must agree to the verdict, and the opinion of the chief carries considerable weight. Any oaths taken are sworn on the leopardskin. If one party refuses to accept his decision, the chief may pass him the leopardskin, in which case, he must give the chief a gift before he will take the skin back. The person in whose favor the decision has been given hands his spear to the chief, who spits on it, and gives it back.

(Evans-Pritchard 1940)

Reflections on the Case: About these cases Evans-Pritchard concludes:

> The five important elements in a settlement of this kind by direct negotiation through a chief seem to be (1) the desire of the disputants to settle their dispute, (2) the sanctity of the chief's person and his traditional role as mediator, (3) full and free discussion leading to a high measure of agreement between all present, (4) the feeling that a man can give way to the chief and elders without loss of dignity where he would not have given way to his opponent, and (5) recognition by the losing party of the justice of the other side's case. (Evans-Pritchard 1940, 164)

Case 3: Assault with Weapon
Lebanon

Yussef, a fifty-seven-year-old Christian, and Ahmad, an eighteen-year-old Muslim, were seen arguing in the fields. The quarrel was violent, and Ahmad abruptly left. Minutes later, a shot was heard. Yussef fell, shot in the leg. Ahmad was seen fleeing with a gun. Yussef was taken by car to a nearby government hospital, accompanied by relatives. Ahmad's family elders conferred with them the same day, requesting that the case be settled in the village, between families, and promising to take the necessary steps. Yussef's family agreed, suggesting that Ahmad be kept hidden until discussions could begin lest young relatives seek revenge.

The police questioned Yussef twice in the hospital. He stated he had hurt himself. Elders from Ahmad's family visited him three times to express concern, test his feelings, and evaluate the injury done. Preliminary conversations within Ahmad's family on the amount to be paid for damages and informal conversations between elders of the two families set a figure and let the family begin raising funds.

Almost two months later, Yussef now out of hospital, the mediators gathered at Yussef's home. He was supported by elders, the Christian mayor, and leaders from other villages — twenty-one men in all. Ahmad's family, the Muslim mayor, and other elders numbered twenty-three. They were seated on two sides of the room.

Ahmad's uncle opened with statements of regret. Ahmad sat silent beside him. Then Muslim leaders recounted the long cooperative history of the two families. Then a brief background to the assault was given with extenuating circumstances explaining the young man's rash behavior but recognizing his primary guilt. Many further statements were shared. Then the uncle of Ahmad summarized:

> We realize that you are esteemed and reasonable men, and in your honorable way have chosen not to make this anger public and have our son arrested and humiliated. And for this act of nobility in your time of pain and difficulty, we are truly

grateful and receptive. God willing, your leg will pain you less as time goes on, and God willing, you will again honor us with your evenings. And because we know that you believe it is true and valued what we say, that argument is the cleanser of hearts, we know you will accept our apologies, sorrows, and good will and let this matter be finished between us.

As the proverb was being used to complete the mediation in a traditional way, a pouch was passed through many hands to Yussef, who placed it unopened under his cushion. This symbolized his acceptance of payment for the injury. Yussef then spoke briefly:

I was shocked that such a thing could happen between Ahmad and me, for I have known him since the day he was born, and in fact, my wife and sister helped his mother in his birth. But anger is a powerful force and we have all been angry. And even though I will always walk with this stick, the deed has been done. There is no reason — God help us all — for bad blood to continue. And so, I and all my family accept your gift and apology. Let us talk no more of this incident.

At this point, Ahmad and his father came to sit before Yussef. A basin and razor were brought. Yussef lathered and shaved the younger man with the straight razor. Then a new white robe was brought from another room in Yussef's house; Ahmad dressed in the robe, which became his symbol and possession. Then he and his father returned to sit among their kinsmen.

The atmosphere was now relaxed. Conversation turned to crops, weather, and politics. Tobacco and coffee were passed around. Three hours had passed and the people began to scatter, although the family remained to discuss the night's events.

(Witty 1980, 54–58, condensed)

Reflections on the Case: Central elements in the management of conflict through mediation are clearly present in this illustrative case. These include: the immediate channeling of the situation by the elders; the initial agreement to use mediation; the patience with a long lapse of time; the oscillating movements of mediators between parties; the knowledge of family history and motives; the equalizing of family status through storytelling; the presence of mayors and elders as legitimate communal authorities; the goodwill in both families to settle by mediation; the openness to hear and review the entire dispute in catharsis and search for mutual satisfaction; the use of ritual apologies, proverbs, and reconciling symbolic actions; and throughout a concern for the saving of face and honor for both parties, their families, their faith groups, and their supporting communities.

Case 4: The Ifugao Monkalun
Luzon, Philippines

The *monkalun* is, literally, "an adviser," "a mediator." He possesses no official office since he is a *monkalun* only when acting as a *monkalun*. He is chosen for this role by the plaintiff in the conflict, not by the public. He is not a judge for he makes no judgments, nor an arbiter since he hands down no settlement. He is a forceful go-between. He has the authority, war knife in hand, to compel the offending party to listen, but he cannot demand an agreement. He is not an advocate for the defendant or plaintiff, but a neutral party. He is a pipeline between the two, for once the issue is taken up, the two antagonists may not confront each other or speak to one another until the issue has been resolved one way or another. So he shuttles back and forth with demands and counterproposals.

Honor is maintained by lengthening the negotiations. Neither accepts settlement easily. If the demands of the plaintiff can be beaten down below those of like cases, the defendant gains in prestige.

The mediation process itself is a period of truce that gives both sides a chance to cool off. It avoids the rash and ill-considered revenge that would follow breaking off diplomatic relationships. But the threat of the sharpened spear is ever present. So the *monkalun* scolds, wheedles, lashes with sarcasm, insinuates the ill-temper of the other side, exaggerates the ferocity of its warriors, scoffs at the weakness of the defendant's supporters, and punctures the thinness of their arguments. Knowing the custom of overstating grievances and expected damages, he works to whittle down the original demands. Finally the damages are determined on the basis of five basic factors: (1) the nature of the offense; (2) the relative class positions of the parties; (3) the solidarity, size, and threat of the two kinship groups; (4) the personalities, reputations, and personal tempers of the two principals; and (5) the geographical positions of the two kin groups.

The uniqueness of the Ifugao mediation process lies in: (1) the action of the mediation may be initiated upon the request of only one party; (2) once requested, mediation is compulsory; (3) the action of the mediator is prolonged until there is sufficient repetition and revision of the settlement; (4) when the settlement has been accepted by the parties it becomes binding upon them; (5) the peace cannot be broken during the mediation truce, nor for an enforced period that follows unsuccessful mediation and the withdrawal of the *monkalun*.

(Barton [1919] 1969)

Case 5: The Injured Water Buffalo
Luzon, Philippines

Among the Kalingas, of central Luzon, Barton found that most dispute negotiation is accomplished through the *pangat* — a powerful individual whose main function is to make peace when trouble arises. The *pangat*, or "peacemaker," offers advice, arranges settlements between persons, and negotiates peace pacts between tribes. *Pangats* are assisted by go-betweens, advocates who arrange settlements by carrying out a mediation process that may take months or years to finalize. Since a settlement is between clans, not between persons, payments of decreasing worth are negotiated for siblings and first and second cousins to ensure that satisfaction is attained and revenge will not follow. The payment of this satisfaction, the weregild, marks the end of the dispute, generally, although a dissatisfied member may still retaliate, and the whole cycle begins again.

In situations of establishing guilt, if evidence and witnesses are lacking, the use of ordeal is common, such as all dipping hands in boiling water to take out an egg with the guilty one being burned.

The water buffalo of Ginaang was injured by an unknown person, so he summoned the two *pangats*. The people of the town assembled, and Ginaancy brought a basket of dry, uncooked rice. While the *pangats* were repeating their prayers before the ordeal, it was observed that one man was trembling. One by one the people came forward, chewed a mouthful of dry rice, and it was always wet. When this man's turn came, his rice was dry. The *pangats* charged him with the offense and he confessed. He was compelled to pay three buffaloes and give the *pangats* two blankets each. (Barton 1949, 230)

The go-between's typical handling of a case of wounding or killing proceeds in reciprocal bargaining:

He first goes to the offender's clan and proposes ritual payments. They readily agree since they fear being killed. He then goes to the victim's clan and suggests that they accept the weregild lest they be further attacked. Then he proceeds from the offended to the offender; the brothers of the offender to the brothers of the offended; the first cousins of the offender will be asked to buy off the first cousins of the offended. There will be buffaloes for the brothers, pigs for the first cousins, blankets for the second cousins, and for the third cousins, a dog or a knife. When agreement is reached, the ritual feast which follows seals the negotiation since one dare never eat with an enemy or it will cause the stomach to swell and death to follow.

(Barton 1949, 166)

Case 6: Sweat Lodge
Ontario, Amerindians

A conflict erupted in a lumber crew when Stanley damaged a beautiful large tree, was criticized by the team leader, lost his temper, and walked off the job. After cooling down, he sought to regain his job, was not welcomed back, and began to polarize the crew against the leaders.

Two attempts at mediation failed to resolve the situation or release the resentments, so one crew member suggested that a sweat lodge ceremony was required. The next evening the crew paid a formal visit to James, the Ojibwa spiritual leader. They presented a gift of tobacco, reported the problem, and requested that he conduct a sweat lodge ceremony. After deliberation, he agreed and gave instructions for preparation.

The site chosen was on the shore of a remote lake, two miles from the nearest road. After two days of preparation, the group gathered at sundown and took their places in the circle in the lodge. After a short address and prayer by James, red hot rocks were passed through the small door by the fire keeper. Water was thrown on them, and the group began to sweat.

James invited any who wished to speak to do so. One told of his struggle with alcohol. A second shared family conflicts; a third dealt with his work attitudes and actions.

Then more rocks, water, and sweat followed. Now James began to interpret the meaning of what was happening. All participants were equal; all crouched in fetal positions; all were being cleansed of negative thoughts and selfish concerns; all would leave born anew into harmony with all God's creation and creatures. Then all left the lodge and swam in the ice-cold lake.

The next morning when the crew met before work, they opened with the pledge to be as concerned about the needs of each other as about production and work progress. Each promised "more works and less smoke." A new crew leader was chosen, and the remaining differences were negotiated to each person's satisfaction.

The sweat lodge, a hut made of sixteen willow branches planted in a circle, plaited into a dome and covered with blankets, was centered over a pit filled with hot rocks, brought from the fire outside by a doorman with a rock fork.

The Sioux symbolism of purification called all the powers of the Great Spirit, the elements of earth, fire, water, rocks, and sky, and the mystery of the changing seasons as witnesses to the participants' honesty, cleansing, and transformation. The lodge faces east toward the "fire of no end"; the wood is laid in the four directions of north, south, east, and west. The pit (the center of the universe), the low door (human finitude), the sage around the perimeter (holy incense), the path to the fire (the sacred path of life), the seating (sunwise), the shared pipe (peace and harmony), the raising of the door flap four times (the light of wisdom), and the prayers (to see with the eye of the heart as well as the physical eye) all symbolize the sacredness of life.

The sweat lodge ceremony, called a purification ritual, is a petitioning of the Great Spirit for mutual direction, for communal reconciliation and relational healing.

(Bast 1987, 4–10)

Chapter Eight

Conflict: Cycles, Pathways, and Patterns

If a quarrel gets too hot for you, pretend it is a game.
　　　　　　　　　　　　　　　　—Hausa proverb

UNIVERSAL INSIGHT
(The Bottom Line)

> The more we run from conflict,
> The more it masters us;
> The more we try to avoid it,
> The more it controls us.
> The less we fear conflict,
> The less it confuses us;
> The less we deny our differences,
> The less they divide us.

FOLKTALE: THE MYSTERY OF JUSTICE
Ethiopia

A woman one day went out to look for her goats that had wandered away from the herd. She walked back and forth over the fields for a long time without finding them. She came at last to a place by the side of the road where a deaf man sat before a fire brewing himself a cup of coffee. Not realizing he was deaf, the woman asked: "Have you seen my herd of goats come this way?"

The deaf man thought she was asking for the water hole, so he pointed vaguely toward the river.

The woman thanked him and went to the river. And there, by coincidence, she found the goats. But a young kid had fallen among the rocks and broken its foot.

She picked it up to carry it home. As she passed the place where the deaf man sat drinking his coffee, she stopped to thank him for his help. And in gratitude she offered him the kid.

But the deaf man didn't understand a word she was saying. When she held the kid toward him he thought she was accusing him of the animal's misfortune, and he became very angry.

"I had nothing to do with it!" he shouted.

"But you pointed the way," the woman said.

"It happens all the time with goats!" the man shouted.

"I found them right where you said they would be," the woman replied.

"Go away and leave me alone, I never saw him before in my life!" the man shouted.

People who came along the road stopped to hear the argument.

The woman explained to them: "I was looking for the goats and he pointed toward the river. Now I wish to give him this kid."

"Do not insult me this way!" the man shouted loudly, "I am not a leg breaker!" And in his anger he struck the woman with his hand.

"Ah, did you see? He struck me with his hand!" the woman said to the people. "I will take him before the judge!"

So the woman with the kid in her arms, the deaf man, and the spectators went to the house of the judge. The judge came out before his house to listen to their complaint. First, the woman talked; then the man talked; then people in the crowd talked. The judge sat nodding his head. But that meant very little, for the judge, like the man before him, was very deaf. Moreover, he was also very nearsighted.

At last, he put up his hand and the talking stopped. He gave them his judgment: "Such family rows are a disgrace to the emperor and an affront to the church," he said solemnly. He turned to the man. "From this time forward, stop mistreating your wife," he said.

He turned to the woman with the young goat in her arms. "As for you, do not be so lazy. Hereafter do not be late with your husband's meals."

He looked at the baby goat tenderly: "And as for the beautiful infant, may she have a long life and grow to be a joy to you both!"

The crowd broke up and the people went their various ways.

"Ah, how good it is!" they said to one another. "How did we ever get along before justice was given to us?"

FOLKTALE: THE WISE JUDGE
India

A large earthen chatty, or jar, half filled with corn, was standing in the courtyard of a farmhouse, when a horned ram thrust his head into it to satisfy his hunger. Owing to the size of the neck of the chatty, he could not withdraw his head. The farmer and his servants were perplexed. "What's to be done now?" they asked each other. At last they agreed that the problem was so great, only the village headman, the lumbardar, *could resolve it.*

The lumbardar *arrived on his camel, but found the archway to the courtyard was low. "I cannot get in there to judge," he said from the top of his camel. "You must knock the doorway down." So the arch was destroyed and the wise man entered.*

Having dismounted and gazed profoundly at the imprisoned ram, he said, "This is a mere trifle. Fetch me a sword." With a single blow he severed the animal's head. "Now there," he cried, "there is your ram, and here is your crock of corn. Take them away."

All the village, who by now had assembled, murmured their praises of his wisdom.

But a servant protested, "Wait, great one, the ram's head is still in the jar. Now what are we to do?"

"True," said the lumbardar, *"to you this affair seems difficult, but to me, one thing is no more difficult than another." With this he raised a large stone, dashed the jar to a thousand*

pieces, spilled the grain over the courtyard, and dusted off his hands. And all the people clapped in admiration just as they had before.

"Thank you, thank you, master," cried the farmer. "You have solved a great difficulty which confounded me and all my servants. You must take the carcass of the ram with you as payment."

True, his gateway was destroy, his jar broken, his grain spilled, his ram killed, and the meat all taken by another, but his problem was solved.

(Lee 1931, 645–47)

FOLKTALE: DIVIDING THE CHEESE
Cape Verde Islands

Two cats stole a cheese. One wanted to divide it. The other was distrustful; he said, "No, let us get the chief of the monkey tribe to divide it." The cats went to the monkey chief and asked him to be the judge. "Yes, with pleasure," answered the monkey. He sent them for a scale. He took a knife. Instead of cutting the cheese in halves, he made one piece larger than the other. As he put them on the scale, he said, "I didn't divide this well." So he took a full bite out of the heavier side.

"What are you doing?"

"I'm going to eat on this piece to make it even with the other."

As he ate it, it became lighter than the other piece, so he changed over, and began to eat the other to even the balance.

The cats saw that the monkey intended to eat all the cheese. They said, "Sir judge, let us have the balance of the cheese, and we will divide it ourselves."

"No, a fight might arise between you, then the king of the animals would come after me."

He went on eating, first on one side, then on the other. They soon saw that nothing would be left. One cat turned to the other, and said, "It had been better for us to have divided our cheese ourselves."

After the monkey had eaten it all, he said, "Let us all go in peace, and never again let your interest blind your understanding."

(Lee 1931, 51)

———————

Of the five basic conflict options — avoidance, accommodation, coercion, compromise, and collaboration — the most frequent, the most commonly chosen, is avoidance. A wealth of proverbs bears witness from cultures around the world. A few of these are:

Of the thirty-six ways of handling a conflict situation, running away is the best. — China

Trumpet when in a herd of elephants, crow in the company of cocks, bleat in a flock of goats. — Malaya

Love has no dispute. — Kenya

Money softens a dispute like water softens clay. — Nigeria

The second word [the answer] makes the quarrel. — Japan

When one doesn't want, two don't quarrel. — Brazil

A meager peace is better than a fat quarrel. — Latvia

A good silence is better than a bad dispute. — Russia

The squirrel does not talk back to the elephant, it just goes back into the hole. — Angola

It is best to let an offense repeat itself three times. The first may be an accident, the second a mistake, only the third is likely to be intentional. — Kongo

Silence produces peace, and peace produces safety. — Swahili tribe

All is never said. — Ibo tribe

In playing chess, there is no infallible way of winning, but there is an infallible way of not losing — that is not to play chess. — China

If a quarrel gets too hot for you, pretend it is a game. — Hausa tribe

Conflict that cannot be avoided is often concealed and then expressed in covert strategies. In every culture, there is recognition of surface conflicts masking deeper differences, of primary and secondary disputes.

"The teeth of the elephant are deep in the throat," the Nepalese proverb warns. The presenting issue, the trunk and tusks, may look formidable enough, but may be only the presenting problem. The real grinding conflict lies hidden, beneath the surface, unseen, "deep in the throat."

A woman may break her neighbor's cooking pot in a Botswana village dispute as a means of obtaining access to a public forum of dispute negotiation where a more fundamental grievance can be aired. A man may wrongfully detain someone else's billygoat overnight to provoke a village hearing, at which he can then introduce a serious grievance on respective rights over arable land and a well. The goat issue will be quickly solved but the conversation will turn eventually to the real issue over which the men are at odds (Roberts 1979, 53).

The conflict being manifested may often involve symbolic components of the underlying conflict, but the former is considered safer and less threatening, so it is exposed. A conflict between father and son over the keys to the car seems safer to dispute than the underlying struggle of competing power tactics between strong personalities; the criticism of the daughter's short skirt may be less

Table 12
The Various Options for Conflict,
Viewed as a Continuum, Are:

AVOIDANCE	REPRESSION	DISPLACEMENT	MANAGEMENT	RESOLUTION	UTILIZATION
Conflict is handled by denying its existence or by attempting to evade it through strategies of overlooking, ignoring, etc.	Open conflict is avoided by explicit action to suppress or punish its expression.	Conflict is avoided by projecting a part or the whole onto another party or onto a different issue with the same party.	Conflict is directed in a limited or sequential manner or with diminished intensity by mutual agreement.	Conflict is terminated by changes that alter its causes or modify its driving forces.	Conflict is utilized not only to achieve a new integration of goals and values but to effect creative change in the system itself.

A conflict situation may evoke
any of these various responses
and be directed toward these
ends.

threatening than discussion of the mother's attempts to control and define her daughter's sexual behavior. In counseling theory these two levels are often called "the presenting problem" and "the psychological dynamics"; in group work they are called "the stated or public agenda" and "the hidden agenda." Doubtless all conflicts are multilevel. The Amerindian disputes with American governmental fishing quotas are only symptomatic of the fundamental conflict over the white man's control, exploitation, and destruction of Native American traditions and identity.

Any movement from the overt, or manifest, levels of a conflict to the expression or definition of the covert levels will increase emotional intensity, create threat, and stimulate internal conflict with resulting defensive behavior.

The various options for conflict, viewed on a continuum as in table 12, contrast the more covert strategies of avoidance, repression, and displacement with the overt styles of management, resolution, and conflict utilization. Traditional cultures show a preference for the first three, but every society has some patterns similar to all six. Western societies that publicly value options four through six actually utilize much more of the first three than of the last three. We are all more alike in our fear of tensions and avoidance of alienation than we are different.

Cultures that prize harmony and uniformity — smoothing solutions — are more likely to turn toward avoidance, repression, and displacement as preferred options; cultures that place a high value on confrontation and open dialogue stress the desirability of conflict management, resolution, and even conflict utilization to provoke change. In the former, conflict is seen as an abnormal eruption disturbing the norm of harmonious relationships; in the latter, conflict is a normal interruption in the cyclical process of social change.

Interpersonal conflicts, group conflicts, and community conflicts can be viewed from either a harmony model or a conflict model.

The harmony model sees uniformity, unity, and concord as the natural, normal state of affairs in community and holds that this is occasionally, if unavoidably, interrupted by conflict events.

The conflict model sees cycles of latency and expression, of concord and conflict, of differences lying dormant for long periods and then erupting as unexpected events.

The cyclical view does not see conflicts as inevitably repetitive and redundant (although some are), but as normal patterns of social metamorphosis and evolutionary change that may be creative or destructive.

The linear view of social process is more common in Asian countries that place a high value on harmony and conformity. The cyclical conflict model, more common in the West, sees the sequences of concord becoming strained, confusion following, then conflict emerging, leading to confrontation and hopefully conciliation, which when confirmed by celebration of the new understandings achieved results in a renewed and strengthened concord (see fig. 22).

This presents a model of a productive conflict cycle that utilizes the conflict to strengthen the concord of the community. The goal is not to "manage" the conflict as much as to channel it, not to "resolve" it in a unilateral fashion, but to utilize it for the strengthening of the whole community. These are optimum outcomes, and

Figure 22
The Cyclical Conflict Model

may rarely be reached, but intentionally working toward such goals can increase the productivity and decrease the destructive impact of conflict even though its results may be mixed.

Conflict proceeds according to each culture's rich deposit of conflict myths, and moves along predictable patterns with historical precedents. These patterns, like river beds in the bottom of the cultural sea, channel the energies suppressed beneath the surface so that they flow forcefully toward creating change, or branch into diffused tributaries and permeate the entire ocean floor of the culture's or group's processes.

Turbulence may erupt in unpredictable places with treacherous undertows. When a group develops trusted channels for conflict energies over a long period of time, these ways of directing conflict toward resolution become familiar and provide security in the disruptive and explosive periods of community unrest or fragmentation.

The cyclical movement from concord to confusion is inevitable as the tensions already present in concord begin to surface. Most persons fear confusion and immediately seek to place blame, isolate the "problem makers," or attack the identified foes. Or they may choose denial, repress signs of unrest, avoid facing the difficulty, and return to a concord of pretended uniformity. The person who can tolerate confusion and allow it to disrupt old assumptions about the balance of relationships can take the first steps toward defining the conflict accurately as it enters stage three. The various kinds of conflict — goal, pathway, resource, value, or personality conflict — each takes a different course and each presses toward an appropriate resolution. Discovering the primary focus of the conflict — the contrast in desirable ends or goals of persons or groups, the distribution of scarce resources of materials, time, or persons, the difference in ways of reaching a goal or means of accomplishing the same desirable end, the contradiction of different values held by the parties, or the irritation and frustration of different personality styles and traits — can both clarify the nature of the conflict that is to be confronted and then help direct the negotiation processes of the conciliation period.

Confrontation, as a direct address between parties, is an optional step in conflict resolution and is rarely utilized in most of the world, as we will note later. In Western cultures it is viewed as the optimal, not optional, step for complete resolution and utilization of an interpersonal or group conflict. As a Western theorist notes:

If all goes well, confrontations not only allow for the exchange of essential information but also increase the authenticity of the relationship and the personal integrity experienced in the relationship. If they are not well managed, confrontations can further polarize the individuals, increase the costs of the conflict, or discharge the principals from further efforts to resolve the conflict. One task of conflict management is to maximize the potential gains from a confrontation and to minimize the risks for the participants. (Walton 1969, 145–46)

In Western society, the presence of a third party may safeguard the integrity of the confrontation process to ensure that both sides feel secure, that each is fully heard, that perspectives are honored as having equal weight, and that all data — factual and emotive — relevant to conciliation have been made available from each to each. In the third world, this process more often takes place between third parties without the principals being present, as we shall explore later.

Conciliation is grounded in mutuality. Each principal must accept the other as acting in good faith. Each must be open to an outcome that is oriented toward both relationships and goals — that is, there must be a concern for the ongoing relationship as well as a commitment to one's own ends or goals. Parties enter conciliation recognizing that the outcome may favor either side or may result in some ratio of sacrifice of either or both goals. The negotiation may end in convergence or divergence. There may be agreement, compromise, or collaboration, or the issues may lead toward separation, division, and termination of contact.

Celebration, the missing step in much conflict, is the crucial element that confirms the learnings that have resulted from the preceding steps. If one ends conflict with regrets for its having occurred or with shame for the existence of tensions, any positive insights and experiences gained are erased by the negative reinforcement given to the whole process. Both persons must review the solution found, reaffirm the relationship, release the resentments that remain, reach out to each other in deeper respect, and finally accept the rewards — as well as reward themselves — for having persevered through the various stages to completion. Only with positive reinforcement do new behaviors become internalized and retained in one's behavioral repertoire.

Now the conflict is full circle, but it is not over. The return to concord contains issues that may become the basis for new tensions and renewed negotiations in the future, but the pathways for creative resolution have been strengthened; the relationship has been proved through the restructuring and recovenanting of the conflict resolution; and the possibilities for more authentic, genuine relating have been enlarged and deepened.

Cyclical conflicts rarely proceed throughout these stages without turning negative for brief or extended periods. Frequently the negative spiral disrupts all communication and turns persons away from each other in flight or against each other, provoking a fight.

The negative spiral results from two factors that dog us in stressed relationships. These negative tendencies are:

First, issues tend to multiply. This may occur when a party introduces new issues for strategic reasons — to overwhelm, to strengthen a weakening position, to divert attention, to undermine the other's self-esteem, and so on. Or the attitudes and actions of the other person may themselves become further issues by alienating, exciting antagonism, adding unfair judgments, and so on. Or the conflict behavior used by one party may frustrate the other. If one yields sacrificially it may evoke guilt in the other and thus anger. If one postpones out of fear or confusion when the other is dependent on an immediate resolution, the conflict is exacerbated as these become further issues.

Second, conflict resolution tends to move toward being nonreciprocal. Motivation is rarely equal on both sides, and a positive gesture by one is often premature or intimidating for the other. The balance of power between the two is rarely the same, so moves by either become laden with secondary meanings. Contrasts in the amount of anxiety, differences in verbal and argumentative ability, contrasting needs for time and reflection, and different needs for closeness or distance in negotiation are some factors that can contribute to one side offering and the other refusing a movement toward resolution and a spiral of negativity.

Negative spirals must be interrupted and the process deescalated and reversed as both parties commit themselves again to seek a mutually satisfactory resolution.

Groups or communities that have frequent small conflicts that test and clarify the conflict process develop trusted pathways — most frequently similar to the cycle outlines — that serve them well in times of stress. Many small conflicts make it unlikely that a large, destructive conflict will occur. If it does, the group has patterns and skills for dealing with it available in recent experience. In a group that suppresses the routine conflicts in an attempt at total harmony, no functional pathways for conflict channeling may exist, and the conflicts that do occur will not only be large, unmanageable, and destructive; they will inevitably flush out other buried conflicts that have accumulated over time. These attach themselves (as multiple issues, grievances, and complaints) to the main conflict, further confusing the situation and making accurate definition of issues difficult or sometimes impossible when secondary issues usurp the stage and become the central focus of negotiation.

The conflict cycle (fig. 22) that reflects Western values is directed toward reaching a satisfactory resolution for both the individual and the group, or toward both individuals involved and their social context. Neither the person nor the group dares be sacrificed. In settings of conflict in which one must yield, the Western pattern tends to support the satisfaction and needs of the individual over the group. Individual goals tend to be honored before family goals, and personal fulfillment tends to overshadow marital commitment. In most of the world, personal fulfillment is a penultimate goal that is desirable but not necessary; the ultimate goal is the harmonious life of the institution — marriage, family, community. If the individual must adapt, adjust, or sacrifice, it is seen as both inevitable and necessary. Optimum resolution of conflict takes both person and group with equal seriousness in every culture, but each group has its own sense of balance. In various cases presented in this chapter, one may note the strong coercion of the individual in order to maintain the group stability (see the case of Chendrayya, below).

Conflict Myths in Western Cultures

I. CONCORD: Harmony is normal; conflict is abnormal.

Concord is the normal, natural, neutral state of human community; thus any disruption is abnormal, pathological, lamentable.
No.
In every state of concord the conditions of future conflict lie embedded. These are the occasions of creativity in healthy community.

II. CONFUSION: Confusion is irrational; clarity is rational.

Confusion is intolerable, threatening, inferior, a state to be feared, fled, denied.
No.
Confusion is suspending judgment, deferring closure, maintaining openness. The ability to sustain confusion is the beginning of wisdom.

III. CONFLICT: Conflict is undesirable; when unavoidable, it is deplorable.

Conflict is a destructive process in human relations and is best suppressed or oppressed.
No.
Conflict is both inevitable and resolvable. It is the opportunity to restructure relationships, realign tasks, redistribute resources, renegotiate covenants, and realize new levels of communication.

IV. CONFRONTATION: Confrontation is defining rightness and wrongness.

Confrontation is fixing blame, defining who is right and who is wrong.
No.
Confrontation is both caring and clarifying; it is concern for relationship with concern for goals.

V. CONCILIATION: Differences must be decreased, similarities increased.

Conciliation creates conformity, uniformity, commonality, and agreement.
No.
Cooperation, collaboration, and co-creation can reduce stress, increase respect, and enhance distinctiveness and differences.
Differences are the occasion of conflict, similarities the cause.

VI. CLOSURE: Conflict concludes in commitment to maintain future peace at any price.

Effective resolution requires the commitment of both parties to permanent solutions.
No.
Conflict closure channels and covenants differences, celebrates the understandings achieved, and fosters appreciation of the new pathways for managing differences.

VII. CONCORD: Concord is final; harmony is total; differences are ended.

Concord is a state achieved; permanency is guaranteed; peace is achieved.
No.
Concord is covenanted, but it is human, fallible, and will need to be renewed and remade again and again.

The Western model is based on (1) acceptance of conflict as a normal, useful process; (2) the openness of systems to modification and change through negotiation ("everything is negotiable"); (3) the value of direct confrontation and conciliation processes; and (4) the acceptance of the process as a necessary renegotiating of contract, redistributing of opportunity, releasing of tensions, and renewal of relationships — it is therefore worthy of celebration.

Traditional models stand in sharp contrast on each of these points; their basic assumptions about conflict are frequently the converse of those just articulated. Painting with a very broad brush, we can say that traditional conflict beliefs present a full reversal of each of the Western values; or, speaking historically, Western values have inverted traditional beliefs.

In a traditional hierarchical society, (1) conflict is seen as a destructive disturbance of the peace and all parties are at fault until harmony is restored; (2) the system is not to be adjusted to the needs of members, but members are to adapt to traditional values; (3) third-party solutions are necessary, and confrontations are destructive and ineffective; and (4) the participants are sanctioned; the responsible parties are disciplined; the process is viewed as unfortunate; and celebrations are of the community's success in regaining harmony, not of the participants' contribution to the community's change and growth.

TRADITIONAL CYCLES — POSITIVE AND NEGATIVE

The concord of uniformity in a traditional society assumes a solidarity of agreements and unanimity achieved through hierarchy, conformity, and the practice of harmony. The sanctions and controls built into the community ensure the suppression of differences that would threaten the historic heritage of patterns of social, economic, and political processes.

Figure 23 offers two of many possible directions in which the cycle of disruption may move. These two offer typical patterns of positive management of conflict and negative suppression of

Figure 23
The Concord-Conflict-Concord Cycle

CONCORD, CONFORMITY
In a community based on unity and harmony, the sanctions and controls demand conformity. Tensions, differences, and value contrasts are suppressed or repressed in unconscious depths.

POSITIVE CONFLICT CYCLE

CONSULTATION
The community looks for leaders or mediators to achieve contact, carry messages, and negotiate issues.

CONCILIATION
The go-between (person or process) works for compromise, collaboration, convergence, or divergence.

CONFIRMATION
The compromise is contracted or the parties agree to collaborate in an acceptable solution. They celebrate the renewal of concord.

CONFLICT
Conflicts begin to form. These include: personality conflicts, pathway conflicts, resource conflicts, value conflicts, goal conflicts.

CONFUSION
Confusion rises in a community as the balance of unity is lost, suppressed tensions emerge, and the possibility of breaking conformity or demanding change threatens the "peace."

NEGATIVE CONFLICT CYCLE

CONSOLIDATION
The opposition is overcome and driven underground, or the resistance gains power, creates schism, and a new concord is consolidated.

COERCION
The establishment seeks to coerce conformity. The innovators demand change.

CONSPIRACY
The party in power conspires to crush resistance and impose conformity; the opposition seeks to precipitate a crisis.

COVERT CONFLICT
Conflict, although suppressed, continues to grow beneath the surface, to reduce trust, and to create divisions.

CONSTERNATION
Consternation emerges as suppressed tension surfaces and there is the threat of nonconformity, free thought, or rebellion; or it rises as people reach limits of yielding to dominance or oppression.

NEGATIVE CYCLE −

+ POSITIVE CYCLE

the conflict with a reimposing of the controls and no resolution of the issues. The negative cycle (A-F) is marked by frustration of the party not in power (which may be a minority or a majority), which lacks the recognized forms of power (legitimate power, coercive power, traditional office power, control of information, expert power, reward power). This period is shaped by the consternation of leadership, which is threatened by the unrest but is not confused by what is taking place. Confusion requires some openness to admit new and surprising data and some attempt to understand the dynamics of the tensions present beneath the surface. In hierarchical systems the definition of the situation tends to be a given and requires little alteration in the cyclical periods of unrest.

The conflict, suppressed by the structures of power, continues to grow, polarize positions, create factions, reduce trust, and accentuate divisions between persons and parties. When control strategies drive a conflict underground it becomes more diffuse, more destructive, more unmanageable. The accumulated feelings, when they do erupt, are more intense and often out of control because their full content, long buried, is unknown to the participants themselves.

Conspiracies ensue — by the leadership to initiate means of crushing resistance, by the opposition to precipitate a crisis since that alone might force the issue to the surface and demand a hearing.

Coercion — the use of pressure by repressive violence or violent resistance — inevitably follows. Passive resistance through nonparticipation and active nonviolent resistance through noncooperation are alternatives at this stage. Gandhi's *ahimsa* (nonviolence), Lech Walesa's noncooperation through solidarity, Martin Luther King, Jr.'s active march for justice, and Desmond Tutu's vocal use of moral resistance are a few of the many models (see Sharp 1973 for a historical survey).

Consolidation follows in one of two forms: (1) The establishment overcomes the opposition and drives it and its demands underground. (2) The resistance, having gained coercive power, seizes control or creates a schism, and consolidation of power follows. Both situations result in concord: the old state of concord retrenched, or the revolutionary concord following the alteration in values that has motivated the change.

The destructiveness of the negative cycle, most frequently a malevolent cycle, is visible in the violations of human rights required by the means utilized by both those in power and those seeking the power to change. The vertical solutions that prohibit lateral or horizontal negotiations serve to perpetuate the status quo of tradition. This offers security, stability, and continuity between generations. It does not allow for the movement of people very far from the given station in life. In India, this process functions alternately with the positive cycle. Caste and class are maintained by the negative process; gradual steps toward opportunity occur as the positive cycle is allowed to function in communities where movements toward increases in human rights are initiated. In Africa, the move toward technological change and the shift of populations from rural to urban settings break the grip of tradition and provide the opening for alternate directions for conflict.

The positive cycle (1–6) flows from *concord* into the *confusion* necessary to allow for a reconsideration of things assumed. From the unfreezing of structures and the rising awareness, *conflicts* can take definite and intentional form. In most of the world, *consultation* follows instead of the confrontation more common in the West. In this phase mediators, go-betweens, and neutral parties with trustworthy credentials — elders, peers, family leaders, other leaders from neighboring settings — are invited to achieve contact between the two or more sides and to carry messages, offers, ultimatums, and compromises in the bargaining rituals familiar to the particular culture. This *conciliation* is a means of seeking mutually satisfactory solutions of compromise, cooperation, collaboration, or co-existence, and distance carries the process forward toward conclusion. As the contracting is achieved, *confirmation* — either in the signals from the primary parties that a new level of trust has been constructed, or in the new terms of settlement that can be celebrated — completes the cycle and returns the sense of continuing *concord*.

In the case of Chendrayya, which follows, the power of a communal process that has predominantly negative-cycle elements illustrates the consternation of the caste, the immediate driving of the conflict into covert holding patterns, the conspiracy of those in power who consult privately and collude to coerce a preferred outcome, the consolidation through binding contracts, and the community reward of celebrating with the accrued funds.

The case is described by Lakshayya (the headman of the Washerman caste) and has to do with an unfaithful wife.

Case: Chendrayya
India

One of our local bachelors got into trouble with the wife of another Washerman named Chendrayya. It was common knowledge, but no one, not even his friends, would tell Chendrayya; they did not want to get into trouble or make him feel bad. Chendrayya suspected something. He tried beating his wife; but she denied everything. Finally, one day Chendrayya left as though he were going to work but turned the corner and hid behind a mud wall. When he saw the bachelor sneak into his house, he crept up to the house and snapped a big lock on the door (like most houses this one had no windows or back door). Then he went to call the police. They were only too willing to arrest the culprits and lock them up in jail. When I heard about this affair, I said to myself that nothing good would come of it if the case went to court. I went to Krishna Chari (the village headman) and told him we should settle the matter within the village. He agreed and gave me a note for the *patwari* (village land officer). The *patwari* and I went to see the police. They agreed to release the couple to us for seventy rupees, which I paid.

Since the matter was serious, I locked the couple up in my house. I needed the support of my caste and the village so I called in more than forty men from many castes. Elders from the Barber, Muslim, and *Harijan* castes were also present. The problem was a difficult one. The guilty couple loved each other. On the other hand, the wife had several children including an infant boy two months old, and the bachelor was too poor to support a wife. If we granted a divorce, the husband would take the children, a solution that would be hard for the unweaned infant. We decided that for the children's sake the husband and wife should remain together. The husband was the key to the problem. He was proud and did not want his wife back. If we could first persuade him, the rest would be easy. I bought drinks around and we went to the husband's house. He said, "My wife slept with another man." "Did you have any proof?" we asked. "I caught them both in my house and called the police," he replied. As soon as he admitted calling the police we found fault with him. He had insulted the caste by ignoring the elders and going directly to the police. Moreover, he had charged an innocent woman without witnesses. We knew the wife was guilty, but we did not dare admit it. We fined the man five hundred rupees for dishonoring the caste. By now he was quite humble and ready to take his wife back, and we agreed to drop the fine if he did so.

Next we dealt with the woman. To make certain that the trouble would not be repeated, we made her sign a paper that if she were caught with the bachelor again she would have to pay the caste five hundred rupees. Finally we got to the bachelor who was the cause of the trouble. We fined him one hundred fifty rupees and made him sign a bond as well. I took seventy rupees to repay what I had given the police, and the rest we used for celebrations.

(Hiebert 1971, 110–11)

Reflections on the Case: The negative concord-conflict-concord cycle is clearly embedded in this community's way of dealing with differences.

The suppression of conflict is so effective that nothing can surface until one party conspires to precipitate a crisis. As long as the conflict is in the suspicion, argument, name-calling, and concealed-deceit stage, both parties gain by upholding the status quo.

The concord of communal harmony is so powerful that

all persons in conflict are considered guilty of disturbing the peace, and hence are under caste suspension until judgment is passed. They are seated apart from those gathered to discuss the case. After a successful settlement, however, all parties to the case are seated at the end of the row of elders, and a jug of palm beer is passed around, symbolizing the restoration of the offenders to caste fellowship. If there is no settlement, there are no drinks. (Hiebert 1971, 111)

The coercion by the elders serves to reimpose the traditional harmony. A situational ethic allows the elders to draw on their knowledge of the persons, their family history, and the past relationships of all involved. Since all parties must continue to live together in the same village for the rest of their lives, a good settlement that leaves the social fabric seamless is highly desirable.

The power of the elders is not in physical force, but in social sanctions that can ostracize the culprit from village life, economic opportunity, and religious services; it is a social death. This requires the united front of communal concord to effect a sweeping exclusion, so consensus in a binding concord is necessary. For outer-directed personalities, the style that negates full resolution of justice issues for each person in favor of communal concord is finally satisfactory.

GETTING IN, GETTING THROUGH, GETTING OUT

The same case situation can be untangled by use of a model drawn phenomenologically from the folk wisdom and practice of a people in a traditional culture on the opposite side of the world.

In an outstanding phenomenological study of conflict processes in a Costa Rican village, John Paul Lederach teased out the language, affects, and stages of conflict in a coastal village. The central concept that emerged is that of "getting located, locating oneself, defining the situation and one's relationship to it." We make sense of confusing conflict situations by coordinating locations. "That involves finding *where* one is, where others are, and where the issues stand. Thus dealing with conflict is like map making and map reading" (Lederach 1988a, 93–94).

The subtleties and nuances of this careful field study are charted by figure 24, which breaks the process into three major stages: (1) getting in to the conflict-resolution process, (2) getting

Figure 24
A Phenomenological Model of a Conflict Process

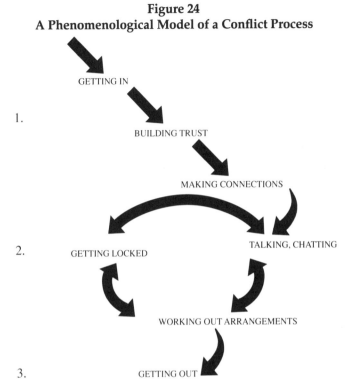

The process is in three stages: (1) *getting in* to the conflict-resolution process, (2) *getting through* by figuring out locations (i.e., mapping, which leads to) (3) *getting out* of the conflict.

(Lederach 1988a)

through by figuring out locations, which then leads to, (3) getting out of the conflict. From this analysis there are five theses that emerge:

1. Conflict is created and managed usefully when there is a context of interdependence that provides a basic field on which persons can seek to map locations and relationships.

2. Meanings in a conflict situation are created and assessed

through a process of locating persons and/or issues and coordinating these so that data perspectives and persons intersect and interconnect.

3. Coordination, locating things, takes place by evaluating and accounting priority, impact, and significance of issues, events, and roles, so locating is a mechanism of valuing.

4. Any "thing" or element in the conflict can be valued in multiple ways, so persons must manage multiple meanings and locations in their "map making" and creation of a common map of the conflict.

5. Shared meaning emerges in circular phases. Individual valuations are made (maps drawn), then shared to test with others (maps shared), and finally become a social reality (a common map drawn) (Lederach 1988a, 151–52).

This traditional model has high applicability in cultures throughout the third world. The case of Chendrayya, analyzed previously by the cyclical model, can be understood phenomenologically by use of these stages. The elders get into the conflict situation by taking ownership back from the police; trust is built by summoning representative headmen and making connections. Once gathered, the group talks through the dilemma and defines each person's location and situation. Arrangements are then worked out — by negotiation, imposition, threat, and coercion. Having gotten through, the group gets out of the conflict process by a communal celebration that returns the community to its normal processes. The applicability of this model, its flexibility in definition, prediction, and direction of a conflict, and its economy and simplicity give it broad intercultural usefulness.

DEVELOPMENTAL MODEL OF CONFLICT

Conflicts have a predictable series of developmental stages in both traditional and modern cultures, argues P. H. Gulliver in his ground-breaking book on disputes in intercultural perspective (Gulliver 1979). From his work in legal anthropology in Africa, Gulliver has defined a sequential model of conflict stages. He begins by defining disagreements, disputes, and negotiations.

Disagreements, whether large or small, inevitably arise in any relationship if only because no set of social rules can prospectively provide for every eventuality. These disagreements are commonly resolved within the relationship by private dyadic or triadic problem solving initiated by the parties themselves. The disagreements are resolvable or tolerable or the relationship is terminated, but no dispute arises.

Disputes occur when the two parties are unable or unwilling to resolve their disagreements. Either one or both are unwilling to accept the status quo, agree to the demand, or deny the demand made by the other. The crisis precipitates the dispute. The dispute moves the impasse into the public domain.

To convert dyadic disagreement into a dispute, three things are required. First, one party precipitates a crisis and seeks to bring the matter into a public domain. Second, the other party must be willing or be induced to agree to and to participate in negotiations. Third, other persons take cognizance and become involved as supporters, representatives, and third parties, and processes of meetings are agreed on.

Negotiations are interactions between disputing parties (without the compulsion of an adjudicator) through which they seek to arrive at an interdependent, joint decision that resolves the issues between them. The outcome is satisfactory enough, or perceived as the best possible in the circumstances, so that agreement can be reached. The two share information and make modifications of their expectations until agreement is reached (Gulliver 1979, 74–80).

In Gulliver's eight-phase model of negotiation (fig. 25), the first phase is the "search for an arena." In this stage the disputants arrive at some agreement in locating where the dispute will be negotiated. Is this a formal court battle, or will the dispute be settled informally over the back fence? Will the village elders become involved or only the immediate family? The choice of a particular arena includes not only the physical location, but also the "kind of social and cultural rules, assumptions, and predispositions an arena prescribes" (Gulliver 1979, 125).

The second phase is "agenda definition." In phase one the disputants come to some agreement about the site for working at the

Figure 25
A Disagreement in Ongoing Social Life
Precipitates a Dispute

A → to → C
1   Search for an arena
    (a place where negotiations may occur)
      A → to → C
      2   Agenda definition
          (nature of dispute; what issues are to be faced?)
            A → to → C
            3   Exploring the field
                (emphasis on difference, setting maximal limits)
                  C → to → A
                  4   Narrowing differences
                      (emphasis on tolerable agreement)
                        C → to → A
                        5   Preliminaries to final bargaining
                            (search for bargaining range, trading possibilities)
                              A → to → C
                              6   Final bargaining
                                  (exchange of specific, substantive proposals)
                                  (demand, offer, bid, and their counters)
                                    C
                                    7   Ritualization of outcome
                                        (public announcement, observation,
                                        recognition)

                                        8   Execution of outcome
                                            (allocation and administration of rights
                                            and resources)

A = predominance of antagonism
C = predominance of coordination

A DEVELOPMENTAL MODEL OF NEGOTIATION
(The stages may be sequential, or at any point may return to the previous antagonistic status quo in a breakdown of negotiation, or to a previous stage.)

(Gulliver 1979, 122)

dispute; in the second phase agreement must be reached regarding the actual issues of the dispute. What are the important issues and how are they to be defined?

In the third phase, "exploring the field," each party presents its own case and assertively rejects the case of the other. A show of strength is made, and even overt antagonism is evidenced and tolerated as each party actively demands its own terms and rejects outright the terms of the other. There is open, direct concentration on differences. If any reconciliatory tone has been seen in phases one and two regarding arena and definition, that tone is not seen in this stage.

The seemingly irreconcilable issues seen in phase three begin to narrow in phase four: "The emphasis changes from differences, separateness, and antagonism toward coordination, collusion, and even cooperation" (Gulliver 1979, 141). After the maximal limits are established in the previous phase, some movement toward negotiation is seen. The real priorities start to appear; the differences between parties seem to be fewer and less pronounced; and the tone of the negotiation softens.

The gradual shift in concerns leads to phase five: "preliminaries to final bargaining." "These preliminaries are concerned with one or more purposes: the search for a viable bargaining range, the refining of persisting differences, the testing of trading possibilities, and the construction of a bargaining formula" (Gulliver 1979, 153). Preliminary bargaining at its best almost eliminates the need for final bargaining as it clears the way for it to take place.

In the "final bargaining" phase the substantive issues are dealt with in terms of demands, offers, bids, indications of compromises, and concessions. This phase is characterized by "incremental convergence." Concessions are given and sought. The cost of not reaching agreement is usually much higher by now than the cost of an agreement within the range established.

Phase seven is "ritualization of outcome." Formal affirmation is given when an agreement is reached. In some cultures this occurs by eating or drinking together. In other settings documents are signed in the presence of witnesses.

Finally, there is execution of the outcome or agreement. The land border is re-marked, an apology made, or a fine paid.

The following case, condensed from Gulliver's account, illustrates his developmental model, phase by phase, with an East African conflict over land boundaries.

The case can be usefully explored by use of Gulliver's stages (as done below with certain modifications — i.e., below I examine seven, rather than eight, stages), by application of Lederach's "getting in, through, and out of conflict" model, or by application of the positive and negative cyclical model offered earlier.

All models are heuristic, temporary, and dispensable. They serve to assist us in making peace with our confusion as social contracts break down and new understandings must be negotiated that provide justice for all concerned.

Case: Land Dispute
Arusha Tribe, Tanzania

Lashiloi and Kinyani were unrelated neighbors, each fifty. Each had indisputably inherited his farm from his own deceased father. Between their farms lay a smaller plot, long disputed between them, now vacant because of the tenant's death (see fig. 26). Each wanted the farm, each claimed it had been owned by his grandfather and thus was coming to him. There were no written records, no surviving witnesses.

Tensions rose; there was conflict over Lashiloi's goats trespassing on Kinyani's land; Kinyani beat Lashiloi's son for damaging a watergate; Lashiloi accused Kinyani of using witchcraft against him; Kinyani claimed Lashiloi owed an unpaid debt.

Phase 1. Lashiloi forced the crisis by initiating a public dispute at the age-group meeting. Kinyani denied the claims and refused to negotiate with this group as mediators. Instead he went to a patrilineal counselor who then arranged a patrilineal moot for elders and counselors from both clans; an arena had been chosen; they met on the vacant plot.

Phase 2. An opening controversy over the agenda led to the accumulation of sixteen issues, the two land claims made by the principals, six further complaints by Kinyani, and eight further complaints by Lashiloi.

Phase 3. Reciprocal changes, complaints, testimonies of the oldest men present, further testimony by middle-aged spokespersons, ventilation, and blaming — all these tested the whole field of the controversy.

Phase 4. Kinyani's counselor offered a package deal; Lashiloi's counselor refused; then issues began to narrow, prioritize. After some concessions, a return to acrimony, and further debate and

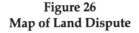

Figure 26
Map of Land Dispute

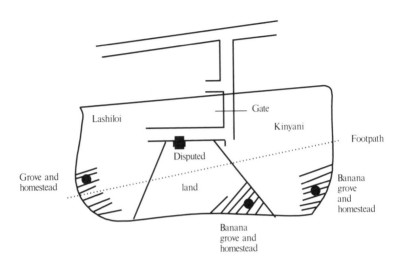

stalemate, Lashiloi's counselor offered a compromise — to divide the land along the footpath. This gave Kinyani a home site for his son and Lashiloi the agricultural land he desired.

Phase 5. Final bargaining now resolved the subsidiary issues and redefined some of the changes so that they were mutually acceptable. Resentment was still high at each other's rigidity. Then one of Lashiloi's supporters made a speech on reconciliation calling on each party to give a little. The group agreed and pressed the two men to soften their demands.

Phase 6. Gradually the two disputants made reciprocal concessions. Trade-offs and compromises were worked out. A day was set for exchange of all items and termination of the conflict.

Phase 7. On the agreed day, the two met with counselors and family members; a goat was sacrificed; beer was given and drunk together; then the counselors announced that there was no longer any quarrel between the neighbors. Each now owned the land; there was nothing to fear from any changes or from any resorting to uses of supernatural powers. The two men drank beer from the same gourd; then all drank beer and consumed the rest of the goat.

The dispute was between neighbors who recognized that in the end, neighborliness had to be reestablished and a solution had to be found. Both were willing to give ground, but neither wished to initiate the process or yield more than necessary.

(Gulliver 1979, 234–52, abridged)

Chapter Nine

Reconciliation: The Many Faces of Forgiveness

A sin covered is half-forgiven.
— Arab proverb

The one who forgives gains the victory.
— Yoruban proverb

UNIVERSAL INSIGHT
(The Bottom Line)

The one who throws the stone forgets;
The one who is hit remembers forever.
— Angolan proverb

FOLKTALE: LETTING GO
Japan

Tanzen and Ekido were once traveling together down a muddy road. A heavy rain was falling; the mud was deep.

As they passed through a village, they came upon a lovely young woman in a silk kimono and obbe sash, unable to cross the muddy intersection.

Tanzen stopped, bowed, and asked, "May I be of help?" Then he lifted her in his arms and carried her gently across the streets.

Ekido did not speak again to Tanzen until they had arrived at a lodging temple late that night. Then he could no longer restrain himself. "How could you do such a thing?" he asked. "We monks do not go near females, especially not young and lovely ones. It is dangerous. Why did you do that?" "I left the girl there," said Tanzen. "You are still carrying her!"

FOLKTALE: THE ADOPTION OF THE ENEMY
Lesotho

In the early 1800s there was a time of great unrest and conflict in southern Africa. Dutch and English settlers were at war with each other and against the black tribespeople, who were also in conflict against each other. Homelessness, poverty, and starvation were epidemic. Cannibalism was occurring in this time of extreme hunger.

The Lesotho people were a small tribe living in a mountain fortress with their leader, Moshoeshoe (Mo-shwa-shwa). The grave threat to their survival led them to migrate to a place of greater safety. As they were making this long trek by foot, with the older people bringing up the rear of the caravan, a group of cannibals attacked the stragglers and killed a number of them for food. Among those eaten were the grandfather and grandmother of chief Moshoeshoe.

When the chief learned of this tragedy, he sent his warriors to capture the cannibals, but with the injunction that they should not harm any of them since "they are the grave of my ancestors." When the captured cannibals were brought to the fortress, they discovered that Moshoeshoe had killed a cow and prepared a feast for them. The murderers were seated as the honored guests at the head of the feast. At the end of the feast, Chief Moshoeshoe rose to offer a field, a cow, and a plot of land to build a house for each member of the cannibal clan. "Now you have no more reason to practice cannibalism," he said. "Since you're the grave of my ancestors, you belong among us." Two peoples became one people, through forgiveness.

(Meyer 1984)

In forgiving, we Irish are historians; we focus on the injustices of the past. We remember the injuries, review the violations, ruminate on the hurts. We are like the Jews. We do not want the world to forget what we have suffered.

The English want to forgive by forgetting the past, focus on the future. Close the door on the oppressive memories, start fresh from this moment, with the situation that now exists. They are like the Germans who do not want to recall the holocaust and think it ill-mannered of the Jews to continue to do so. (Corry 1989)

The person who throws the stone, forgets; the one who is hit, never forgets. That is the wisdom of the Angolan proverb. When the embarrassment and guilt of having been the oppressor, the exploiter, or the perpetrator weigh down a national conscience, then a forgiveness of forgetfulness — denial, distancing, and distortion — is profoundly attractive. When the anger of having been oppressed, exploited, and violated cries out for correction, then forgiveness that deals with the past — resolving resentment, reviewing injury, and reflecting on what restitution, repayment, or repentance is appropriately owed — will constantly stir memories.

Forgiveness has many faces. Each culture shapes its understandings of forgiveness from its central values. Harmony calls for a forgiveness of overlooking; justice for a forgiveness of repentance; solidarity for a forgiveness of ostracism; honor for a forgiveness of repayment; dignity for a forgiveness of principled sacrifice. Each group gives forgiveness a face composed of multiple values, framed by its unique history, and formed by its collective ledgers of justice and injustice received and given, harmony and disharmony chosen or imposed, and honor or dignity won or lost.

Forgiveness and reconciliation are difficult for all human beings. In some cultures mutual horizontal reconciliation is preferred; in other cultures vertical acceptance or lateral inclusion is the norm. Where structures are hierarchical, such as traditional China, forgiveness may be either an overlooking of an act, or a vertical, one-way form of meriting acceptance by earning honor or respect. Or as in Japan, the choice may be between excusing and ostracism. In Indian cultures, the choice is between an all-inclusive acceptance of good and evil alike or violent retaliation. Where reparation is a central motif, it may be a choice between repayment, retaliation, or generous acceptance of the injury, as in Muslim thought, where honor is the crucial moral arbiter. Or, as in Greek culture, forgiveness may be the recognition that sufficient punishment has been exacted. The nature of forgiveness and reconciliation, both in form and content, varies so widely across cultures that multiple models are necessary if we are to capture the unique character and process of restoring severed relationships in each particular context.

The function of a model is to simplify the complex by inten-

Figure 27
Polarities of Response to Perceived Wrongdoing

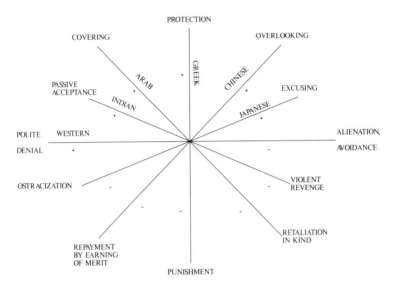

A model of cultural preferences for responding to wrongdoing. The minus sign indicates negative acts that sever or exact a cost from a relationship; the plus sign indicates ways of continuing a relationship through smoothing or accommodation.

tionally sacrificing particulars in order to highlight uniqueness. Figure 27 highlights central cultural motifs or paradigms of reconciliation in representative civilizations to contrast how these dominant polarities appear as a central tendency in each context. The variations within each culture are frequently as great as the differences between them, yet the cultural preference can be visualized in order to examine the general trajectory of the group's behavioral patterns. The references to Chinese, Indian, and Arab cultures, for example, are meant to be illustrative, not definitive. There are over twenty-five distinct Indian cultures, twice as many

Arab cultures, and three times as many Chinese cultural groups, so any general comment about patterns is intended to invite increased awareness of contrasts, not a detailed analysis of distinct dynamics.

The polarities highlighted — such as the accepting poles of overlooking, denying, protecting, or excusing and the rejecting poles of ostracism, alienation, retaliation in kind, and violent revenge — exist in virtually all cultures. The midpoint of uniting acceptance and justice in the creative and costly synthesis we call forgiveness is rare. No culture has any advantage in practicing it. It is painfully difficult for all. It requires bringing together the two most common ways of coping with injury — anger and denial — and turns anger toward breaking down walls rather than erecting them. It reverses denial into acceptance of pain and the pursuit of creative change and growth.

OVERLOOKING OR REPAYING

Chinese proverbs offer wisdom on the impact of wrongdoing and the difficulty of reconciliation:

"If you take one step in the wrong direction, a hundred steps in the right direction will not atone for it."

"Retribution must come sometime, if not to you, then to your children."

"Death is not enough to atone for the guilt."

"He who is held in contempt by all dies without being ill."

But on the generosity that can overlook a mistake, Chinese proverbs counsel:

"Blame yourself as you would blame others; excuse others as you would excuse yourself."

"What is hateful to yourself do not do to others."

This two-level process — overlooking and accepting, or exacting repayment to earn reacceptance or regain honor — is authentically Chinese. Offenses to responsibility, veracity, or property may be excused, but an insult to face, pride, or dignity may be unforgivable. A Chinese proverb states: "A murder may be forgiven, an affront never!"

In traditional Confucian Chinese cultures, the two polarities of reconciliation are to overlook a fault or to exact repayment, specifically, to regain honor by earning reacceptance. Overlooking is seen as being tolerant, liberal, and generous; it involves not holding an offense against the other (*fun syu*) or excusing the other (*yuen leung*). The repayment pole is modeled from the vertical relationships of father-son, parent-child, and God-human, which demand the erring person merit acceptance, earn release from shame, and regain status by obedience, service, and compliance (*se min*). Confession seems totally unacceptable since one does not reveal personal failure to others, just as one does not reveal family problems or secrets to the world. Confession is a brazen publication of an evil act and an irresponsible abdication of the duty to earn acceptance where one has betrayed trust or failed others' expectations.

The "rectification" processes of coerced confession introduced during the Cultural Revolution sought to reverse and thus destroy the power of "face." As people were forced to offer self-critiques, confessing faults and recanting, they suffered the humiliation of both exposure and repayment rituals. Often these statements were torn up in their faces and a second, third, or fourth writing was demanded. "They are ripping the faces off of them until there is nothing left. Once that has been done they can remodel where the old face was," said one official to journalist Dennis Bloodworth (Bloodworth and Ping 1977).

In traditional thought and practice, social face (*mein-tzu*) stands for one's reputation, prestige, success, and ostentation. It is the maintenance of status and the performance of expected roles. Moral face (*lien*) represents the confidence of society in the integrity of one's moral character. A professor who gives a poor lecture loses social face; if the lecture is discovered as plagiarized, moral face is lost (Ho 1974, 240).

Social face (*mien-tzu*) is a matter of reputation and appearance, but honor (face as *lien*) is an affair of conscience and integrity. A loss of social face is a smudge in the makeup, but a loss of honor is a cancer in the skin. The Chinese person thinks not only of saving, gaining, or losing his or her own face, but also of the face of others since "faces" are interdependent. So tolerance, forbearance, and overlooking of faults are necessary for living together. This forgiveness that excuses another is the acceptance of daily difficulties and differences. "The wise person is like a vast ocean within, and nothing can stir or trouble the waters," a Chinese pastoral counselor quoted, explaining this capacity to overlook.

The vertical, one-way nature of the forgiveness given to the person who regains acceptance by earning the other's respect is not seen as a mutual, reciprocal process; it is a unilateral, largely nonverbal action of mercy given to the repentant offender or of recognition offered when restitution has been made.

Two-way, reciprocal, mutual forgiveness is a concept that does not accord with the vertical patterns of filial piety, or fit the hierarchical social structures that are supported and enriched by four thousand years of tradition. Forgiveness, say Chinese pastoral theologians, is in most cases a specifically vertical, nonverbal transaction that leads to reconciliation; it is a reconciliation of mutual care for social face in lesser infractions, and of earned and merited justice in larger injuries (Choi 1984).

COVERING OR RETALIATING

In Arabian cultures, the two polarities of forgiveness are the covering of wrongdoing on the more permissive pole, and retaliation in kind at the other pole.

"A sin covered is half-forgiven," states an Arab proverb expressing the deep sense of loyalty and caring for fellow group members that are understood as essential human behavior. "To take care of one's own people, irrespective of merit or order of priority, is a basic duty; it is fulfilling a part of one's elementary role" (Hamady 1960). This loyalty is expressed in the Arab proverb: "I and my brothers against my cousins; I and my cousins against the world."

To fellow family or group members, the Arab acts in a "subject-to-subject" manner, but outside of kin and the circle of near friends, people are seen more as objects, as outsiders. Relationships within are tough and resilient; without they are easily bruised.

Retaliation, specifically blood-vengeance, is a deeply rooted legal and psychological concept in the Arab heritage. The word *forgiveness* at times means "blood-money" or "ransom" in the Qur'an (Küng 1987, 92). The root word for retaliation can mean "to retell, relive, or re-experience an event." To retaliate means to return like for like, repeating the same action again; the action is retraced, replicated, redone (Reimer 1977, 47).

This urge to reproduce events, more than a need to repeat history, combines a defensive process of undoing with a need for retributive justice. The concrete understanding of fairness calls for exacting like and equal penalty as the condition for fulfilling and thus canceling claims against another.

The Qur'an contains five key passages commanding retaliation yet limiting it to equal retribution. Two of these (2:178 and 5:48) teach exact compensation and exacting retaliation. But in the latter statement, the call is also to go beyond retaliation to the point of forgoing it and forgiving to gain a spiritual reward:

> We prescribed, the life for the life, and the eye for the eye, the nose for the nose, the ear for the ear, and the tooth for the tooth, and for wounds retaliation. But who so forgoeth it, in the way of charity it shall be an expiation for him. (5:48ff.)

And in two other settings, the Qur'an discourages revenge and encourages forgiveness as "a better way." One of the statements reads:

> Repel the evil deed with one which is better, then lo! he between whom and thee there was enmity will become as though he was a bosom friend. (41:34)

In every religious tradition, there is a disparity between the ideal and the actual. In Arab cultures, the predominant practice swings between the poles of covering for "us" and retaliation toward "them." The we-they division holds until violence erupts within the family, and then revenge frequently occurs there as well. But forgiveness remains an option in both the religious tradition and the cultural alternatives. Its nature as overlooking, tolerating, or redemptively reconciling is not often spelled out beyond the final words of instruction in the Qur'an cited above.

Similarities with the Hebrew traditions of reconciliation show common Semitic values. *Lex talionis* (the law of retaliation) as a legal principle is ancient. It is found in the Code of Hammurabi, the Hittite laws, and the Old Testament (Ex. 21:23–24; Lev. 24:19–20; Deut. 19:21; see also Deut. 25:11, 12; Num. 35:16ff.), but is also limited with the teaching of proportionate compensation (Ex. 21:18–27) and with limitations on needless bloodletting.

In the Sermon on the Mount, Jesus does not abrogate the law of retaliation in his reference and citation (Matt. 5:21–45) but rather suggests a new way of understanding it. The principle of angry retaliation is to repay evil for evil. Jesus demands repayment, but with good (Nazir Ali 1987, 146ff.).

ACCEPTANCE OR REVENGE

In India, the polarity of forgiveness stretches from passive acceptance of another's act as his or her karma to violent revenge.

In Hindu thought, the general ethical laws are truthfulness, justice, compassion, amiability, patience, and the procreation of offspring. A general principle arising from these laws emphasizes harmlessness to all creatures as good or virtuous, and injury to them as evil. But in practical application, forgiveness is not extolled as the highest virtue under all circumstances (just as one need not always speak the truth since in certain situations "it is better to speak what is beneficial than what is true"). The law of karma is held in balance with the possibility of forgiveness. Karma, not to be misinterpreted as fatalism, is the law of cause and effect, of sowing in one life and reaping in this life or in lives to follow (Radhakrishnan and Moore 1957, 14).

In accepting the law of karma, you recognize that an injury or a favor from another was the other's karma to give and yours to receive. So why should there be resentment or gratitude? If another strikes you, you might well marvel at the efficiency of nature that brought the two of you together so auspiciously. It was the other's karma to strike someone, and it was yours to be smitten, and both karmas were fulfilled in a single blow. So what is there to forgive? Indeed, an attitude of forgiveness is an attitude of acceptance, of tolerance, of wise recognition that all proceeds by cause and effect. The cause may not be in your awareness, but it is within you, so the effect is to be received with enlightened resignation for what is and acceptance of what can be gained from it.

Gandhi writes of this forgiveness as acceptance of karma.

> The inexorable law of karma prevails, and in the very fulfillment of the law — giving everyone his deserts, making everyone reap what he sows — lies God's abounding mercy and justice. Being oneself ever liable to be judged, one must accord to others what would be accorded to the self, viz., forgiveness. (Gandhi 1970–76, 41:115)

In Indian psychology, forgiveness is largely equated with patience and tolerance toward others. The manifestation of soul-force is in patient endurance of those who are aggressive or destructive. The conquest of evil without is accomplished by the conquest of any impulse to retaliate within. Patience and forgiveness are the result of this powerful control through inner discipline of the self:

> It is difficult for weaklings to practice forgiveness. Any weakling can lose his temper; no strength is needed for that. It requires strength to control one's self. It requires tremendous power to control one's emotions or natural propensities, what they call "normal self-expression." ... Maturity in emotional life means self-control and consequent removal of conflict. In fact, to our way of thinking, a mature person is he who can use his ideal in his interpersonal relationships, however provocative the circumstances may be. (Akhilananda 1952, 60)

Pavhari Baba, an Indian holy man, surprised a thief who was stealing from his cave the few cooking utensils with which he prepared food for the poor. The man dropped his booty and ran. Pavhari Baba shouldered the bundle and ran after him calling: "Here, take this bundle. It belongs to you. Your need must be greater than mine, otherwise you would not have come." The overtaken thief was overcome by tears and begged, "Forgive me, forgive me." Convicted by shame, he renounced the world and became a holy man. Such patient soul-force is true forgiveness in the classic Hindu vision of spirituality. Reconciliation is seen not as integral to the nature of forgiveness, but as a desirable consequence.

> People must spiritualize themselves in order to cultivate this spirit of forgiveness. Spiritualize means conquest of the lower nature and manifestation of the higher nature. It does not matter whether people are Jews, Christians, Hindus, Mohammedans, Buddhists, or any other religionist. The solution is the same for all. One cannot reach that state of spiritual consciousness over-night where one is ready to forgive enemies and destroyers. It requires time. (Akhilananda 1952, 63)

The negative pole of violent revenge is the shadow of this acceptant tolerance. The practice of violence in the resolution of family, clan, or caste conflicts; the institutional violence within the caste system; the massive outbreaks of violence following the partition in 1947; the violent retaliation after the assassination of Indira Gandhi — these all express the pole of revenge that rises as a group response, a corporate sense of acting according to karma in rendering retributive or expiatory justice to the offenders, their kin, their caste, or their community's members.

DENIAL OR AVOIDANCE

In Western cultures, the dominant polarity of responses to perceived wrongdoing is most characterized by gracious denial on the positive pole, and alienation and avoidance on the negative pole.

The response of denial pretends acceptance, tolerance, and closeness, but it inevitably produces distance and superficiality in relationships. The defensive ways of avoiding reconciliation include *denial:* "It was nothing, forget it"; *reversal:* "I'm not angry at his meanness; I'm just concerned"; *superiority:* "Nothing that she could say would affect me"; *isolation:* "Feelings? What feelings? I couldn't care less." All these defenses provide mechanisms for coping that intensify individualism and result in distancing from the other person under the guise of civil, polite "niceness." The functions of American niceness to cover feelings, avoid confrontation, pretend superiority, suppress conflict, and eliminate differences have been noted in numerous studies and analyses (e.g., Bach 1974, 23–25).

The response of alienation and avoidance of relationship is the inevitable solution to tensions in a highly individualized society. "The emotional cutoff" of severing communication and interaction becomes the most frequent means of managing high anxiety in relationships. The most anxious party will terminate all authentic encounter and may effectively avoid all human contact. High social mobility, geographic movement, and the breakdown of extended family relationships all facilitate the use of emotional cutoffs as means of managing tensions, avoiding open conflict, and pretending self-sufficiency in isolated independence of significant others (Bowen 1978, 382).

These Western strategies are symptomatic of the exaggerated independence and rugged individualism consciously prized by some and unconsciously practiced by most persons within the culture. Although the cultural values of direct address of difficulties, confrontation with differences, negotiation of issues, and reconciliation of conflicts are present in the society, the more common behaviors are to practice superficial forgiveness through denial or to reach a one-way resolution through severed relationships ("I forgive him; I just don't want to get involved with him again"). In spite of the presence of values and models of mutual, reciprocal forgiveness and reconciliation, the rarity of their authentic practice points to the preference for individualistic avoidance (Lasch 1979, 51).

EXCUSING OR OSTRACISM

In Japanese culture, the two polarities are the covert style of excusing the shortcoming and the overt practice of ostracism. The most frequently used word to express forgiveness (*yuroshi*) carries the meanings to excuse, to permit, to grant indulgence for another's failure. In individual failings, one may give the other person the benefit of all doubts, excusing the other's behavior rather than exposing the other and forcing a loss of face and so losing face oneself. In the group, one excuses the other's behavior by bearing some responsibility for all group members' actions.

The pride and shame of a group member are shared by the group, and in turn the group's pride and shame are shared individually by its members. Every person seeks to enhance the pride of the group, and to avoid disgraceful conduct that would shame fellow group members. No one who causes the group shame is tolerated. The collective sharing of shame becomes most acute when the dishonorable action by a group member is exposed to outside groups. The worst crime is then to expose the group's shame.

Not only pride and shame but also suffering may be collectively shared in vicarious joint pain. The suffering of one person arouses intense guilt in other group members even when they are not responsible (Lebra et al. 1976, 36).

The collective implications of individual experience are described by Takeo Doi in his discussion of guilt: "Guilt is sharpest when a person is afraid that his or her action may result in betraying the group" (Doi 1973, 49).

Where the transgression can be quietly excused and the shame contained, the action may be forgotten in compassion. But where the loss of honor is not only for the person but also for the group, ostracism is necessary to correct, clarify, and cleanse the group or community's honor.

In ancient Athenian society there was no possibility for forgiveness. An offense was an uncleanness that only exile or death could dispel. Nothing less could cleanse the homeland and atone for the sin (Ricoeur 1967, 41). In Japanese experience, certain acts are beyond excusing; they are literally unforgivable, except through distance, time, and a public period of exclusion as a cleansing of the community.

Mura hachibu (village ostracism) is the appropriate response to one who exposes shame to the outside world. In 1952 a high school girl exposed a case of political scandal in a village election by writing a letter to the newspaper editor. She and her family were excluded from all social interaction with villagers.

Such ostracism may be felt as an invitation to die. The traditional rituals of suicide as an honorable death offer the ultimate of ostracism accepted by the person as a means of regaining honor for self and family.

The structures of guilt in Japanese society are hidden from Western observation, since they occur in the traditions and duties of familial systems, not in religious systems and generalized principles of morality as in the West. "Guilt is related to a failure to meet expectations in a moral system built around family duties and obligations" (DeVos 1967, 262).

Failure, laziness, and rebellion are felt to injure the parents and thus lead to feelings of guilt. This responsibility to parents is analogous to the sense of accountability to God in Western thought. The suffering of the mother has great power to evoke obedience, and her death is seen as providing great motivation to achieve and succeed, especially in correcting any previous shortcomings: "If one fails to achieve, he has no way to atone. He is lost. The only thing left is to hurt himself, to extinguish himself — the one whose existence has been hurting his parents and who now can do nothing for them. Suicide is an answer" (DeVos 1967, 272–73).

When the failure is less complete, the child can strive for acceptance by pouring all energies into attaining the goal of highest value by working hard, being virtuous, becoming successful, attaining a good reputation, and winning the praise of society. By this she or he brings honor upon the self, on the parents, and to the *ie* (household lineage). Thus the child becomes a credit to the parents and to the familial line, and grows into a parent who will demand such obedience in turn from the next generation. The forgiveness thus gained is vertical, from superior to inferior, from parent to child. It is attained by meriting respect, achieving praiseworthy status, and earning one's place once more in spite of the resistances and ambivalences of the soul.

The concepts of forgiveness in Japanese thought thus move from the pole of compassionate forgetting, excusing, and accepting (these being motivated by either loyalty or the evidence of having earned honor) to the opposite pole of exclusion in ostracism, social death, or an invitation to die. The creative transformation of wrongdoing into healing of persons and relationships in forgiveness occurs more rarely in traditional Japanese thought.

The Japanese have an almost magical regard for the power of an apology. An apology brings reconciliation in most daily situations. The feeling and expression of *sumanai* are the only acceptable means of admitting one's guilt and asking pardon.

An American psychiatrist, through some complication in carrying out immigration formalities, found himself being rigorously questioned by an official. However often he explained that the problem was not really his fault, the official would not be appeased. Finally, as a prelude to further argument, he said, "Well, I'm sorry, but..." only to be interrupted by the official, whose expression had suddenly changed. The matter was dismissed. The "I'm sorry" that he had spoken was far from the Japanese use of *sumanai*, but the official had obviously taken it as such and upon a perceived admission of guilt, ended the interchange (Doi 1973, 50).

ABSORPTION OR REVENGE

In Korean thought, the alternatives for alienated or injured parties lie between the pole of absorbing the injury in resignation to the reality of the evil suffered and the opposite pole of active resentment and the urge to take revenge. This double pattern of internalizing pain grows out of the repeated experience of invasion, oppression, and exploitation that the culture has experienced in two thousand years of being repeatedly violated by neighboring countries.

An outstanding Minjung theologian, Nyun Young-hak, has defined this overpowering sense of internalized suffering, rage, and resentment through use of a central word in classical Korean philosophical and theological thought — *han*.

Han is a sense of unresolved resentment against injustices suffered, a sense of helplessness because of the overwhelming odds against, a feeling of acute pain, of sorrow in one's guts and bowels making the whole body writhe and wriggle, and an obstinate urge to take "revenge" and to right the wrong — all these combined. We Koreans often think of ourselves as a "*han*-ridden" people. (Cited in S. Y. Kim 1984, 101)

Han, Koreans note, is the dominant feeling of being oppressed that is shared in common by women, by despised slaves, and by downtrodden people. It calls for release, and seeing no just means of resolution, it demands revenge. It can also be expressed as a deep compassion with others who suffer and a motivation for forgiveness, although such transformation arises from the influences of Christianity in the last century with its sweeping impact on cultural change. It may be this profound sense of *han* that has made the Korean culture more congenial to the theology of the cross than any other oriental culture.

RECONCILIATION RITUALS

When the alienated meet, and at last greet each other, the painful moment must be ritualized to give it security, authenticity, authority, and finality.

Rituals of reconciliation occur in every culture, as simple as a handshake, or as complex as the saying of a Mass.

In a conversation with David Shenk, Joshua Okello, a Kenyan leader, told of a peace ritual that had been performed in a previous generation and that had been explained to him by his father. A protracted conflict between the Masai and the Luo at last came to negotiation between the elders of each tribe. The ritual, or mechanism for bringing about the peace, involved the following.

The warriors, women, children, and elders of both sides converged on the battleground. They chopped down the trees that give a milky soup used to make a poison for coating arrowheads. These trees were piled into a fence along the tribal border. Along this barrier, spears were thrust into the ground to symbolize the war that had divided them. A black dog was slain, cut in half, and its blood poured along the fence. Then mothers exchanged the babies with the enemy tribe and suckled the new generation of their foes. Prayers were offered by the elders and a profound curse pronounced on anyone who should cross that fence to bring harm to either side. After this ritual, it was impossible to fight again. A covenant had been made (Shenk 1979).

"To take revenge is to sacrifice oneself," say the Kongo. Their rituals of releasing anger and recovering relationship express the removal of the insult or injury in concrete symbolism. If the conflict has reached the intensity of injurious words, the mediator may counsel the younger of the parties to ritualize repentance by approaching the other on his or her knees. He or she then places three small piles of dirt on the older person's thighs. These are brushed off one at a time with the affirmation that the words are withdrawn and nothing remains in the heart.

In a parent-child conflict where the parent has, in extremity, pronounced a solemn curse (a malediction by an ascendant in direct bloodline is as powerful as a blessing), a ritual is necessary for repentance. A mediator, such as a grandparent, uncle, or aunt, will ask the child to approach the threshold of the parent's house on knees and elbows. There the penitent puts a bit of dirt on the foot of the parent who in turn may brush it off as a sign of forgiveness (Burke 1988).

"He that forgives gains the victory," the Yoruba say. Their rituals of "head washing" offer an insight into the meaning of forgiveness in Nigeria. E. A. D. Adegbola writes:

> The Yoruba word for forgiveness (*iforiji*) originates from the myth of the first man who bowed down before Odolumare and who was told to stand and go home with his "head still on his shoulders." To forgive is to let the sinner go with his head on his shoulders when it should have been cut off because of his sin. This act of the deities actualizes itself in the experience of the individual sinner when he enters into the ceremony of "head washing," at the time when the history of the first event is repeated above his head.... When the

priest recites the history (*ayajo* = the similar journey), the sinner washes his head, inflicting pain to it, and wishes himself well in confessing his sin. Forgiveness (*iforiji*) in Yoruba religious thought is more than forgetting the past; it is accepting the gift of "a head," a new creation. (Adegbola 1960)

Kenneth Kaunda, first president of Zambia, writes about the power of forgiveness and the great capacity for it native to African cultures:

Forgiveness is not, of course, a substitute for justice. Forgiveness is a gift, not something we earn, but to know the reality of forgiveness we must be prepared to turn our backs on the things we have done which required us to seek forgiveness in the first place. Justice and forgiveness are related this way. To claim forgiveness whilst perpetuating injustice is to live a fiction; to fight for justice without also being prepared to offer forgiveness is to render your struggle null and void. Justice is not only about what is due to a human being; it is also about establishing right relationships between human beings. (Kaunda 1980, 181)

Bellona, one of the Solomon Islands, offers an oral history of five hundred years of interclan warfare that includes twenty-four generations of feuds and reciprocal killings between the Seven Original Clans and the Kaitu Clan. Peacemaking was looked upon by everybody as something temporary, as a kind of armed neutrality. "Peace is but a deception," it was said.

Yet, fifty years ago two districts, which through generations had fought with one another, decided to put an end to their hostilities. A man said to his son, "Ngango and Matangi [the two districts] have been fighting each other for generations, but we are [because of intermarriage between the two districts] like two eyes. If one eye is hurt, the other one cries, so let's stop the fighting between the two districts" (Kuschel in Boucher, Landis, and Clark 1987, 294).

The father and son went from family to family pointing out their interrelatedness, their interdependence. The two eyes began to see, feel, and work together.

From culture to culture, the movement from the bitter urge to revenge oneself to the painful decision to embrace the other as neighbor is crystalized proverbially. Several deserve to be quoted:

"The bitter heart eats its owner." (Bantu)

"The heart knows its bitterness as the owner knows his body." (Hausa)

"Hate has no medicine." (Ga)

"It is better to spend the night in anger than in repentance." (Tamashek)

Roger Rosenblatt did a series of articles for *Time* entitled "Children of War"; the series captures the beauty and strength of reconciliation in a truly extraordinary way. He concludes: "There is a copability quotient that allows children who have suffered the most to have an essential goodheartedness,... a generosity of nature that transcends and diminishes anything they have suffered" (Rosenblatt 1982, 52).

Rosenblatt reports an exchange with a child who had lost both parents to the genocide of Pol Pot's Khmer Rouge:

"Does your spirit tell you to get revenge?"
    "Yes" (solemnly).
    "So, you will go back to Cambodia one day and fight the Khmer Rouge?"
    "No, that is not what I mean by revenge. To me revenge means I must make the most of my life." (Rosenblatt 1982, 52)

This amazing conversion of the meaning of revenge from destructive retaliation to constructive solidarity offers "kindness for cruelty, generosity for spite. In short [the children's] goodness may be a means of survival" (Rosenblatt 1982, 52).

PSYCHOLOGICAL DYNAMICS OF FORGIVING

Three primary controls in the human psyche press toward or away from reconciliation. These emerge from the three basic control processes of the human personality (anxiety, shame, and guilt), which form during the first, third, and fifth years of development of children in every culture. However, the socialization process of each culture utilizes the three in different ways and emphasizes one of the processes beyond the others so that we may speak of anxiety cultures, shame cultures, or guilt cultures. Given that distinction, it is also important to note that all three processes are present in all cultures; all three influence reconciliation dynamics; all three must be resolved in healing injuries between persons and groups.

The three parallel forms of forgiveness that resolve these emotional states are "punitive forgiveness," "inclusive forgiveness," and "reconciliatory forgiveness." It is helpful to have a clear statement of their genesis — the epigenetic process of human development — in order to understand their dynamics. One must choose a language for such exploration, so, arbitrarily, Western psychoanalytic thought will be used here although the patterns can be seen in each ethical, psychological, cultural, or anthropological language.

Punitive forgiveness is a concrete repayment process. As a child risks seeking a forbidden gratification in defiance of the parents' rules, anxiety and anger arise. Anxiety stems from the fear of punishment, anger from the frustration by the parents, but since the child dare not express his or her desire, the anger is turned inward on the self in superego formation. So the child seeks gratification, feels consequent anxiety and anger, and narcissistically asks for forgiveness to relieve the self-punitive process. Each parent is treated as an it, a thing, since the concern is with the self, not the other or the relationship.

Inclusive forgiveness is acceptance, rather than true forgiveness. As the child comes to perceive the parents as persons, the child finds that attitudes are more important than acts, and estrangement becomes more significant than punishment. Now the driving force for resolving the tension is no longer fear of punishment but the deprivation of love. Identification with the parents' values is internalized in the ego ideal, and shame (failure before the ideal) becomes possible. Now violations produce not only anxiety, but also shame in the fear of contempt and abandonment by the parents. The concern for forgiveness is focused on acceptance and inclusion, although the budding superego floods the emotions with anxiety — the fear of punishment — and the child expects, even requests, punishment as the requisite for being accepted. "I'd feel better if you'd spank me and get it over with instead of talking to me about what I did." The child involved in I-it actions of violation expects an I-it punishment in response. But now inclusive forgiveness seeks to accept the offender and restore the loving relationship.

Reconciliatory forgiveness is a transformation of the relationship; it is true forgiveness. As the responsible ego forms, the person is at last capable of truly seeing the self from the other's perspective, so decentering of the self, reversal of one's past behavior in repentance, and reciprocity in relationship become possible. In true forgiveness, the guilt is felt, faced, and followed through to mutual recognition that repentance is genuine, and right relationships — with justice and reciprocity — are now achieved. This transforms the relationship, strengthening the acceptance and re-creating the power differential felt in the wrongdoing to build a true mutuality. These are functions of both *the observing ego*, which can transcend the hurt and guilt and see the two-person situation of pain clearly, and *the responsible ego*, which can test reality in appropriate trusting and risking until relationships of fairness and respect are once more possible.

The superego functions in all kinds of forgiveness. It is dominant in its punitive and rudimentary form in the anxiety of punitive forgiveness; it is secondary in the auxiliary form of inclusive forgiveness since it now shares the controlling functions with the ego ideal; and it is, hopefully, tertiary in reconciliatory forgiveness as the ego — prompted by anxiety, directed by shame, and corrected by guilt — works through the wrongdoing to a new interpretation, a new self and acceptance of the other, and a reconciliation of affect and action.

Forgiveness depends not upon the superego and its anxiety, shame, and guilt, but upon the response of the ego. As Mansell Pattison writes: "The punitive superego does not discriminate among those events which call for forgiveness (real guilt) and those which do not. Forgiveness is not a superego phenomenon. The superego never forgives, it can only be satiated" (Pattison 1973, 252).

If we accept that forgiveness is mutual recognition that repentance is genuine and right relationships achieved, then four corollary concepts need to be clarified: confession, contrition, restitution, and reconciliation.

Confession is not ventilation, dissipation, justification, or flagellation; it is the authentic recognition of responsibility for one's acts and their consequences. Ventilation only discharges the tension but with no intention to change; dissipation may seek to diminish the responsibility by drawing in others to share one's guilt, or to evade the real injury by emphasizing a part of the pain process to cover the rest; justification covertly excuses, explains, rationalizes, and attributes blame or projects hostility into others' emotions; flagellation abuses the self in repayment strategies of undoing or self-destruction. Confession owns and expresses responsibility. Its style, content, focus, degree of disclosure, and appropriate setting vary across cultures from radical openness to intense guardedness, but each culture possesses structures for responsible confession.

Contrition is not punitive self-condemnation, obsessive remorse, manipulative kowtowing, or expiatory groveling; it is appropriate sorrow for one's wrong behavior and consequent grief-work for the injury to the relationship; such grief-work has genuine reconciliation as its goal. In punitive forgiveness contrition becomes self-destructive, depressive, and suicidal rage rather than the regret that facilitates repentance and reconciliation. In inclusive forgiveness contrition becomes expiatory self-negation. In reconciliatory forgiveness it moves along pathways of culturally accepted grief-work.

Restitution is not a repayment to avoid retaliation (anxiety) or return of equivalent value to earn acceptance (shame); it is the reestablishing of mutual justice (resolving guilt and responsibility). The restitution is motivated not by the obsessive mathematics of mechanical reparations, a *lex talionis* in reverse; it is the creative, responsive work of seeking justice between wrongdoer and wronged.

> Restitution re-establishes the conditions of the I-Thou. If I have stolen your purse and then seek forgiveness, I must return the purse. Not because I will not otherwise be forgiven, or because it is demanded by the forgiver. Rather, I return the purse because my love compels me to restore what belongs to Thou. To keep the purse is self-preference and repudiates the love of Thou. Restitution consists of returning to Thou anything I have taken in disregard of Thou. (Pattison 1973, 255)

Restitution rituals, in each culture, offer paradigms of that culture's balance of reparation, inclusion, and reconciliation processes. To appreciate and understand the ritual is to experience the process in depth.

Reconciliation is not a vertical restoration of unjust structures that may have been part of the process of the injury; nor is it a new vertical solution in which the forgiver emerges in a superior position and the forgiven emerges in an inferior position. It is a joint process of releasing the past with its pain, restructuring the present with new reciprocal respect and acceptance, and reopening the future to new risks and spontaneity. In receiving acceptance, the wrongdoer must tolerate the situation of dependence on the love of another. One who fears dependence cannot enter the co-freedom of interdependence. As both persons accept their appropriate ratio of responsibility and share the redistribution of guilt, anger, suffering, and estrangement that have been between them, the situation is reframed, the pain reviewed and released, and the two are reconciled to the past and to each other in the present.

Reconciliation is a refusal of I-it retaliation and a choice of restoring the I-thou relationship of culturally appropriate mutuality in love. Punitive forgiveness leads to overt or covert retaliation; inclusive forgiveness leads to generous, vertical, and benevolent acceptance but without restored mutuality in an I-thou relationship. Reconciliation is authentic meeting and jointly shared meaning in loving relationship.

The many forms of reconciliation and the many faces of forgiveness seen across cultures are created from and corrected by the balance of repayment, inclusion, and reconstruction that is consistent with central cultural values. The intercultural mediator must know both the values of the disputants as well as his or her own values in depth in order to facilitate meeting and the bonding of new meanings in creating relationships.

FORGIVENESS RE-CREATES AS WELL AS RECONCILES

Forgiveness, one of the most difficult human transactions, is frequently defined in ways that render it simpler, less costly. It is commonly equated with releasing anger, restoring respect, and giving acceptance. It is most frequently practiced as overlooking, tolerating, excusing, and forgetting.

Forgiveness can be differentiated from the strategies used for denying the injury, avoiding the broken relationship, or resuming interaction without restoring relationship.

1. Forgiveness is not an arbitrary, free act of pardon given out of the unilateral generosity of the forgiver — forgiveness is an interpersonal transaction between two parties, but a wide ratio of degrees of initiative and responsibility occurs across cultures.

2. Forgiveness is not a superior action that makes the other permanently inferior, indebted, and obligated — forgiveness either restores or achieves a relationship of reciprocity within the cultural patterns of social exchange whether these be hierarchical or egalitarian.

3. Forgiveness is not protecting because of connections, excusing because of loyalties, or setting free because of permissive tolerance — forgiveness takes the integrity of the forgiver, of the forgiven, and of the relationship with equal seriousness. However, the rituals by which each of these is protected, expressed, or honored vary.

4. Forgiveness is not immunity from legal liability, or an amnesty from consequences or penalties, or a blanket pardon from prosecution — forgiveness involves both justice and repentance in re-creating the relationship.

Forgiveness re-creates the relationship as it releases the anger, guilt, and pain from the past, reopens the future by resolving fear and suspicion, and restores the relationship by renegotiating the differences and reclaiming the other as a brother or sister in a reconciled present.

Forgiveness is the mutual recognition that repentance is genuine and right relationships have been restored or achieved. Repentance is not a precondition for forgiveness, and it is not a desired consequence; it is the correcting and clarifying process by which forgiveness occurs.

In the New Testament the two most frequently used words for forgiveness are *charidzomai* (an act of grace) and *aphesis* (a setting free or releasing from obligations or debts). Both words are used to describe the regaining of relationship and the restoring of community that are the primary focus of forgiving in the New Testament. Forgiveness is not a private act done for the healing or salvation of the forgiver, but a transaction whose goal is the regaining of the other (see Matt. 18:15).

Forgiveness takes precedence even over worship. If another has sinned, we are to go seeking restoration (Matt. 18:21–22). If another has a complaint against us, we are to go seeking reconciliation (Matt. 5:21–26). Both parties are obligated by love to take the initiative in restoring community. Forgiveness is an act of integrity requiring the working through of differences, the recognition of genuine repentance, and the celebration of a relationship justly restructured (Matt. 18:15–19; Luke 17:3–4; Gal. 6:1–5).

All forgiveness, whether human or divine, operates from the same model of re-creating or restoring trust in new covenants of relationship. As Saint Paul repeatedly instructs: "Forgive one another as God in Christ has forgiven you" (Eph. 4:32; Col. 3:13). The old vertical and horizontal dichotomies are ended as both become one in a new vision that renders these traditional religious distinctions obsolete.

The biblical model of forgiveness is not vertical — superior to inferior, lord to servant, righteous to unrighteous. Nor is it horizontal — the working out of ratios of responsibility in mathematical resolutions of injury and fault. The one tends toward hierarchy and its violation of communal equality and solidarity; the other presses toward an egalitarian resolution of differences in a flattened humanism of acceptance of each other's failures and faults.

The new vision of forgiveness is given us in neither a vertical nor a horizontal model, but in a circular process of forgiving and being forgiven. It is circular precisely because it is in the circle around the cross — the symbol of a forgiving God incarnate in human pain and suffering — that we give and receive forgiveness.

The English word *forgiveness*, which I am using here for want of a better word, is a contraction, a grammatically incorrect construction. "Ness" is not added to a verb, but to an adjective — for example, goodness, badness. So when we speak of forgiveness we mean *forgivenness* or *forgivingness*, or both.

The vertical societies of the East, with forgiveness patterns that stress the superiority of the forgiver and the obligation of the forgiven, are confronted by this circular process of standing with each other before the forgiving God-in-Christ, standing where healing enemy-love is incarnated, enfleshed, and unforgettably enacted. The egalitarian, individualistic societies of the West are confronted by this vision of truly meeting, melting, and remolding faithful relationship.

The temptation of two-sphere thinking — vertical and horizontal — must be energetically rejected. Vertical relationships of God with humanity come to us through the horizontal structures of life, and the horizontal structures become healing, acceptant, forgiving, and transforming by virtue of the vertical intervention of God's presence. To recognize that grace becomes real in horizontal relationships of love in no way implies that the vertical is absent, or that no act of God occurs in the interaction between faithful persons. The self-revelation of God is fully present in historical structures and is made known through horizontal encounters. The reality of the incarnation is that vertical and horizontal are united in the cross and in the circle around Christ, the suffering servant. There we see what forgiveness costs, how it is entered with integrity by all participants, and what it produces in the creation of a new humanity.

H. B. Dehqani-Tafti, bishop of Iran and presiding bishop of the Episcopal church in the Middle East, has chronicled his life in an outstanding autobiography entitled *The Hard Awakening*.

This book is a text on practical reconciliation. Dehqani-Tafti was constantly harassed by fundamentalist revolutionaries. At one point, they burst into his bedroom and fired four shots into his pillow, barely missing his head, and wounding his wife. Later, Dehqani-Tafti's secretary was tied up and shot. But Dehqani-Tafti entered the deepest valley of his life one day while attending a meeting in Cyprus. On that day he received a phone call from Oxford, England. The broken voice gave the simple message: "Bahram [Dehqani-Tafti's only son] has been shot and is dead."

In the pain of bereavement, perplexity, and outraged justice, the bishop wrote the following words the day before his only son's funeral. Because of danger, he could not attend the funeral, which was held in Iran:

O God,
We remember not only Bahram but also his murderers;
Not because they killed him in the prime of his youth and made our hearts bleed and our tears flow,
Not because with this savage act they have brought further disgrace on the name of our country among the civilized nations of the world;
But because through their crime we now follow thy footsteps more closely in the way of sacrifice.
The terrible fire of this calamity burns up all selfishness and possessiveness in us;
Its flame reveals the depth of depravity and meanness and suspicion, the dimension of hatred and the measure of sinfulness in human nature;
It makes obvious as never before our need to trust in God's love as shown in the Cross of Jesus and his resurrection;
Love which makes us free from hate towards our persecutors;
Love which brings patience, forbearance, courage, loyalty, humility, generosity, greatness of heart;
Love which more than ever deepens our trust in God's final victory and his eternal designs for the Church and for the world;

Love which teaches us how to prepare ourselves to face our
own day of death.
O God,
Bahram's blood has multiplied the fruit of the Spirit in the
soil of our souls;
So when his murderers stand before Thee on the day of
judgment,
Remember the fruit of the Spirit by which they have enriched
our lives.
And forgive. (Dehqani-Tafti 1981, 113–14)

FABLE: A TALE OF TWO HALVES
Asante Tribe

*Once there lived on earth creatures known as Half in Half.
Each of them was only half a human being, with only half the
feelings, half the intuition, half the wisdom of a human soul.
These half-humans spent all their time quarreling and fighting, disturbing everyone in the village, injuring the children
and trampling the crops. Each time one half-human began to
fight another, cries went up to God, "Aneunse Kokroko Fa ne
Fa neko o!" (O God, they are at it again, the half-humans are
fighting again!)*

*So one day, God came down, brought the two halves to-
gether, and a whole human being appeared.*

(Oduyoye 1983, 246)

Bibliography

Abrahams, Roger. 1983. *African Folktales*. New York: Pantheon Books.

Achebe, Chinua. 1958. *Things Fall Apart*. London: Heinemann.

——. 1972. *Girls at War*. London: Heinemann.

——. 1975. *Morning Yet on Creation Day*. London: Heinemann.

Acosta, F. X., and J. G. Sheenan. 1976. "Psychotherapist Ethnicity and Expertise as Determinants of Self-disclosure." In M. Miranda, ed., *Psychotherapy for the Spanish-speaking*. Los Angeles: Spanish Mental Health Research Center.

Adegbola, E. A. D. 1969. "Le fondement théologique de la morale." In Kwesi Dickson and Paul Ellingworth, eds., *Biblical Revelation and African Beliefs*. Maryknoll, N.Y.: Orbis Books.

Adorno, T. W., et al. 1950. *The Authoritarian Personality*. New York: Harper & Row.

Aida, Yuji. 1970. *The Structure of Consciousness Among the Japanese*. Tokyo: Kodansha.

Akhilananda, Swami. 1952. *Mental Health and Hindu Psychology*. London: Allen & Unwin.

Antoun, R. 1972. *Arab Village*. Bloomington: Indiana University Press.

Aronson, Shlomo. 1976. *Conflict and Bargaining in the Middle East*. Baltimore: Johns Hopkins University Press.

Asoera, Lillian. 1989. "Conflicts and Disputes Across Culture." Unpublished paper read at Associated Mennonite Seminaries, Elkhart, Ind.

Assefa, Hizkias. 1987. *Mediation of Civil Wars*. Boulder, Colo.: Westview.

Augsburger, David. 1974. "The Management and Control of Hostility in the Nonviolent-nonresistant." Ph.D. Diss., School of Theology at Claremont, Claremont, Calif.

———. 1986. *Pastoral Counseling Across Cultures*. Philadelphia: Westminster Press.

Averill, James. 1982. *Anger and Aggression*. New York: Springer-Verlag.

Axelrod, Robert. 1984. *The Evolution of Cooperation*. New York: Basic Books.

Ayoob, Mohammed, ed. 1980. *Conflict and Intervention in the Third World*. New York: St. Martin's Press.

Bach, George. 1974. *Creative Aggression*. Garden City, N.Y.: Doubleday.

Bach, George, and Herb Goldberg. 1979. *Creative Aggression*. New York: Avon Books.

Baker Miller, Jean. 1976. *Toward a New Psychology of Women*. Boston: Beacon Press.

———. 1983. "The Necessity of Conflict." In J. H. Robbins and R. J. Siegel, eds., *Women Changing Therapy*. New York: Haworth.

Barnlund, Dean. 1982. *Public and Private Self in Japan and in the United States*. Tokyo: Simul.

Barton, R. F. [1919] 1969. *Ifugao Law*. Reprint, Berkeley: University of California Press.

———. 1949. *The Kalingas, Their Institutions and Custom Law*. Chicago: University of Chicago Press.

Bast, Mahlon. 1987. "Sweat Lodge Case Study on Conflict Mediation." Unpublished student paper, Conrad Grebel College, Waterloo, Ontario.

Bateson, Gregory, and Mary Catherine Bateson. 1987. *Angels Fear*. New York: Macmillan Publishing Co.

Benedict, Ruth. 1946. *The Chrysanthemum and the Sword*. New York: Meridian Books.

Bercovitch, Jacob. 1984. *Social Conflicts and Third Parties Strategies of Conflict Resolution*. Boulder, Colo.: Westview.

Beresford, David. 1989. *Ten Men Dead: The Story of the 1981 Irish Hunger Strike*. New York: Atlantic Monthly Press.

Berger, Peter. 1970. "On the Obsolescence of the Concept of Honor." *European Journal of Sociology* 11:339–47.

Berry, J. W. 1966. "On Cross-cultural Comparability." *International Journal of Psychology* 1:124ff.

Blake, Robert, and Jane Moulton. 1964. *The Managerial Grid*. Houston: Gulf.

Bloodworth, Dennis, and Ching Ping. 1977. *The Chinese Machiavelli*. New York: Dell Publishing Co.

Bochner, Stephen. 1981. *The Mediating Person*. Cambridge, Mass.: Schenckman.

Bock, Philip K. 1970. *Culture Shock: A Reader in Modern Cultural Anthropology*. New York: Alfred A. Knopf.

———. 1988. *Rethinking Psychological Anthropology*. New York: W. H. Freeman.

Bohannan, Paul. 1957. *Justice and Judgment Among the Tiv*. London: Oxford University Press.

Bonoma, Thomas. 1975. *Conflict: Escalation and Deescalation*. Beverly Hills, Calif.: Sage.

Boucher, Jerry. 1969. "Culture and Emotion." In J. Marsella et al., eds., *Perspectives on Cross-cultural Psychology*. London: Academic Press.

Boucher, Jerry, Dan Landis, and Karen Arnold Clark. 1987. *Ethnic Conflict: International Perspectives*. Beverly Hills, Calif.: Sage.

Bourdieu, Pierre. 1979. *Algeria 1960*. Cambridge: Cambridge University Press.

Bowen, Murray. 1978. *Family Therapy and Clinical Practice*. New York: Jason Aronson.

Briggs, Jean. 1970. *Never in Anger: Portrait of an Eskimo Family*. Cambridge, Mass.: Harvard University Press.

Brislen, Richard W. 1981. *Cross-cultural Encounters*. New York: Pergamon.

———. 1986. *Intercultural Interactions*. Beverly Hills, Calif.: Sage.

Brown, P., and S. Levinson. 1978. "Universals in Language Usage: Politeness Phenomena." In E. N. Goody, ed., *Questions and Politeness*. Cambridge: Cambridge University Press.

Burke, Joan F. 1988. "Dossier: L'inculturation de la vie religieuse chez les Soeurs de Notre-Dame de Namur zu Zaire." Unpublished internal report of the Sisters of Notre Dame in Zaire.

Burton, John W. 1972. *World Society*. Cambridge: Cambridge University Press.

———. 1974. *Deviance, Terrorism and War: The Process of Solving Unsolved Social and Political Problems*. Oxford: Martin Robertson.

———. 1984. *Global Conflict: The Domestic Sources of International Crisis*. College Park, Md.: University of Maryland Press.

———. 1987. *Resolving Deep Rooted Conflict*. New York: University Press of America.

Campbell, J. K. 1964. *Honour, Family and Patronage: A Study of Institutions and Values in a Greek Mountain Community*. Oxford: Clarendon Press.

Campbell, Joseph. 1972. *Myths to Live By*. New York: Viking Press.

Camus, Albert. 1950. *Les Justes*. Paris: Gallimard.

Carey, Margaret. 1970. *Myths and Legends of Africa*. London: Hamlyn.

Casse, Pierre. 1981. *Training for the Cross-cultural Manager*. Washington, D.C.: Sietar.

Casse, Pierre, and Surinder Deol. 1985. *Managing Intercultural Negotia-*

tions: Guidelines for Trainers and Negotiators. Washington, D.C.: Sietar International.

Chagnon, N. 1977. The Yanomamo: The Fierce People. New York: Holt, Rinehart & Winston.

Chekhov, Anton. 1982. Chekhov: The Early Stories. Ed. P. Miles and H. Pitcher. London: John Murray.

Choi, Philemon. 1984. Personal Communication. Hong Kong: Breakthrough Counseling Center.

Cohen, Anthony. 1985. The Symbolic Construction of Community. New York: Tavistock.

Coleman, James. 1957. Community Conflict. Glencoe, N.Y.: Free Press.

Collier, Jane. 1974. "Women in Politics." In M. Z. Rosaldo and L. Lamphere, eds., Woman, Culture, and Society. Stanford, Calif.: Stanford University Press.

———. 1979. "Stratification and Dispute Handling in Two Highland Chiapas Communities." American Ethnologist 6, no. 2:305–28.

Colson, Elizabeth. 1971. "Heroism, Martyrdom and Courage." In T. O. Beidelman, ed., The Translation of Culture. London: Tavistock.

Comaroff, John L., and S. Roberts. 1981. Rules and Procedures: The Cultural Logic of Dispute in an African Context. Chicago: University of Chicago Press.

Condon, John, and Fathi S. Yousef. 1985. An Introduction to Intercultural Communication. New York: Macmillan Publishing Co.

Cooper, J. B. 1955. "Psychological Literature on the Prevention of War." Bulletin of the Research Exchange on the Prevention of War 3:17.

Corbin, John. 1986. "Insurrections in Spain." In D. Riches, ed., The Anthropology of Violence. Oxford: Blackwell.

Corry, Geoffrey. March, 1989. Interview with author, Dublin, Ireland.

Cragg, K. 1976. The Wisdom of the Sufis. London: Sheldon Press.

Curle, Adam. 1971. Making Peace. London: Tavistock.

———. 1986. In the Middle: Non-official Mediation in Violent Situations. Leamington Spa: Berg Publications.

Daniel, Norman. 1975. The Cultural Barrier. Edinburgh: Edinburgh University Press.

Darmaputera, Eka. 1982. "Pancasila and the Search for Identity and Modernity in Indonesian Society." Ph.D. diss., Andover Newton Theological School.

Davis, Russell, and Brent Ashabranner. 1959. The Lion's Whiskers. Boston: Little, Brown & Co.

Davitz, Joel R. 1969. The Language of Emotion. New York: Academic Press.

Dean, Arthur H. 1966. *Test Ban and Disarmament: The Path of Negotiation*. New York: Harper & Row.

DeBono, Edward. 1985. *Conflicts*. London: Harrap.

Dehqani-Tafti, H. B. 1981. *The Hard Awakening*. New York: Seabury Press.

Dennis, Philip. 1987. *Intervillage Conflict in Oaxaca*. New Brunswick, N.J.: Rutgers University Press.

Deutsch, Morton. 1969. "Conflicts: Productive and Destructive." *Journal of Social Issues* 25, no. 1 (March): 7–41.

———. 1973. *The Resolution of Conflict: Constructive and Destructive Processes*. New Haven: Yale University Press.

———. 1987. "A Theoretical Perspective on Conflict and Conflict Resolution." In D. Sandole and Ingrid Sandole-Staroste, eds., *Conflict Management and Problem Solving*. New York: New York University Press.

DeVos, George. 1967. "The Relation of Guilt Toward Parents to Achievement and Arranged Marriage Among the Japanese." In Robert Hunt, ed., *Personalities and Cultures*. Garden City, N.Y.: Natural History Press.

Diaz-Guerrero, R. 1959. "Mexican Assumptions About Interpersonal Relations." *Et Cetera* 16:185–88.

Djilas, Milovan. 1958. *Land Without Justice*. London: Methuen.

Dodd, Carley, and Bruno Montalvo, eds. 1987. *Intercultural Skills for Multicultural Societies*. Washington, D.C.: Sietar.

Doi, Takeo. 1973. *The Anatomy of Dependence*. Tokyo: Kodansha.

Doob, Leonard W., ed. 1970. *Resolving Conflict in Africa*. New Haven: Yale University Press.

Dore, Ronald. 1959. *Land Reform in Japan*. London: Oxford University Press.

———. 1978. *Shinohata: A Portrait of a Japanese Village*. New York: Pantheon Books.

Dorson, Richard. 1975. *Folktales Told Around the World*. Chicago: University of Chicago Press.

Duley, M., and M. Edwards. 1986. *The Cross Cultural Study of Women*. Old Westbury, N.Y.: Feminist Press.

Dumont, Louis. 1986. *Essays on Individualism*. Chicago: University of Chicago Press.

Edelmann, Robert J. 1987. *The Psychology of Embarrassment*. New York: Wiley.

Ellis, Pat. 1986. *Women of the Caribbean*. London: Zed.

Ellul, Jacques. 1969. *Violence*. New York: Seabury Press.

Evans-Pritchard, E. E. 1940. *The Nuer*. Oxford: Clarendon Press.

———. 1963. *Witchcraft, Oracles, and Magic Among the Azande*. Oxford: Clarendon Press.

Faul, John, and David Augsburger. 1978. *Beyond Assertiveness*. Waco, Tex.: Word.

Fisher, Glen. 1980. *International Negotiation: A Cross-cultural Perspective*. Chicago: Intercultural Press.

Fisher, Roger, and William Ury. 1981. *Getting to Yes: Negotiating Agreement Without Giving In*. New York: Penguin Books.

Fisher, Ronald J. 1984. *Conflict and Collaboration in Maori-Pakesha Relations*. Hamilton, New Zealand: University of Waskato Press.

Folberg, Jay, and Alison Taylor. 1984. *Mediation*. San Francisco: Jossey-Bass.

Foster, George M. 1967. *Tzintzuntzán*. New York: Elsevier.

Foucault, Michel. 1970. *The Order of Things*. London: Tavistock.

Frenkel-Brunswik, E. 1954. "Further Explorations by a Contributor to *The Authoritarian Personality*." In R. Christie and M. Johoda, eds., *The Authoritarian Personality: Scope and Method*. Glencoe, N.Y.: Free Press.

Friedman, Maurice S. 1983. *The Confirmation of Otherness in Family, Community, and Society*. New York: Pilgrim Press.

———. 1985. *The Healing Dialogue in Psychotherapy*. New York: Jason Aronson.

Galtung, Johan. 1975–80. *Essays in Peace Research*. 5 vols. Copenhagen: Christian Ejlers.

Gandhi, Mahatma. 1970–76. *The Collected Works of Mahatma Gandhi*. 78 vols. Ahmedabad: Publications Division, Government of India.

Gbadamosi, B., and U. Beier. 1968. *Not Even God Is Ripe Enough*. London: Heinemann.

Gibbs, J. L., Jr. 1973. "Two Forms of Dispute Settlement Among the Kpelle of West Africa." In D. R. Black and M. Mileski, eds., *The Social Organization of Law*. New York: Seminar.

Gillin, John. 1956. "The Making of a Witch Doctor." *Psychiatry* 19:131–36.

Glazier, Jack. 1973. "Conflict and Conciliation Among the Mbeere of Kenya." Ph.D. diss., University of California, Berkeley.

Glenn, Edmund, and Christine Glenn. 1981. *Man and Mankind: Conflict and Communication Between Cultures*. Norwood, N.J.: Ablex.

Glenn, E. S., D. Witmeyer, and K. A. Stevenson. 1977. "Cultural Styles of Persuasion." *International Journal of Intercultural Relations* 1, no. 3 (fall): 52.

Goldman, Robert. 1980. *Roundtable Justice: Case Studies in Conflict Resolution*. Boulder, Colo.: Westview.

Gudykunst, William, and Stella Ting-Toomey. 1984a. *Communicating with Strangers*. Reading, Mass.: Addison-Wesley.

———. 1984b. *Methods for Intercultural Communication*. Beverly Hills, Calif.: Sage.

———. 1988. *Culture and Interpersonal Communication*. Beverly Hills, Calif.: Sage.

Gudykunst, William, and Young Yun Kim, eds. 1984. *Methods for Intercultural Communication Research*. Beverly Hills, Calif.: Sage.

Gulliver, P. H. 1963. *Social Control in an African Society*. London: Routledge & Kegan Paul.

———. 1971. *Neighbors and Networks*. Berkeley: University of California Press.

———. 1979. *Disputes and Negotiations: A Cross-cultural Perspective*. New York: Academic Press.

Hall, E. T. 1976. *Beyond Culture*. New York: Doubleday.

Halle, Louis J. 1971. "International Behavior and the Prospects for Human Survival." In John F. Eisenberg and Wilton S. Dillon, eds., *Man and Beast: Comparative Social Behavior*. Washington, D.C.: Smithsonian.

Hallie, Phillip. 1979. *Lest Innocent Blood Be Shed*. New York: Harper Colophon.

Hamady, Sania. 1960. *Temperament and Character of the Arabs*. New York: Twayne.

Hanami, Tadashi. 1984. "Conflict and Its Resolution." In Ellis Krauss, Thomas Rohlen, and Patricia Steinhoff, eds., *Conflict in Japan*. Honolulu: University of Hawaii.

Hare, A. Paul. 1985. *Social Interaction as Drama: Applications from Conflict Resolution*. Beverly Hills, Calif.: Sage.

Hare, A. Paul, and Herbert Bluberg, eds. 1968. *Nonviolent Direct Action: American Cases: Social-psychological Analyses*. Washington, D.C.: Corpus Books.

———. 1977. *Liberation Without Violence: A Third Party Approach*. London: Rex Collings.

———. 1980. *A Search for Peace and Justice: Reflections of Michael Scott*. London: Rex Collings.

Harré, Rom, ed. 1987. *The Social Construction of Emotions*. Oxford: Blackwell.

Harris, Phillip. 1987. *Managing Cultural Differences*. Houston: Gulf.

Heelas, P. 1986. "Emotion Talk Across Cultures." In Rom Harré, ed., *The Social Construction of Emotions*. Oxford: Blackwell.

Henderson, D. C. 1965. *Conciliation and Japanese Law: Tokugawa and Modern*. Seattle: University of Washington Press.

Henderson, George. 1979. *Understanding and Counseling Ethnic Minorities*. Springfield, Ill.: Charles Thomas.

Henry, J. 1936. "The Linguistic Expression of Emotion." *The American Anthropologist* 38:250–57.

Hertzfield, M. 1980. "Honor and Shame: Problems in the Comparative Analysis of Moral Systems." *Man* 15:339–45.

Hiebert, Paul. 1971. *Konduru*. Minneapolis: University of Minnesota Press.

Hill, Frederick. 1972. *Conflict Utilization: The Role of the Black Professional*. Washington, D.C.: Black Affairs Center.

Ho, David Y. J. 1974. "Face, Social Expectations, and Conflict Avoidance." In John Dawson and Walter Lonner, eds., *Readings in Cross-cultural Study of Counseling*. Hong Kong: Hong Kong University Press.

Hoebel, E. A. 1968. *The Law of Primitive Man*. New York: Atheneum.

Hoopes, David, and Paul Ventura. 1979. *Intercultural Sourcebook*. Washington, D.C.: Sietar.

Horowitz, Donald L. 1985. *Ethnic Groups in Conflict*. Berkeley: University of California Press.

Howell, S. 1981. "Rules Not Words." In P. Heelas and A. Lock, eds., *Indigenous Psychologies*. London: Academic Press.

Isard, Walter. 1982. *Conflict Analyses and Practical Conflict Management Procedures*. Cambridge, Mass.: Ballinger.

Jandt, Fred. 1985. *Win-win Negotiating*. New York: Wiley.

Johnson, L. Gunnar. 1976. *Conflicting Concepts of Peace in Contemporary Peace Studies*. Beverly Hills, Calif.: Sage.

Kalish, Richard, and David K. Reynolds. 1981. *Death and Ethnicity*. Farmingdale, N.Y.: Baywood.

Kaplan, Robert B. 1966. "Cultural Thought Patterns in Intercultural Education." *Language Learning* 16, nos. 1 and 2.

Kaunda, Kenneth. 1980. *The Riddle of Violence*. San Francisco: Harper & Row.

Kayano, Shigeru. 1966. "Ainu Folktales." Unpublished folktales from Nibutani, Biratori-cho, Hokkaido, Japan. Recorded August 18, 1966, at Nibutani. Trans. Marvin Miller.

Kim, Sang Yil. 1984. *Hanism as Korean Mind*. Los Angeles: Eastern Academy of Human Sciences.

Kim, Y., and William Gudykunst. 1988. *Theories in Intercultural Communication*. Newbury Park, Calif.: Sage.

King, Ursula. 1989. *Women and Spirituality*. London: Macmillan Publishing Co.

Klama, John, et al. 1988. *Aggression*. Essex: Longman Scientific.

Klare, Michael, and Peter Kornbluh, eds. 1988. *Low Intensity Warfare*. New York: Pantheon Books.

Kluckholn, Clyde, and Henry Murray. 1948. *Personality in Nature, Society and Culture*. New York: Alfred A. Knopf.

Knappert, Jan. 1970. *Myths and Legends of the Swahili*. Nairobi: Heinemann.

Knauft, Bruce. 1985. *Good Company and Violence*. Berkeley: University of California Press.

Kochman, Thomas. 1981. *Black and White Styles in Conflict*. Chicago: University of Chicago Press.

Krauss, Ellis, Thomas Rohlen, and Patricia Steinhoff, eds. 1984. *Conflict in Japan*. Honolulu: University of Hawaii Press.

Kumar, U., and B. Srivastava. 1979. "Desirable and Actual Modes of Conflict Resolution of Indian Managers." In L. Eckensberger, et al., *Crosscultural Contributions to Psychology*. Amsterdam: Swets and Zeitlinger.

Küng, Hans. 1987. *Christianity and the World Religions*. London: Collins.

Kurokawa, Minako. 1969. "Beyond Community Integration and Stability: A Comparative Study of Oriental and Mennonite Children." *Journal of Social Issues* 25, no. 1.

Lake, Frank. 1986. *Clinical Theology*. Abridged by Martin Yeomans. London: Darton, Longman & Todd.

Lamphere, Louise. 1974. "Strategies, Cooperation, and Conflict Among Women in Domestic Groups." In Michelle Rosaldo and Louise Lamphere, *Women, Culture, and Society*. Stanford, Calif.: Stanford University Press.

Lasch, Christopher. 1979. *The Culture of Narcissism*. New York: Norton.

Leakey, Richard, and R. Lewin. 1977. *Origins*. London: MacDonald and Jane's.

————. 1979. *People of the Lake*. London: Collins.

Leary, Timothy. 1958. *The Diagnosis of Interpersonal Behavior*. New York: Ronald Press.

Leas, Speed. 1985. *Moving Your Church Through Conflict*. Washington, D.C.: Alban Institute.

Lebra, Joyce, et al. 1976. *Women in Changing Japan*. Boulder, Colo.: Westview.

Lebra, Takie Sugiyama. 1984. "Nonconfrontational Strategies for Management of Interpersonal Conflicts." In Ellis Krauss, Thomas Rohlen, and Patricia Steinhoff, eds., *Conflict in Japan*. Honolulu: University of Hawaii Press.

Lederach, John Paul. 1986. "Assumptions." *MCS Conciliation Quarterly* (Summer): 2–5.

————. 1988a. "Of Nets, Nails and Problems: A Folk Vision of Conflict in Central America." Ph.D. diss., University of Colorado.

————. 1988b. "Yes, But Are They Talking? Some Thoughts on the Trainer as Student." *MCS Conciliation Quarterly* (Summer): 10–12.

Lee, F. H. 1931. *Folktales of All Nations*. London: George Harrap.

Leis, Nancy. 1974. *Ijaw Women*. New York: Holt, Rinehart & Winston.

Levine, E. S., and Anado Padilla. 1980. *Cross Cultures in Therapy: Pluralistic Counseling for the Hispanic*. Monterey, Calif.: Brooks/Cole.

LeVine, Robert, and Donald Campbell. 1972. *Ethnocentrism: Theories of Conflict, Ethnic Attitudes, and Group Behavior*. New York: Wiley.

MacDonald, Sharon, et al. 1987. *Images of Women in Peace and War*. London: Macmillan Publishers.

McGinn, Noel, Ernest Harbury, and Gerald Ginsburg. 1965. "Responses to Conflict by Middle Class Males in Guadalajara and Michigan." *American Anthropologist* 67, no. 6:1483–94.

MacGregor Burns, J. 1977. "Wellsprings of Political Leadership." *American Political Science Review* 71 (March).

Mack, R. W. 1965. "The Components of Social Conflict." *Social Problems* 12, no. 4:388–97.

Maidment, Robert. 1987. *Conflict: A Conversation About Managing Differences*. Reston, Va.: National Association of Secondary School Principals.

Marvin, Garry. 1986. "Honour, Integrity and the Problem of Violence in the Spanish Bullfight." In D. Riches, ed., *The Anthropology of Violence*. Oxford: Blackwell.

Mbiti, John S. 1969. *African Religions and Philosophy*. London: Heinemann.

Mbog, Makang ma. 1969. "Essay on the Dynamics of Psychotherapy in African Tradition." *Psychopathologie Africaine* 3.

Mead, Margaret. 1968. "Alternatives to War." In Morton Fried, Marvin Harris, and Robert Murphy, eds., *War: The Anthropology of Armed Conflict and Aggression*. Garden City, N.Y.: Natural History Press.

Megargee, Edwin. 1966. "Undercontrolled and Overcontrolled Personality Types in Extreme Anti-social Aggression." *Psychological Monographs* 80, no. 3.

Metge, Joan. 1986. *In and Out of Touch: Whakamaa in Cross Cultural Context*. Wellington, New Zealand: Victoria University Press.

Meyer, Brenda Hostettler. 1984. Folktale recorded in Lesotho. Mennonite Central Committee, Akron, Pa.

Mitchell, C. R. 1981. *Peacemaking and the Consultant's Role*. New York: Nichols.

Moore, Christopher. 1985. *Mediation*. San Francisco: Jossey-Bass.

Moore, Erin. 1985. *Conflict and Compromise: Justice in an Indian Village*. Berkeley: University of California Press.

Mpolo, Masamba ma, and Wilhelmina Kalu. 1985. *The Risks of Growth Counseling and Pastoral Theology in the African Context*. Nairobi: Uzima.

Mulder, Niels. 1978. *Mysticism and Everyday Life in Contemporary Java*. Singapore: Singapore University Press.

Nader, L., and H. F. Todd, Jr. 1978. *The Disputing Process: Law in Ten Societies*. New York: Columbia University Press.

Nakhre, Amrut. 1982. *Social Psychology of Nonviolent Action*. Delhi: Chanakya Publications.

Nazir-Ali, Michael. 1987. *Frontiers in Muslim-Christian Encounter*. Oxford: Regnum.

Newcomb, T. M. 1959. "Individual Systems of Orientation." In S. Koch, ed., *Psychology: The Study of a Science*. Vol. 3. New York: McGraw-Hill.

Oduyoye, Mercy Amba. 1983. "Reflections from a Third World Woman's Perspective." In Virginia Fabella, ed., *Irruption of the Third World*. Maryknoll, N.Y.: Orbis Books.

Oquist, Paul. 1980. *Violence, Conflict, and Politics in Colombia*. New York: Academic Press.

Osgood, Charles. 1962. *An Alternative to War or Surrender*. Urbana: University of Illinois.

Osgood, Charles, et al. 1975. *Cross Cultural Universals of Affective Meaning*. Urbana: University of Illinois.

Pattison, Mansell. 1973. "The Development of Morality in Children." In Ellis Nelson, ed., *Conscience*. New York: Newman.

Paz, Octavio. 1961. *The Labyrinth of Solitude*. New York: Grove.

Peristiany, J. G. 1965. *Honour and Shame: The Values of Mediterranean Society*. London: Pelican.

Pierson, Ruth R. 1987. "Women in War, Peace and Revolution." In Sharon MacDonald, et al., *Images of Women in Peace and War*. London: Macmillan Publishers.

Porter, Jack N. 1987. *Conflict and Conflict Resolution: A Sociological Introduction*. Lanham, Md.: University Press of America.

Postma, Minnie. 1964. *Tales from the Basotho*. Austin: University of Texas Press.

Pukui, M., E. Haertig, and C. A. Lee. 1972. *Nana Ike Kumv (Look to the Source)*. Honolulu: Hui Hanai.

Radcliffe-Brown, A. R. 1964. *The Andaman Islanders*. New York: Free Press.

Radhakrishnan, Sarvepalli, and Charles Moore. 1957. *A Sourcebook in Indian Philosophy*. Princeton, N.J.: Princeton University Press.

Ramírez, S. 1961. "El Mexicano: Psicología de sus motivaciones." In *Pax-Mexico*. Mexico City: Nevarez.

Rasmussen, Knud. 1927. *Across Arctic America*. New York: Putnam.

Rawls, John. 1971. *The Theory of Justice.* Cambridge, Mass.: Harvard University Press.

Reay, M. 1974. "Changing Conventions of Dispute Settlement." In A. L. Epstein, ed., *Contention and Dispute.* Canberra, Australia: A.N.V. Press.

Redfield, Robert. 1964. "Primitive Law." *University of Cincinnati Law Review* 33:1–22.

Reimer, Carlton. 1977. "The Qur'anic Concept of Retaliation." *The South East Asia Journal of Theology* 18, no. 2:46–51.

Riches, D., ed. 1986. *The Anthropology of Violence.* Oxford: Blackwell.

Ricoeur, Paul. 1967. *The Symbolism of Evil.* New York: Harper & Row.

Ridd, Rosemary, and Helen Callaway. 1986. *Caught Up in Conflict: Women's Responses to Political Strife.* London: Macmillan Publishers.

Roberts, Simon. 1979. *Order and Dispute.* Harmondsworth, England: Penguin Books.

Rohner, R. P. 1976. "Sex Differences in Aggression: Phylogenetic and Enculturation Perspectives." *Ethos* 4:57–72.

Romanucci-Ross, Lola. 1986. *Conflict, Violence, and Morality in a Mexican Village.* Chicago: University of Chicago Press.

Rosaldo, Michelle. 1980. *Knowledge and Passion: Ilongot Notions of Self and Social Life.* Cambridge: Cambridge University Press.

Rosaldo, Michelle, and Louise Lamphere, eds. 1974. *Women, Culture, and Society.* Stanford, Calif.: Stanford University Press.

Rosenblatt, Roger. 1982. *Time,* January 22, 52.

Rummel, R. J. 1976. *Understanding Conflict and War.* New York: Wiley.

Saadawi, Nawal El. 1980. *The Hidden Face of Eve: Women in the Arab World.* London: Zed.

Sabbah, Fatna A. 1985. *Woman in the Muslim Unconscious.* New York: Pergamon.

Samuelson, Loris J. 1976. *Soviet and Chinese Negotiating Behavior.* Beverly Hills, Calif.: Sage.

Sanday, Peggy R. 1981. *Female Power and Male Dominance.* Cambridge: Cambridge University Press.

———. 1986. *Divine Hunger: Cannibalism as a Cultural System.* Cambridge: Cambridge University Press.

Sandole, Dennis J. D., and Ingrid Sandole-Staroste. 1987. *Conflict Management and Problem Solving: Interpersonal to International Applications.* New York: New York University Press.

Scarman, L. 1977. "Human Rights." *University of London Bulletin* 39.

Schieffelin, E. I. 1983. "Anger and Shame in the Tropical Forest: An Affect as a Cultural System in Papua, New Guinea." *Ethos* 113:181–91.

Schneider, Jane. 1971. "Of Vigilance and Virgins: Honor, Shame and Access to Resources in Mediterranean Society." *Ethnology* 10:1–24.

Schreiner, Olive. [1911] 1978. *Women and Labour*. London: Virago.

Schroeder, Richard, and Robert LeVine. 1984. *Culture Theory: Essay on Mind, Self and Emotion*. Cambridge: Cambridge University Press.

Sharp, Gene. 1973. *The Politics of Nonviolent Action*. 3 vols. Boston: Porter-Sargent.

Shenk, David. 1979. "Conversation with Joshua Okello." Unpublished paper presented at Eastern Mennonite Board of Missions.

Shon, S., and D. Ja. 1982. "Asian Families." In M. McGoldrick, et al., *Ethnicity and Family Therapy*. New York: Guilford.

Shook, E. Victoria. 1985. *Ho'oponopono*. Honolulu: East-West Center, University of Hawaii.

Singer, Kurt. 1949. "The Resolution of Conflict." *Social Research* 16, no. 2 (June): 230–45.

Singer, Marshall. 1987. *Intercultural Communication: A Perceptual Approach*. Englewood Cliffs, N.J.: Prentice-Hall.

Sites, P. 1973. *Control: The Basis of Social Order*. New York: Nunellen.

Song, C. S. 1979. "New Frontiers of Theology in Asia." *South East Asia Journal of Theology* 20, no. 1:13–33.

Stagner, Ross. 1967. *Psychological Aspects of International Conflict*. Belmont, Calif.: Brooks/Cole.

Stewart, Lee, and Stella Ting-Toomey. 1987. *Communication, Gender, and Sex Roles in Diverse Interaction Contexts*. Norwood, N.J.: Ablex.

Stulberg, Joseph. 1987. *Taking Charge/Managing Conflict*. Lexington, Mass.: Lexington Books.

Tanner, Nancy. 1981. *On Becoming Human*. Cambridge: Cambridge University Press.

Tanner, N. M., and A. L. Zihlman. 1976. "Women in Evolution." *Signs* 1:585–608.

Tavris, Carol. 1973. *The Female Experience*. Del Mar, Calif.: Communications Research.

——. 1982. *Anger: The Misunderstood Emotion*. New York: Simon & Schuster.

Thomas, E. Marshall. 1969. *The Harmless People*. Harmondsworth, England: Penguin Books.

Ting-Toomey, Stella. November, 1982. "Toward a Theory of Conflict and Culture." Paper presented for the Speech Communication Association, Louisville, Kentucky.

Ting-Toomey, Stella, and Felipe Korzenny. 1989. *Language, Communication, and Culture.* International and Intercultural Communication Annual Series, vol. 13. Beverly Hills, Calif.: Sage.

Toupin, Ahn. 1980. "Counseling Asians: Psychotherapy in the Context of Racism and Asian-American History." *American Journal of Orthopsychiatry* 50 (January): 76–86.

Touval, Saadia, and I. William Zartman, eds. 1985. *International Mediation in Theory and Practice.* Washington, D.C.: Westview.

Troeltsch, Ernst. 1960. *The Social Teaching of the Christian Churches and Groups.* New York: Macmillan Publishing Co.

Tseng, W., and J. Hsu. 1971. "Chinese Culture, Personality Formation and Mental Illness." *International Journal of Social Psychiatry* 16:5–14.

Turnbull, Colin. 1961. *The Forest People.* London: Picador.

————. 1972. *The Mountain People.* London: Picador.

Turner, Victor. 1971. "An Anthropological Approach to the Icelandic Saga." In T. O. Beidelman, ed., *The Translation of Culture.* London: Tavistock.

Ury, William, Jeanne Brett, and Stephen Goldberg. 1988. *Getting Disputes Resolved.* San Francisco: Jossey-Bass.

Valentine, C. A. 1963. "Men of Anger and Men of Shame." *Ethnology* 2:441–47.

Veda, T. 1962. "A Study of Anger in Japanese College Students." *Journal of Nara Gakugei University* 10:341–48.

Wagner, Roy. 1981. *The Invention of Culture.* Chicago: University of Chicago Press.

Walton, Richard. 1969. *Interpersonal Peacemaking.* Reading, Mass.: Addison-Wesley Publishing Co.

Warner, C. T. 1986. "Anger and Similar Delusions." In Rom Harré, ed., *The Social Construction of Emotions.* Oxford: Blackwell.

Wehr, Paul. 1979. *Conflict Regulation.* Boulder, Colo.: Westview.

Weyer, E. M. 1932. *The Eskimos.* New Haven: Yale University Press.

Williamson, John. 1983. *Case Studies of Conflicts in the Context of Development in Rural Nepal.* Kathmandu: United Mission.

Wilson, Marie, and Ian Crawford. 1988. "The Circle of Reason." *The New Internationalist* 186 (August): 18–19.

Wilson, S. 1988. "Conflict Among the Gitksan." *The New Internationalist* 18, no. 3 (March): 18–20.

Witty, Cathie. 1980. *Mediation and Society: Conflict Management in Lebanon.* London: Academic Press.

Wolf, Margery. 1972. *Women and the Family in Rural Taiwan.* Stanford, Calif.: Stanford University Press.

Wolfgang, Aaron. 1985. *Intercultural Counseling and Assessment.* Lewistown, N.Y.: C. J. Hogrefe.

Wolfson, Kim, and Martin Norden. 1984. "Measuring Responses to Filmed Interpersonal Conflict: A Rules Approach." In William Gudykunst and Young Yun Kim, eds., *Methods for Intercultural Communication Research*. Beverly Hills, Calif.: Sage.

Woolf, Virginia. 1938. *Three Guineas*. Harmondsworth, England: Penguin Books.

Wright, Quincy. 1942. *A Study of War*. Chicago: University of Chicago Press.

Wu, John C. H. 1967. "Chinese Legal and Political Philosophy." In Charles Moore, ed., *The Chinese Mind*. Honolulu: East-West Center, University of Hawaii.

Yeda, A. 1962. *The Unknown Japan*. Tokyo: Sophia University Press.

Young, M. 1971. *Fighting with Food*. Cambridge: Cambridge University Press.

Young, Oran R. 1967. *The Intermediaries: Third Parties in International Crises*. Princeton, N.J.: Princeton University Press.

Zartman, William, ed. 1978. *The Negotiation Process: Theories and Application*. Beverly Hills, Calif.: Sage.

Index

Acknowledgment of Copyrighted Sources